SUSTAIN YOUR AUTHOR CAREER

USING THE ENNEAGRAM TO CULTIVATE OUR
GIFTS, DEEPEN OUR CONNECTIONS, AND
TRIUMPH OVER ADVERSITY

CLAIRE TAYLOR

Cover Design © FFS Media LLC

ISBN: 978-1-959041-09-2

www.ffs.media

Author photograph by Anna Monette

CONTENTS

Section 1: YOU'RE IN THE RIGHT
PLACE   1
Section 2: UNDERSTANDING THE
ENNEAGRAM   14
Section 3: WHAT MOTIVATES YOU?   54
Section 4: TROUBLESHOOTING
YOUR BLOCKS   94
Section 5: BUILDING AUTHOR
RESILIENCE   233
Section 6: HOW WE GROW   273
Section 7: PROGRESSING
FROM HERE   313

Acknowledgments   345
About Claire Taylor   349

SECTION 1: YOU'RE IN THE RIGHT PLACE

It was New Year's Eve of 2018 as I sat on the couch in my therapist's office, clutching my face. I'd taken two unexpected weeks off from my writing business over the holidays as a result of burnout from a year of rapid-releasing eleven books. During that "vacation," the most upsetting thing had transpired: I'd seen the best sales month of my career.

You might be wondering, *Isn't that good news?* It's a logical question, because doing less work for more money is a dream for many of us. But to me in that moment, it was upsetting as hell. My head felt like it might explode. My world was being turned upside down.

"What if there's no connection between how hard I work and the results I get?" I said.

My therapist, unexpressive as ever, replied, "What if?"

I'd started seeing this therapist years earlier because she specialized in treating perfectionism and other forms of anxiety through mindfulness and humor. I'd also received the recommendation from a friend who is one of the most chronically depressed people I've ever met, so if she was able to keep him afloat, I figured I might actually get my money's worth. I've been labeled a perfectionist ever since I was old enough to grip objects and compulsively sort them by color, so that's what I'd come to see her about. That and the random anxiety attack I'd had in my closet a few years before, which was, like, a totally normal thing, yeah? Practically a rite of passage! Oh, and the depression, but I had a liberal arts degree and married a man with a liberal arts degree, so most of the people I knew were depressed. That was as common as being an introvert in my world.

I'm sure you already see what's going on here. I had problems. Some small, others big. And the big ones went even deeper than I ever knew.

Working hard as an author, churning out books and white-knuckling my way through creative dry spells, depression, anxiety, was an ability I'd prided myself on up until that visit in 2018. My attitude was essentially *I may not have the resources, genius, or attractive looks of others, but I can write better books than them if I work hard enough at it.*

Being an independent author played into this belief perfectly. The cause and effect of *working hard more money* was a comfort to me that I didn't recognize as such until it was pulled out from under me that December.

My therapist's question, as much as it caused me to wig out for a while, turned out to be the best she could've posed in that moment: "What if?" What if working myself to exhaustion wasn't necessary? What if the industry—and the world—really did have so many factors influencing every outcome that my decisions, no matter how educated or even "perfect" they seemed to be, had almost no effect on the monetary outcome?

Making a windfall of book sales with minimal effort might seem like a victory, but it was coming at the cost of my sense of control over the external world. And now I had some big, scary questions to ask myself, starting with "What if?"

It's a question authors are used to asking in the context of the story we're crafting but one that very few of us are willing to apply to the story of ourselves and our author career.

What if... *there's no right way to do any of this?*

What if... *I never have a breakout success?*

What if... *hustling at this pace doesn't lead to anything but burnout?*

These questions can be destabilizing because they threaten our view of how the world works. If our view of how the world works is faulty, though, perhaps *that* is to blame for the struggles in our career rather than anything else. That's a scary prospect, because it implies we have much *more* responsibility for whether our careers are filled with joy or misery than we may have thought.

In the years following that particular therapy visit, I held the question of "what if" ahead of me like a lantern, lighting my way through the dark, asking it again and again. That lantern led me deep into study on a framework called the Enneagram and shined light onto how authors across the industry are suffering from a variety of predictable and *preventable* miseries. I've seen how much each of us holds on to, and I've also experienced and witnessed the liberation of letting it go.

This book is the result of my personal experience with that exploration, years of guiding authors like you on their way, and training from many others who traveled by the flickering flame of curiosity before me.

I invite you to follow me on this adventure through the following pages, where I'll show you how to build your own lantern to navigate the ever-changing terrain of being an author in the modern age.

THIS BOOK'S PROMISE

This book is for *any* author making *any* amount of money who loves storytelling and wants to continue doing it for decades to come in one form or another.

That's because this is a book about how to not only survive but—you guessed it—*thrive* as a creative human being when so much is outside of our control, when the world seems like it's on a downward slide around us, and when we're starting to wonder why we even bother.

As you'll discover, I don't see a separation between a healthy life and a healthy author career. The skills and mindset that we need to stay in a business that tests us in the ways that publishing does are the same skills and mindset that build a healthy life in *all* areas.

Everyone I know, with no exception made for authors, goes through periods of life that are a daily struggle. That struggle is certainly made harder when financial burdens are heaped on top, but take those financial burdens away, and one is not simply *in the clear*. There are certain kinds of struggle that happen inside of us independent of our financial situation. We all recognize that truth deep down, even though some might think, *I would rather be sad and wealthy than sad and poor*. Me too, friend. Me too. I've experienced depression both with money and very much without it, so I can say that it's easier to bear when I have some cash on hand. Money alone has never made me *thrive*. However, doing the kind of work I'll guide you through in this book has.

I don't want your author career to feel like something you "get through." I don't want you waiting until some arbitrary publishing goal is reached to feel good about who you are. I want you to feel complete, worthy, confident, and joyful every day for the rest of what I hope is a long, long life. I want you to build a life that's worth living for a long time.

Whether we like it or not, how we feel about our career has a massive impact on how we feel about ourselves and our lives. Even if you don't consider writing your primary career, if you publish books, you have an author career. You may have another career running parallel, or you may already be in retirement, and that's okay. This is still a book for you. Because when I talk about an author career, I'm not only talking about the business side or even the audience-facing side of it. I'm also talking about your sense of connection to the art and process of storytelling. When that connection is injured, a writer's life can disintegrate. To have written and published more than one book tells me that there is something special about you that sets you apart from the rest of the population. You are a writer at your core. You need this process so badly that you're willing to push through the painful parts for it. That's love. That's romance. But if you've picked up this book, it's likely that you feel some sort of rift between you and the writerly life you imagined enjoying. I want to help you keep that romance alive, because if you lose it and fail to reconnect, you'll be confined to a life of grieving that part of yourself. I don't know of anyone who gave up writing for good and ever quite got over it.

We will fall in and out of love with our writing, sure, but I want you to finish this book feeling secure that you know *how* to find your way back to writing, time and again.

With that goal in mind and heart, this book offers practices that will support you in the important areas of:

1. Understanding what motivates you in your life and creative practice
2. Gaining clarity on what you can and cannot control in your author career
3. Troubleshooting for when you hit a block or fall out of love with your manuscript
4. Building resilience so you can always get back up one more time than you fall down
5. Learning how we grow into flexible decision makers, so the industry doesn't leave us behind

Once we've explored these topics together, we'll look at how you can use these concepts moving forward in your career beyond the pages of this book.

HOW IS THIS DIFFERENT FROM *RECLAIM YOUR AUTHOR CAREER*?

You might be wondering what the difference is between the book you're about to read and my previous book, *Reclaim Your Author Career*.

In most ways, the concepts in this book build upon the previous one. That doesn't mean you have to have read *Reclaim Your Author Career* to benefit from the information in this book, but I'd like to think that if you've read that one first and then you read this one, the benefits are multiplicative.

Because both books use the framework of the Enneagram to organize the information and explain the deeper structures that we'll be diving into, there will be unavoidable information overlap as we cover the basics. The great news is that we can read the same useful tidbit about the Enneagram at two points in our life and gain two separate insights from it, depending on what parts of ourselves we're able to perceive in that moment. Because of that, I suggest you don't skip over the section on Understanding the Enneagram, even if you feel confident in your understanding of it.

Reclaim Your Author Career shows you how to think of your career in terms of concentric circles that align with who you are at your core. The focus of that book is to get you thinking in this mode, and to encourage you to build the structures of your career from *you* up rather than what's often encouraged, which is trying to shape yourself to some universal "optimal" author strategy.

I stand by that framing as a useful way to organize our thoughts around our values, persona, themes, and protagonists. Certainly it's not the only way to build a career, but I've been pleased to see how many authors have found it revolutionary as well as liberating.

Getting in alignment is just the start. Learning how to *stay* in alignment or *return to* alignment is a whole other set of skills.

Sustain Your Author Career is all about developing those skills and creating practices that support them. It's about creating a sustainable author career.

But here's the thing about that:

> **You cannot have a sustainable writing career unless your patterns of thinking, feeling, and acting are sustainable.**

In this book, we're going to take a deep, honest look at what patterns have been repeating inside of you and your career thus far, mostly outside of your awareness, and how we can tweak them to make sure they elevate you toward lasting success, joy, and fulfillment rather than drive you off a cliff.

As I write this at the start of 2024, the publishing industry seems to be facing an inordinate amount of volatility and an unprecedented number of increasing challenges for selling books. Almost every platform is pay-to-play, no one can agree on whether AI is our savior or destroyer, sales are down across the board, and, oh yeah, we're all still traumatized by and grieving what we lost to that virus thing that rocked our world.

I see some authors starting to get their feet back under them, but for many, we aren't working with the same energy we had five years ago, so it's intimidating if not demoralizing to see the monumental climb we have ahead of ourselves to stay in the game, let alone get back to the place many of us once were in terms of sales.

The industry has been trending this way for a while, but there seems to be a critical mass of authors who are really feeling it lately. Whereas five or more years ago there seemed to be no lack of "overnight" success stories, what we're seeing much more of now is authors who were making five, six, and seven figures a year in book sales exhausting all of their usual tactics while their sales continue to slide month after month.

This dire outlook is not meant to scare you. It's meant to validate what you've probably suspected for a while. Maybe you didn't want to admit it, or your defense mechanisms have you doing a whole song and dance to keep from looking directly at it. If that's the case, then my pointing it out might be triggering for you. I urge you to keep reading anyway. Our sore spots are great entry points for inquiry into what's happening just out of sight in our mind, heart, and body.

I could certainly write a whole book *speculating* on the various causes of the recent market shifts, but I think the last thing we all need is another person with some credibility publicly guessing, stoking anxiety, and confusing correlation with causation. So instead, this book is to help you gain the skills and confidence you need to keep on writing, without sacrificing your mental and emotional well-being, despite the external circumstances of the market. If I achieve what I've set out to, this book will be one that you refer back to for years to come.

In short, this is a book about how to not give up.

WHO AM I?

I've been an indie author since 2014, and my books have been my main source of income since early 2017. I knew from the start of my publishing journey that I wanted to publish independently. It's in my nature to not let anyone tell me what to do once I feel sure about my path forward. I've certainly let people influence my life decisions in many ways through the years, but fiction has always been the place where I put my foot down. It's where I get to take a stand and tell stories that ring true to me but will undoubtedly upset some people.

When I publish this, it will be my forty-fourth published book. I write mainly in humor and mystery. Some of my series are money makers, and some of them are not, but I needed to write them anyway. There are all sorts of legitimate reasons to write a book, and I've used many of them at this point.

Writing fiction as a profession has been my dream since I was ten years old, and I protect that dream as fiercely as I would protect a ten-year-old family member.

But then this other thing happened a few years into my publishing experience. I dove deep into this concept called the Enneagram, and it basically took over my brain. I started using it to write my characters and then to build my own career in an aligned way. If only that had been enough! If only I could've stopped the spread of Enneagram there! But no. The Enneagram kept spreading throughout my life. I began using it to advise *other* authors on how to write stronger characters, and eventually they wanted to know how it could be applied to their career as well. And so it was that the Enneagram did what any useful idea does: it continued to spread.

Flash forward to today, and I've created multiple Enneagram-related courses, blogs, videos, and now books. I offer Enneagram coaching for authors through my Story Alignment and Author Alignment services, my Liberated Writer 5-Week Course, and in-person Liberated Writer retreats.

Along the way, I became an Advanced Certified Instructor in the Enneagram Spectrum of Personality Styles taught by Dr. Jerome Wagner and an Accredited Practitioner of the Integrative Enneagram.

My interest and curiosity lead me down a rabbit hole, and when I finally popped my head up, I discovered that I knew my shit. Neat.

I don't see a point in learning useful things if I don't share those useful things with others. So that's what I do. I learn from amazing teachers, I apply the knowledge to my own life, and then I compulsively consider and explain the applications for anyone else who will listen to me.

Today, that person is you. I'm so glad you're here.

CONCEPTS IN ACTION

Throughout this book, there will be sections where I explain what the Enneagram concept we're exploring might look like for each of the nine types, in both life and publishing.

However, even those specifics can feel general at times because they lack the *context* of a specific writing or marketing conundrum. In such cases, I'll describe more specific examples from my work with authors at the end of sections. I want to show you the concepts in action.

These "Concept in Action" sections will not include the person's real name, and some of the specific details that could help you identify the author will definitely be changed. That's the reality of working with visible people in a relatively small industry: you might be able to piece together who I'm talking about if I'm not careful. Especially you mystery writers.

The last thing I ever want to do is make a client feel like I'm telling their secrets. I value the trust my clients put in me, especially since so much of the work we do together touches on incredibly personal and deep parts of ourselves. Discretion on my part is crucial.

So, if you're a client of mine reading this, and one of these Concept In Action sections sounds oddly familiar, there's a distinct possibility that it's not because it's about you. Rather, it's incredibly likely that the nature of the problem we discussed together is related to your type, and I coach many people of each type who fall into traps of a similar nature. Either way, seeing a familiar problem written out can help us look at it with new eyes, so I hope that each of these Concept in Action sections will be of great use to folks of *all* types, but especially folks of the type represented in the story.

And now, let's get to the good part. Let's dig into the Enneagram and all of the gifts this framework has to offer.

SECTION 2: UNDERSTANDING THE ENNEAGRAM

ENNEAGRAM BASICS

The Enneagram is a personality framework that is unlike any other because of what it measures. People often ask me how it corresponds to MBTI types, and the answer is: it doesn't. It's not measuring the same thing at all. It's also not measuring the same thing as DISC, Big 5, Clifton-Strengths™, True Colors, or any other test (some of which are developed solely as marketing lead magnets to get your customer info and useless for transformational purposes).

The Enneagram sorts people into nine distinct types, sometimes called "styles" or "lenses." The criteria for sorting are simple: a person's core fear and core desire.

Fear and desire are the basis of the thing we call "motivation." The word "motivation" is derived from the same root as the word "move." Motivation moves us. What we fear and desire most determines where we put our attention and, subsequently, what we do, think, and feel.

You might see how this is incredibly useful to know as a writer, particularly if you write fiction. How do you get your characters from one place to the next? What is the right motivation to move them where you want them to go?

This doesn't only apply to physically moving a character from one setting to the next. When we talk about motivation, we're also talking about moving someone emotionally and intellectually.

In Enneagram-speak, the results of motivation are often referred to as "cognitive, emotional, and behavioral" patterns or "schema."

The Enneagram describes how we are motivated in three ways: thinking, feeling, and doing.

The interconnectedness of these three parts is important to remember as we do this work. Changing your thinking patterns will create a shift in your emotional and behavioral patterns. Changing your emotional patterns will lead to new thoughts and actions, as well. And changing your behavioral patterns can alter your thinking and emotional patterns.

We're at our best when there's coherence between our thinking, feeling, and doing. This is what's described as alignment. But it's entirely possible that one of these three elements of our life is out of alignment. We do things based on faulty beliefs or we ignore our feelings because we think we shouldn't feel or act on them. This is where we begin to run into problems that the Enneagram is incredibly useful for diagnosing, and we can use it to map our path back to alignment.

The good news is that we have three pathways to change: our thoughts, our emotions, and our actions. We can shift our thinking, our feelings, or our behaviors, and such an adjustment will result in the awakening and influencing of the other two avenues.

The bad news is that we have three ways that we can fall out of alignment with ourselves: thoughts, feelings, and actions. But again, we have this handy tool to assess where we went off track, and then we can get ourselves back on.

My favorite description of the Enneagram comes from a teeny-tiny book that packs a punch, called *The Essential Enneagram* by David Daniels, MD, and Virginia Price, PhD:

> *The Enneagram is a powerful and dynamic personality system that describes nine distinct and fundamentally different patterns of thinking, feeling, and acting. (p.1)*

Of note here is the word "patterns." Certain patterns of thinking, feeling, and behaving are more commonly seen in certain types, but not everyone within a particular type will have all identical patterns. *And* there is crossover in these patterns between the types, meaning when you observe a particular pattern of behavior in someone, you cannot with certainty guess their type. That would require you to look inside their mind to see what thoughts and emotions are driving the action. It would also require that you observe those patterns for an extended period of time to find a *pattern among the patterns* to ensure you're not observing a one-off expression.

Perhaps you're starting to understand why it can be a lengthy process before settling on our type.

Price and Daniels go on to explain:

> *Each of the nine patterns is based on an explicit perceptual filter and associated driving emotional energy.*

The concept of note in this is the idea of a **perceptual filter.**

What is that, and why would we have it?

Consider this: there is a massive amount of information coming at you all the time. This information includes visual (sight), auditory (hearing), olfactory (smell), tactile (touch), gustatory (taste), and the often overlooked vestibular (movement) and proprioceptive (body awareness) information.

Now imagine you're speaking with another human being. For auditory information alone, you're processing their tone, volume, pacing, and pitch.

Most of us do this without even "thinking" about it; that is, unless there's ambiguity or conflicting information between those auditory inputs, we follow along easily (obviously there is some variance in this depending on your auditory processing capacity).

How we can function even a little bit in the sea of inputs from a single interpersonal interaction is that our brains are incredibly adept at filtering out irrelevant information from our senses. (Our degree of competency with this can fluctuate and be affected by attentional and sensory disorders, but even if we fall into that category, let's give our brains credit for how much of this they are still able to do! It's remarkable.)

But what data is relevant and what is irrelevant? That will depend largely on your core fear and core desire.

Two people of different Enneagram types, when presented with all the same heaps of sensory information in a situation, will filter out different bits of data. Consequently, they will pay attention to different information.

In effect, those two people, who could be standing side by side and receiving virtually identical information from a source, will have a totally different experience of the interaction based on what their brains are sorting as relevant and irrelevant.

One person may be thinking, *This was the most unproductive meeting I've ever attended,* while the other thinks, *This was such a necessary meeting to clear the air!* The first person likely categorizes productivity in deliverables while the other defines it by the social cohesiveness that's accomplished.

Both of those definitions can be easily traceable to the person's core fear and core desire.

That's because our attention flows toward our fear first.

When introducing this concept while I'm on stage, I like to show a slide with a picture of a king cobra, a cute baby, and a chocolate fountain. Then I ask everyone in the audience to imagine they are in a closed room with these three things. Where does their attention go?

The answer is obvious: the deadly snake. You're going to keep your eyes on the deadly snake. You may risk taking your eyes off it for a second to grab up the baby in your arms to protect it, but only as long as you have to, so that you can stop giving any attention to the baby and focus back on the cobra.

You could be the most hard-core chocoholic in the world, and the most thought you might space for that fountain would be *Once I deal with this snake situation, I'm going to chug the shit out of that liquid chocolate.* But still, the snake comes first.

Whatever your core fear may be, as defined by your Enneagram type, that is your king cobra. It's the threat you build a life around avoiding. When you find yourself in proximity to it, it will take all your attention. Only when you can ease your fear of it will you be able to focus on the cute babies and chocolate fountains of the world, whatever those look like for you.

But here's the thing: you may not yet know what your king cobra is. That doesn't mean it hasn't been getting your attention. It's merely been working below your consciousness to guide you toward building a life that feels like protection.

This is why learning about your type is liberating. You learn what your king cobra is, and then you learn to recognize when it's actually just a little garter snake that is minding its own business and no threat to you at all. And sometimes, if you're really committed to this process, you can become a snake charmer, so even when it *is* the king cobra, you can feel relaxed in its presence.

This is how we use the Enneagram. We begin by identifying our fear, learning about our desire, and seeing how the patterns of attention arising from those may not be getting us to the place we dream of being.

And then we notice, notice, notice. For the rest of our life.

The trick about the Enneagram is that it applies to *all* decisions we're making. This includes the many decisions we make in our writing life.

Here are some of the many creative decisions you'll have to make:

- What genre do I want to write?
- What tropes should I include?
- Should I write standalones or series?
- What themes should I write to?
- How long will I make this book?

And here are some of the many business decisions you'll have to make:

- Who do I market to?
- How do I structure my business?

- How many books will I put on my production calendar this year?
- How many days per week will I work?
- Who will I collaborate with?

Your core motivation (your fear/desire combo), along with where you are in your development of your type, has likely been guiding your decisions without your realizing it. Sometimes those subconscious decisions made by our motivation limit us and are in response to outsized fear. In learning to notice these decision points (that often don't even feel like decisions because we make them so quickly), we can better assess where our fear is outsized and keeping us from what we truly want, and where we're following the truest form of our core desire.

By understanding why we make the kinds of decisions we make, and by reclaiming control over those decisions, we build the writing life we *intended* to build, one that will leave us feeling satisfied and fulfilled along the winding road.

WHY WE LEARN ALL 9 TYPES

I've observed an impulse in myself and others, at least initially, to hyperfocus on our dominant type (sometimes called "core type") when we first learn it. There's something beautiful and human about that. "Oh, hello there, self. Nice to meet you." It's wonderful to see ourselves as we are like never before. To be truly seen is such a pleasure, even if the viewer is our self. But it feels more than that, doesn't it? It can almost feel like the universe has finally seen you. That you are generally "being seen." Yes, it can feel exposing, too, but there can be relief found in truth, even if we don't necessarily like what we're seeing. As they say, the truth will set you free.

Once we get a taste of being seen in the intimate way that the Enneagram is known for, it's normal and healthy to want more. That desire for greater understanding of self is what leads to learning, which leads to growth.

However, there is a limit to how much we can learn about ourselves when we *only* learn about our lens. It's almost impossible to spot the things we take as givens or inalienable truths of the world until we learn more about people who function on entirely different fundamental premises.

Americans assume that we all understand what we're talking about when we talk about biscuits (my favorite Raymond Carver story) ... until they talk about biscuits to a Brit.

The most effective way to see that our fundamental premises about life are not universal is by learning about people who do not share these fundamental premises.

Your brain has been telling you that your Enneagram type's collection of established patterns is the *only* safe collection of established patterns if you want to avoid your core fear. That belief has been keeping you trapped in the same patterns, even after they stop being effective.

But when we learn about how the other types operate in such different ways and are able to witness real-life examples of them thriving in their lives without falling victim to our core fear, we can begin entertaining the idea that we could let go of some of our own patterns and the worst might not come to pass.

Until our minds, hearts, and bodies feel safe loosening their grip on our established patterns, there's not much growth and transformation available to us.

This is why learning about the other eight types is just as important to this process as learning about our own type.

Not to mention it'll make writing characters of different types much, much easier.

If you've ever wondered, *Why won't she just do the responsible thing?* or *Why won't he just lighten up?* then it's time to learn about the other eight Enneagram types. That's where the answers lie.

She won't do the "responsible" thing because her attentional patterns draw her toward the thing that will put her in the power position, and those two things are not the same.

He won't "lighten up" because his attentional patterns draw him into worry about y'all ending up in a tough spot where you part ways and he's left without support.

So, if you know about your type, that's a start. But you haven't even begun to unwrap the gifts of the Enneagram until you've learned about all nine types.

WHAT ARE THE TYPES?

I've delayed describing each of the nine types this far into the book because so much of our focus flows instinctively toward "Which type am I?" and can skip right on past "How do I use this tool for growth?"

But now that you know some of the basics of how the Enneagram works and how you can make it work for you, it's time to talk about each of the types. You may already know (or believe you know) your Enneagram type. Or maybe you're still unclear on it. Not a problem. You can read this book as many times as you need, and as you go through it, you will likely have a particular type emerge as a leader for your dominant type. If that happens, you can always go back and reread chapters through that new understanding.

Just so you know, it's not the end of the world if you mistype yourself for a while. I've seen people mistype themselves in all kinds of ways, and it can be an incredibly informative experience in and of itself. If we're clever and introspective, even mistyping can provide us with gems of insight. Why did you think you were that type? Is that the type of one of your parents that you've learned to adapt yourself to? In what ways have you been discouraged from seeing other parts of yourself and encouraged to act like that particular type?

The useful reflections we can mine from a mistyping are practically endless.

With that in mind, let's take a look at the nine types of the Enneagram.

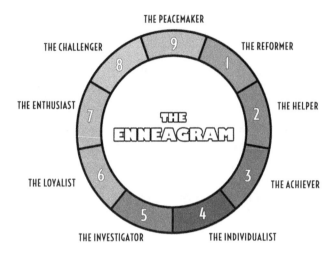

You see that every type has a descriptor associated with it that helps us remember the nature of that type. The above graphic includes the descriptors from the RHETI (Riso & Hudson) model because I think they're the most positive and accurate.* These are also the most commonly used among Enneagram specialists, though there are other ones you'll see crop up based on which school of Enneagram you're working with.

For instance, the Type 5 is called the Investigator (RHETI), the Observer (the Narrative Enneagram), the Wise Person (the Enneagram Spectrum of Personality

---

* You can read much more about how the RHETI model describes each of the nine types at www.enneagraminstitute.com or in Riso and Hudson's book *The Wisdom of the Enneagram*.

Styles), and the Quiet Specialist (the Integrative Enneagram).

Regardless of what descriptor you use, the defining qualities of the Five stay the same, because the type is based on an established core fear and core desire that drives the attentional patterns. This is why you frequently hear people refer to the numbers, and why learning the basics based on the numbers can be incredibly helpful for learning. The numbers are universal across the schools

Below are the core fears of the nine types.

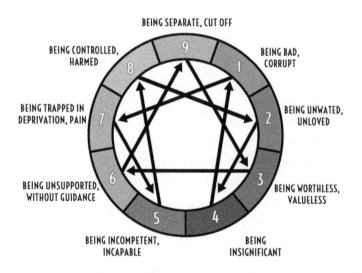

And here are the core desires.

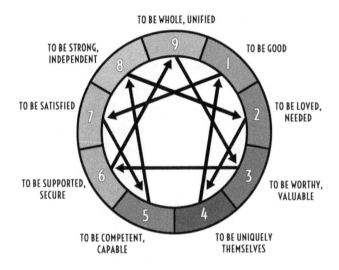

TO BE WHOLE, UNIFIED

TO BE STRONG, INDEPENDENT

TO BE GOOD

TO BE SATISFIED

TO BE LOVED, NEEDED

TO BE SUPPORTED, SECURE

TO BE WORTHY, VALUABLE

TO BE COMPETENT, CAPABLE

TO BE UNIQUELY THEMSELVES

You'll notice that the fear and desire are flip sides of the same coin. For instance, a Four wants to feel significant and fears lacking significance. Similarly, the Eight wants to feel powerful and be in control, and they fear being powerless and controlled by others.

In *Reclaim Your Author Career*, I provided brief descriptions of each type that reflect some of the common patterns that arise from the core motivations. Similar descriptions can be found all over the internet.

So, I've taken things a step further in this book with the descriptions below. Because we're focusing so specifically on your author career and making sure that *you* are sustainable, I've included descriptions that include how your Enneagram type shapes you as a *writer*. From studying the

Enneagram and working with authors for years, I've watched nine distinct types of writers emerge.

The thing about people is that we're usually shit at naming what gifts and energy we're bringing into a room with us (or into a story with us, as the case may be). There's a tendency to assume that what comes naturally to us isn't as valuable as what we have to work our asses off to develop. But if you have a big heart, why would you downplay that? What if, instead, we each leaned into our gifts and natural energy? What if that was the best way to ensure that every much-needed quality was present when we gathered?

So, allow me to introduce you to the kind of writer you are and where your natural energy and attention are flowing, so you can emphasize your gifts rather than devaluing them.

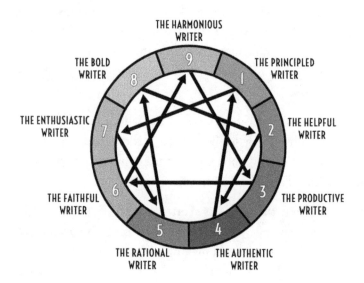

Type 1: The Principled Writer

A.K.A. The Reformer

You bring a strong sense of purpose to everything you do, and writing is no exception. Your need to rationalize what you do leans you toward enjoying a balanced and clear structure in your writing. You like to understand what each scene is intended to contribute in order to justify it being there. Your tendency is to sort things according to right and wrong, which makes the morally gray areas in your stories capture your attention and call for you to dig in and sort things out for yourself, the characters, and the readers. Your high standards of quality can become a siren's song to do *just one more revision pass*, yet you still expect yourself to publish as quickly as people who do one round of revisions or none at all. When you see a person or institution do something blatantly wrong and not suffer a consequence for it, you may find your whole day is derailed, and the need to mete out that correction or punishment yourself can become overwhelming. You channel your idealism into your stories through characters of impeccable integrity and stories of right battling wrong, light overcoming darkness. There are days when that critical voice inside your head is so loud that you want to give up, agree with the jerk, and crawl under the covers rather than getting your writing done. You worry a lot about publishing something that hurts or harms people you care about and triggers a pile-on, because your core fear of being bad or corrupt is always expecting to be confirmed by others. You have a vision of a better world, and it's your mission to move yourself and others toward it, whether you enjoy it or not. Others in the industry respect your self-composure and integrity and come to you for wisdom when they're feeling lost.

Type 2: The Helpful Writer

A.K.A. The Helper

You don't understand how the world can be so harsh. When those around you need help, you're the first one to offer it. Sometimes even when they don't need help, you're the first one to offer it. After all, what good are you if you're not helping? This sentiment carries over into your writing, as you enjoy weaving stories that heal and inspire readers to love themselves and others more deeply. Your protagonists often struggle to love themselves, become overwhelmed with everyone they care for, and must learn how to ask for help. This is your way of helping others explore the concept along with you, since you and that protagonist have a lot in common. You can anticipate the needs of your readership before they even know what they need, and when you deliver that, they become loyal and wild about your work. Your desire to help those around you often eats into your writing time, though, and you find yourself thinking, *I don't have time to write,* instead of *I need more boundaries around my time,* and *I don't have the energy to write,* instead of *I need to learn how to ask for help sooner.* You genuinely love helping others, and that makes you a social fulcrum in the publishing industry, but the meanness and pile-ons, sometimes between two authors you like, break your heart and drain you quickly. If writing books becomes a Herculean labor, it's probably because you're caring for too many people and not refilling your heart or protecting your time, though the lack of productivity is likely to cut directly to the heart of your self-worth. Other writers come to you with their problems because they know you're always ready to lend them a compassionate ear and maybe even a warm meal.

Type 3: The Productive Writer

A.K.A The Achiever

Productivity comes naturally to you. Where you feel friction in your writing process, you seek out ways to refine, adjust, and make yourself into a well-oiled machine to keep the books coming. The authors who don't do the same seem lazy and full of excuses to you, and you don't mind leaving them in the dust. You know how to perform well within whatever system you find yourself, including the publishing industry, and you're ready to do whatever it takes to reach your goals. You have a gift for anticipating the desires of your readers, including whom they would like *you* to be, and you understand that fulfilling those desires is the easiest way to achieve your publishing dreams. For that reason, writing to market or trend doesn't ruffle your feathers, but rather looks like a golden opportunity to sell the most books with the least resistance. Because you can anticipate your audience's desire, you know how to get their attention. If you're not careful, you'll end up chasing attention and forgetting to check if it's converting into book sales effectively. It can be hard for you to turn off the performance at the end of the day, though, and you may find that the self-promotion isn't limited to your books and author career, and you feel the need to sell who you are to your friends as well. That mask can become exhausting, but if you're not sure how to take it off, you end up spending more and more time in the arena of publishing where it benefits your bottom line. If you don't think you can make good money writing a series, the odds of your writing that series are next to nothing, even if you think it would be fun. You have no problem promising to deliver on a project before you know how you'll get it done, because you trust in your work ethic and savvy to find a way to at least meet the bare minimum of what's required. Other authors are in awe of what you've accomplished, and when they need help figuring out a path forward or how to communicate with their audiences, they seek your counsel.

Type 4: The Authentic Writer

A.K.A. The Individualist

The world is a messy and complicated place, and you don't consider yourself an exception. Your persistent and unnamable sense of longing compels you to capture the beauty and ugliness of the world in your stories. It's not just that conforming to popular tropes and genre structures is unpleasant for you—it seems contrary to your point of writing. You want to touch something authentic in yourself and your world, and that means going beyond the familiar territory. Your attention flows to the deeper parts of life, and the shallow is anathema unless you can find the complexity in it. Is it any surprise that you find yourself a little lost in your stories sometimes, unsure of the next step forward? The complexity you bring to your writing doesn't always convert into a clear marketing message that allows the right readers to understand that the book is for them, and so you might not be interested in even bothering with marketing as a result. You feel emotions, especially the heavier ones, strongly, and you channel that in your stories through lots of dark moments and darker humor. You like things messy because chaos seems to shake out the truths and expose the frauds around you, and you see a *lot* of frauds in this industry. Like Holden Caulfield, you sometimes feel surrounded by phonies who aren't willing to go deep and explore the murkiness of life. You're usually the oddball of the group, even at author events, and you prefer to be around authors who don't act like they have it all together. That being said, you are slightly fascinated by the ones who do seem to have it together, and you wonder what's broken in you that you can't be like that. When one of your writer friends feels down, they trust they can share the dark parts of their life with you without judgment.

Type 5: The Rational Writer

A.K.A. The Investigator

You wish you had more time on this earth to read, learn, and indulge your curiosity. When you find a topic interesting, you naturally fall headfirst into it and become an expert without thinking twice. Your stories are enriched with details from these often-obscure interests, and readers finish your books feeling smarter. You live your life rationally, trying to correct for the occasional emotions you feel that could bias your logical thinking, and your sympathetic characters tend to be highly rational as well. Emotionality tends to be reserved for unlikeable or even villainous characters. You enjoy solving the problems in your author business, so you don't often ask for help from others. Learning how to do it yourself not only keeps you from having to pay someone else to do it, but soothes your fear of being incompetent or incapable of handling things on your own. The idea of having a public persona on social media holds almost no appeal, as you don't like to be reachable at all hours of the day. Centering your books rather than your personality in your author brand is much more appealing. You create a fortress around yourself to protect from energy leaks, but the walls keeping your energy in are also keeping potential energy and inspiration out, which can leave you feeling empty and eventually make the writing process feel hollow. While you enjoy observing others, the demands of interpersonal relationships can feel like they're draining the life from you, so you're incredibly picky about whom you network with. and you need that energy for your learning and research. Fellow writers come to you when they need information or an objective opinion from someone they trust won't gossip about it after.

Type 6: The Faithful Writer

A.K.A. The Loyalist

The world is a scary place, and the best way to get through it is by making friends. Your stories undoubtedly center around groups of people coming together to support each other for a common cause. It's what your heart and soul need, and so you create it in your stories. You're probably drawn to stories of rebels banding together to overthrow an abusive authority. You feel drawn toward an interconnected business model with other authors, too, supporting each other through cooperatives, shared worlds, or even trading services. The biggest obstacle you face in getting the words down is wondering if you're doing it "right." When that doubt creeps up, you can start seeking certainty that can never be found, or looking to more confident industry voices for guidance. You often sort your contemporaries into allies and enemies, testing alliances for signs of betrayal. You're a responsible person by nature, understanding that adhering to the rules and expectations of the industry is the easiest way to keep a low profile and avoid ending up with a target on your back. Your fear of being on the wrong end of an industry witch hunt can overwhelm you if you give it the smallest bit of oxygen. You wish everyone could approach life more cooperatively rather than scheming and exercising rugged individualism. Your readers feel like they're on even ground with you, and you struggle to think of yourself as their leader. You struggle to trust authority even as you attach yourself to specific industry authority figures to guide you. The way forward out of doubt for you is always through faith—faith in yourself, in your friends, in humanity, in the universe, or a higher power. Your friends know that you have their back and will be there to wholeheartedly cheer them on and possibly even go into battle alongside them if need be.

Type 7: The Enthusiastic Writer

A.K.A. The Enthusiast

There are so many exciting stories to write and not enough time! The world is full of possibilities, and you sometimes struggle to balance experiencing the world and sitting down to write your escapist stories. The problem arises when the storytelling gets tough and the fun and novelty of the book wear off. Forcing yourself through that part of the process until you get to the fun part again pales in comparison to the dopamine hits instantly available to you through your phone, knocking out some pretty marketing graphics or a video, or hanging out with friends. Jumping between series leaves readers feeling jilted, and over time, the pressure to wrap up some of the many things you started can become overwhelming. When you do show up for your readers, your enthusiasm and joy are contagious, and they quickly sign up for whatever ride your book promises. It's in your nature not to stay down for long when you've been knocked on your butt—there are too many stories to write, and too many author events to experience. Other authors know you're always up for an adventure, and they reach out to you when they need to get away from their troubles for a little while and feel charged up and enthusiastic about their work again.

Type 8: The Bold Writer

A.K.A. The Challenger

You didn't become an author to be told what to do and how to run your business. You know what you want to accomplish and build, and you're going to do whatever it takes to get there, come hell or high water. Life is a battle that you intend to win, and your weapons are a strong will, honesty, and fearlessness. You write stories about people who overcome incredible odds with strength and grit or who boldly challenge injustices that no one else is willing to take on. Whether you mean to or not, you end up as a leader and authority figure to the authors you know, and of course you do; you can't abide being a follower or submitting to the authority of someone else. You're not for everyone, and that's okay. You didn't start writing to make friends, and you're aware of where your money comes from: your ideal readers. You tend to work as solo as possible, as offers of help or collaboration with other authors feel like a threat to your autonomy and independence. However, once do find "your people," you take them on as your responsibility and will defend their interests as you would your own. When abusive power rises to the top of the industry, your first impulse is always to challenge it and destroy it. Your author friends know you have their back in a fight, and they're put at ease by the fact that you say what you mean, no mincing words or double-speak.

Type 9: The Harmonious Writer

A.K.A. The Peacemaker

The universe is a single, rich story, and this comes through in the epic tales you weave. Your focus on harmony and the things that connect us are woven through your complex story worlds... and can also make it difficult for you to tolerate conflict in your own story. You enjoy writing about found family, a band of misfits coming together, and accepting communities. Inclusivity comes so naturally to you that readers can expect it in everything you write. The fear of offending your readers, however, might create friction when it comes to getting the words written and cause you to tone down or omit moments that would better serve the story if you left them as they were. You don't understand why everyone is always at odds with each other when they're more the same than different. Your easygoing attitude can lead you to lose track of how long it's been since you sat down and wrote, and sometimes you can't find the motivation to write at all, telling yourself that it doesn't matter to the bigger picture whether you publish another book or not. Your peaceful presence makes it easy for other authors to be around you, and you may have a lot of friends in the industry without even trying. Industry drama, however, can cause you to check out completely. You're able to see everyone's point of view, so you don't understand why people can't find a peaceful resolution with each other instead. Other authors come to you when they need calm from the storm or a nonjudgmental friend to listen to their woes.

Did you see a description that clicked with your writing life? If so, that's probably your Enneagram type. If a couple resonate, and you're not sure which one is you, go back and look at the core fears of each. Now, imagine a scenario where you can only avoid ONE of those fears. Which one are you going to avoid? If you can think of a situation that's already happened and look at the choice you make there, that's going to be solid data, since we sometimes fool ourselves about who we would be in a hypothetical situation. But if you can't conjure something from the past, use your storytelling abilities to concoct one. For instance, if you had to pick between being in a position where you're harmed or controlled (the Eight fear) or lacking value (the

Three fear), which one scares the shit out of you the most? This simple head-to-head approach can usually clear things up pretty quickly.

I'll admit, there's an inherent problem with using descriptions like the ones above to type. Each type has three "subtypes," and one of those subtypes is considered the countertype, which means it doesn't look *quite* like you'd expect someone of that type to look. If you're a countertype, then descriptions like those above can be a little trickier. So, if none of those seem to describe you, or a single type's core fear resonates but the description is only about fifty to seventy percent accurate, then you're probably a countertype.

I won't be going into the subtypes in this book, but thankfully Beatrice Chestnut, PhD MA, has all the resources you could ever want for this particular deep dive. You can check out her book *The Complete Enneagram: 27 Paths to Self-Knowledge*, or just google your Enneagram type with "subtypes" to find some general descriptions. The essential problem with the above descriptions of the nine types, or any description of them, is that there is no way to write one that includes specific cognitive, emotional, and behavioral patterns without having about ten to thirty percent of readers who are that type decide it doesn't describe them.

The existence of countertypes is just one of the reasons mistyping is so common. So, if you mistype yourself at any point of this exploration, don't worry. There's no shame in it. And it can teach you important things about yourself. I won't hit you with too much woo-woo stuff in this book, but one belief that I've had confirmed again and again in my work is that people find their type when they're ready to do the work on it, not a moment sooner or later than that. Sometimes mistyping is a crucial learning step of the journey to our true type, and there is no path around it, only through.

That being said, we do try to avoid mistyping as often as possible. In the following Concepts in Action, you'll see how nuanced the typing process can be and how useful having someone else work with you on it can be.

CONCEPT IN ACTION:
A Harmonious Writer (9) mistyping as an Authentic Writer (4)

Mario came to see me because he was completely out of motivation to write. He just couldn't bring himself to get going on it.

He mentioned on his intake questionnaire that he believed he was a Four, the Individualist, but he could see himself in all of the types. My default is to believe people about what type they say they are unless something really stands out to me that implies they might be another type instead. Going into the call, I had a little niggle in the back of my mind that doubted whether Four really matched, so I kept an eye out as we talked.

"Maybe you need a break," I suggested. "Is that possible for you to take?"

"All I've done is take breaks lately."

"Walk me through what happens when you sit down to write."

"I can't even get myself to do that. Every time I think about it, I end up scrolling on my phone or turning on Call of Duty."

As ridiculous as it sounds, I couldn't see Call of Duty being the game of choice for a Four. I know, I know. But it was another crumb that made me think there might be another type's patterns beneath this.

"Every time I think about writing, I wonder what the point is. It really doesn't matter if I write another book or not. Nobody would even notice."

"Have you been struggling to find readers?" I asked.

"No. I have plenty of those. Every time I get an email from them asking for the next book, it makes me want to hide away and play more video games."

The contradicting ideas of "nobody would miss me" and "people are literally begging me to write the next book" told me that we were dealing with some deep patterns here that were superseding reality. And the particular pattern made me wonder if Mario wasn't a Nine, the Peacemaker.

I see authors getting stuck between whether they're a Nine or a Four fairly frequently. It usually comes down to "I see a lot of myself in each type." Also, both are withdrawing types and pull back from others to meet their own child-hood needs (more on this in the next section). Nines have a pattern of enmeshment with others that can make it tricky for them to separate their qualities from those of people around them. They can usually tell they're not Eights, but other than that, they kinda see every type in themselves.

Meanwhile, Fours have a pattern of identifying with their emotions, so as they go through the range of human emotion, their sense of who they are can go for a ride. This can make it tricky for Fours to decide which version of themselves should take the test and read the type descriptions. They may feel more like a Five one day and a Seven the next. Add in the creativity needed to write a variety of characters, and the typing difficulties increase.

I asked Mario to tell me what about the Four sounded like him. He said he withdraws to his own world a lot, his family always called him the artistic one, and he tends to see all sides of things.

It was time to start in on some differentiating questions.

"How do you feel when you see authors you consider to be contemporaries having an easy time writing and publishing when you don't?" I asked.

He shrugged. "Fine. I'm happy for them. I know that doesn't sound believable, but I do. I'm glad they're not feeling what I'm feeling right now."

I wasn't seeing the Four's vice of Envy anywhere in that answer.

I asked him what his three highest scores were on the free test when he took it, and he said Four, Nine, and Six, in that order.

"What are your emotions like? Do they come in big highs and lows generally, or are you more even-keeled?"

He said definitely more even-keeled. Especially lately.

Another point in the Nine column.

I suggested Mario read up about the Type 9 and let me know if any of it also sounded true for him. Approaching his specific problem by addressing the wrong type's patterns wouldn't work. I was fairly certain he was a Nine, but I don't want to get ahead of myself.

Once he read a few sections about the Nine, he said that was definitely him. It was describing his experience scarily well.

From there, I was able to point out to him that he is in a Nine pattern of "it doesn't matter, I don't matter," while the reality was telling me that his next book really did matter to the readers. He laughed when he saw the contradiction he was holding in his mind. That laugh was the most energy I'd seen from him on the call. A part of him had woken up. We were on the right track.

I asked him what it felt like in his body when the pattern of "it doesn't matter, I don't matter" surfaced. "I get tired. I feel like I want to take a nap for the rest of the day."

I asked if he was getting enough quality sleep or had any health issues that would otherwise make him tired, and he said his sleep was fine, as long as he didn't stay up too late playing Call of Duty, and he didn't have any health problems that he knew of.

"The next time you feel tired, pause and ask yourself if the pattern is coming up. If it is, do something to make yourself feel alive in your body." He said he liked push-ups, so we went with that. Anything to interrupt the pattern that led to the lethargy.

Would that get the book written? No. But until he could interrupt the pattern enough to lessen its grip on him, he would definitely not get more words written. This is slow work, and when we're deep into our patterns, we have to disrupt them before we can build new ones that help us achieve our goal.

When I checked in with Mario a week later, he said he was starting to notice the pattern more (though he had fallen victim to the Call of Duty pattern a few times, which I expected would happen so long as he had access to the game). The few times he'd done the push-ups instead of jumping right into distractions, he felt much better. He'd even managed to sit down at the computer after one of the times and get some words in. It felt great.

I told him to remember that feeling and keep in mind the steps to get there. He could repeat them any time he noticed the initial pattern. The more he did that, the easier it would be and the sooner he would feel like his old, productive writer self. The choice was his now, because he *saw* the choice.

CONCEPT IN ACTION:
A Productive Writer (3) mistyping as a
Principled Writer (1)

Madeleine was tired, but couldn't slow down the runaway train that was her author business. She wanted help looking at all of her projects and deciding which ones to cut. I became tired just looking over her project list. She already had over eighty books published, and so she'd decided to spend more time marketing her backlist.

She had not taken any time away from marketing her front list to do it. So, now she had more work.

When someone finds themselves in this spot, the fix is never as simple as someone like me saying, "Stop doing these two projects." First of all, Madeleine was unlikely to agree with my suggestions, or else she would've already cut those projects. But mostly, the problem was being caused by an underlying fear pattern, and unless we addressed that pattern, she would keep filling her schedule until she was at this stress point, over and over again.

Madeleine had said on her intake form that she had taken a test and was a One, the Reformer. But on her form I noticed a few sentences that didn't seem One-ish. She was much less worried about meeting her own quality standards (as a One would) and much more worried about her books being "good enough" for her readers. She struggled with perfectionism, which Ones tend to, but certainly don't have a monopoly on.

Perfectionism is an easy habit to pick up, especially for women in a society that gives us little grace when we make mistakes. Also, in my experience, daughters of narcissistic mothers or daughters of less healthy Type 1 mothers frequently develop perfectionist tendencies. I didn't know anything about Madeleine's mother, though. She might've been a lovely woman.

"Why did you decide to take on all the backlist projects now?" I asked.

"I see other authors with fewer books than I have making more money, and they all seem to be focusing on backlist."

"And what emotions come up for you when you see other authors with fewer books making more money than you?"

"I feel like I'm not good enough. That I'm a complete failure. I should be able to get my backlist selling without it running me into the ground."

The inadequacy and feelings of failure sounded like the patterns of a Three to me more so than a One.

I asked her how attached she was to the idea of being a One. She said it fit her really well... but did I think she was something else?

When I suggested she might see some of herself in the Three, her reaction was immediate. "Oh God, no. I'm not the salesy type. I hate putting my face on social media or asking people to buy my books. I really don't think I'm a Three."

That didn't rule it out for me.

"What do you mean when you say you don't feel good enough?"

"I feel like I'm letting everybody down. That readers and other authors expect me to be a certain way, and I just keep disappointing them and falling short. I don't have the sales that other authors do, and trying to keep up wears me out. I don't get any fuel from competition."

Madeleine's objections to exploring the possibility that she might be a Three were all based on stereotypical *traits* that are often associated with the Achievers, but what I kept hearing from her was that she wasn't living up to the standards of *others*. She felt like a failure because she couldn't deliver to people the kind of person they wanted her to be.

If she were a One, I would've expected to hear more talk about how she was disappointing herself and not living up to her own *internal* high standards of conduct, responsibility, and performance.

"How much extra time do you spend getting your books up to a higher standard of quality than your readers even care about?" I asked.

"What do you mean?"

"How much do your readers care about typos, say?"

"Not very much at all."

"So how much time do you spend weeding out typos before publication?"

"Hardly any," she replied.

"It doesn't bother you to publish books knowing there are typos in there?"

"No. I have a lot of typos in my books. I'm not a strong speller, and my proofreader is okay but not great."

It was time: "There's a subtype of Three that I want to tell you about. You tell me if any of it resonates."

I told her about the Self-Preservation Three subtype, about how the pattern of Vanity expressed itself by working hard not to appear vain. How it looked a lot like a One, but at the end of the day gave more attention to being seen as a good person by others than meeting an internal standard of goodness. As I explained the difference between the One and the Self-Preservation Three, I could see it click.

"Okay," she said, "I think I'm that. And my mother is *definitely* a One."

CONCEPT IN ACTION:
A Faithful Writer (6) mistyping as an
Enthusiastic Writer (7)

Danielle was jumping ship on her genre. She wanted me to talk her out of it.

Danielle had only recently taken a free online Enneagram test, and her top score was a Seven. She thought that fit pretty well, considering she was bailing on her genre. She, like many people, associated being a Seven with avoidant personality traits. She saw her genre shifting possibly as the "shiny object syndrome" that Sevens often deal with.

I asked her to describe what was going on. "I started writing reverse harem when it was a piping-hot genre in Kindle Unlimited. My sales are dipping big time lately, and I hear all the other RH authors talking about theirs taking a nose-dive too. I want to bail and start building in a new genre before my sales bottom out."

I could see where this reasoning might *appear* like shiny object syndrome or losing interest as soon as the pain point hit. But it didn't sound like that to me.

"Do you still enjoy writing RH?" I asked.

"Oh yeah, it's my favorite thing to write. But if it's not selling, I need to find something else that is and start building that."

I certainly saw the future-focused orientation of the Seven in that response, but there was another future-focused type that stood out to me as well: the Six.

You wouldn't think that a Six and Seven get confused in typing, but it does happen, especially if the Six is a counterphobic type, meaning they tend to confront what scares them more often than run from it. That doesn't mean they *never* run from it by, say, jumping ship on a genre that's on a downward slide with readers.

"What's your relationship to risk?" I asked. "Are you risk averse?"

Danielle said, "Not at all. When something scares me, I run toward it. I went skydiving, did a backpacking trip on my own for a month, and I was the one who first asked my now-husband on a date."

Again, I saw how some of the behaviors Danielle described might sound Seven-ish. Sevens are often down for any novel experience, even something like skydiving. They're also known for their love of travel, as it puts all kinds of novel experiences within arm's reach. Sevens, as assertive types, would also likely ask someone out if they wanted to take that person out.

But the motivation behind these things wasn't novelty for Danielle as much as it was to confront her fears.

"Would you consider yourself an optimistic person?" I asked.

"Not really."

"Would other people describe you that way?"

"Definitely not."

That was the final nail in Seven's coffin for me. I described the counterphobic Six to her and asked if she recognized any of that. She pointed out a few things in her history that she thought were clearly based on her being a Seven, but once I reflected some of her own words back to her about how she did those things *because* they scared her, she gave in and agreed. "I guess I really wanted to be a Seven. It sounds way more fun."

I wasn't surprised to hear this. A lot of people hopefully mistype themselves as Sevens, since it's known as the "fun" type. Sixes don't tend to want to see themselves as Sixes because being "the anxious one" doesn't draw people in as much as being the "up for anything" type. As someone of the "anal retentive" and "self-critical" type, I totally get that. But we do ourselves a huge favor when we deal with the reality rather than our wishes.

Looking at her genre switch through this new lens allowed us to have a much different discussion. She was probably pushing her limits by being exclusive to Amazon in the first part. Sixes are naturally more sensitive to risk, and even more so when they have all their eggs in one basket. They keep a vigilant eye on that basket for any signs of it tumbling over.

Rather than talking Danielle out of starting in a new genre, I *encouraged* her to start investing energy in a backup plan. It didn't necessarily mean writing a new genre, but maybe taking a single one of her RH series out of Kindle Unlimited and working toward selling it direct would offer her the security her nervous system needed to get back to focusing on her writing. Sixes can work on building up a higher risk tolerance, but in a case like this, her lower risk tolerance was probably working in her best interest, so why change a good thing?

Once she started piecing together an action plan for creating more stability for her RH pen name, her attention stopped drifting toward other genres. And so this Faithful Writer could comfortably remain monogamous with her existing readership while continuing to enjoy her polyamorous heroines.

SECTION 3: WHAT MOTIVATES YOU?

WHAT YOU SWEAR MOTIVATES YOU... MIGHT NOT

I have invested a lot of time and energy in my life being suspicious of my motives, so I have a story, a warning, and some hard-earned wisdom to share with you about this process before we start to go deep on it.

Here's the story. It's one my father tells about me at least once a year. It's that when I was a child, I would cry to get what I wanted, and then as soon as I got what I wanted, I would stop crying. This is a common thing to see in children, and when you boil it down, it's really just two pieces of information: I became upset when my needs weren't met. When my needs were met, I stopped being upset. From everything I've learned about emotional regulation in my life, the story *I* would weave from this is likely that I was a child who was able to express emotions appropriate to the situation and didn't get trapped in negative emotions once the situation changed.

That's not the story my father has come away with from the same set of facts, though. The story I grew up hearing about myself since I was a very young child, and still hear frequently today, is that I've used emotions to manipulate those around me from a young age. Never mind that the idea that little children even *can* "manipulate" fully grown adults is ass-backward. Never mind that children must rely on the adults around them to meet their needs. Never mind that society actively reinforces the idea that women and girls are inherently manipulative to avoid asking men and boys to take full accountability for their actions. I had a need, and I cried when it wasn't met and stopped crying once it was met, so I was born manipulative.

Internalizing this story about myself—that I used emotional expression as a weapon from the moment I involuntarily entered this world—led to a whole array of unfortunate emotional patterns as it filtered through my Enneagram lens of wanting to be a good person and fearing that I was corrupt at my core. I spent three decades crying only when I was alone because that was the *only* way I could trust that I was genuinely sad and not crying to manipulate someone around me, as I'd been led to believe I had a natural propensity to do. I struggled to express many emotions—joy, sadness, disappointment, love, gratitude, insecurity—subconsciously equating all displays of emotions with this dark, insidious desire inside of me to manipulate perfectly capable adults around me. I've played small and neglected to exert a positive influence on the world around me, lumping in *influence* with my definition of *manipulation*. The list goes on, but essentially, I've spent a lot of—way too much—time and energy on this earth questioning my own motivations.

Am I doing this nice thing for my friend because I love them, or am I doing it because it makes me feel good to be the kind of person who does this?

Why do I keep telling this specific story when I'm out with friends? What am I trying to tell them about myself, and why do I feel the need to do that?

I will say that as unfortunate as it is that so many younger versions of me were stripped of their ability to trust that they were a good person who deserved to express emotions, my uncertainty about my true motivations led me to engage with the Enneagram. And now you're reading this book, and I hope it's useful for you to engage with your motivations in a healthier way than I learned to engage with mine.

So, that's the story. Here's the warning: if you find that this work is leading you to a place of mistrusting your own motivations *to the point of paralysis*, take a break from it and find someone like a therapist or Enneagram coach who can help guide you along. While we may have some revelations along the way that what we thought was motivating to us was not truly motivating, the point of this work is not to trust yourself *less*. There may be a brief dip in our trust of our motivations as we unravel some of this, but if it seems more than temporary, or you lose faith that there's something better and more solid for you to anchor yourself to on the other side, it's time to tell your ego to take a back seat and then seek the support you need. A little curiosity about why we do what we do can go a long way, but if you find you're *overly* suspicious of yourself, then you've taken a wrong turn and may need someone with experience to help you find the path again.

And now for the wisdom: every Enneagram type has a way of pursuing what it wants. Fulfilling our desires can certainly look like attempts at manipulating others, and that's just life, baby. Every type does this a little differently, and it's nothing to get too worked up about. Living in a society means living in a web of people trying to get their needs met and exerting influence over others. Isn't that interesting? Don't beat yourself up for trying to get your needs met, is what I'm saying. If you realize you're being manipulative in ways that go beyond influence into coercion, then sure, take a beat to reconsider. But allow yourself some grace here.

In short, it's important to allow yourself to be motivated in a self-serving way from time to time without heaping on judgment about it. For instance, do you help others because you love them or because you like the way you feel about yourself when you help them? What if it's both? Could you be okay with that? Can you exist peacefully beside that tension?

The possibility of mixed motivations, rather than pure ones, is a tension that will likely exist in us until we die, so part of the work is learning to be okay with that. We may never reach a global consensus on whether selfish intentions are acceptable so long as they lead to positive outcomes for others, yet we can still find harmony inside of ourselves despite that.

Holding that tension lightly, we can then drill down to gain more clarity on our own primary motivations and those of others around us. After all, sometimes our motivations are mostly fear- or ego-based, and we convincingly fool ourselves about them to justify cruel behavior. That's probably not something we want to let slide in ourselves. But again, curiosity rather than suspicion may be the trick to doing this without being sucked into a black hole.

The goal is to look for that balance between being honest with ourselves about why we're doing what we're doing and not demanding certainty in our knowledge of it to the point of driving ourselves insane. Instead, choose curiosity. Form educated theories. Explore them. Run experiments. Assess the data then form even more educated theories.

For instance, if you find that you hate marketing and have a block against it, you can look to the parts of this process you love—maybe writing the scene where the hero and heroine finally reconcile—and extract what about that moment really fires you up. Your Enneagram type will be a decoder ring for this process. Then, once you understand why you're motivated to write the reconciliation scene, you can take the essence of it and ask, "How can I inject this into my marketing to make that part of selling books enjoyable and invigorating for me?"

The process of better understanding what drives us can be a healthy step toward sustainability—or a new and interesting punishment. It's up to us to keep a close eye on it and ask for support from others when we sense we might have slipped from curiosity to suspicion. And if we stay awake to that possibility, then we can dive deep into this and uncover some seriously precious gems for our author career and beyond.

MONETARY MOTIVATION

One of the common mistakes that authors make is believing that money itself motivates them. It does not.

"But it does! You're wrong! Checking my sales each days keeps me motivated!"

I hear you. When the money dips, your adrenaline shoots up, which can give you energy and focus. When the money pours in, watching those stats is a nice dopamine hit.

That's not what I mean when I say that money itself isn't motivating. What I mean is this: *what it means to you* to have money is what motivates you to chase money.

This probably sounds like meaningless semantics, but I promise it's not.

What we must look at is how we let the money we have (or don't have) make us feel about ourselves. Many if not most people don't consider it in these terms, and it's to their detriment. If you equate money with freedom, for instance, then whatever money you *don't* have could very well feel like a lack of freedom. The obvious solution? Keep chasing money until you're finally free. Woohoo! What could possibly go wrong?

Or, if you equate money to worth, then when your royalties dip, you better step it up and make some more moolah, whatever it takes, so you can stop feeling like a worthless pile of garbage.

I mean, yikes, right? When we see it spelled out like that, the unhealthiness of this mode of thinking is obvious. But also... it's sort of the standard for us, isn't it? Until we notice we're doing it, we keep doing it. Our subconscious minds work in quite overly simplistic and binary terms. Part of being a thoughtful adult is working to bring those beliefs to the forefront so we can inspect them with more nuance and stop being controlled by fear-based misconceptions.

That said, not having money for the essentials of living can certainly cut into our daily happiness. I would be a real asshole to ignore the impact of poverty on our mental, emotional, and physical health. I would also have to have suffered amnesia, since I've been in the spot where I'm staring a hole into my balance sheet, trying to bully it into having enough money for me to buy groceries. And compared to many people in the U.S. (where I'm writing this from) and around the world, my situation was more like Poor Lite. I had friends who weren't as poor and could've spotted me if I needed. I had a college degree. I had options, even if I didn't have money in my account. Not everyone has that.

Poverty is a tremendous strain on our body, mind, and heart, so until we remedy the larger systems that keep people economically stuck, and until we can collectively muster the humility of "there but for the grace of God go I" to create more social safety nets for our downtrodden fellow humans, it's important that we don't stray into piling responsibility onto the individual to dig themselves out of poverty that didn't result from their individual decisions. A health crisis when we're uninsured between jobs, chronic illness, generational poverty, trauma, being a victim of crime, and so many other things outside of our control can land us in financial situations that are almost impossible to dig ourselves out of.

If the money you're making from your writing is not meeting your basic needs, then you will need to find another source of income to avoid the chronic stresses of poverty. This is not the book to help you find an individual solution to that systemic issue.

There are, however, quite a few authors who have enough money to meet their basic needs and are still deep into craving more money. Maybe the money for essential needs comes from their royalties, another job, a spouse, an inheritance, or some other source. But they are able to pay their bills fairly consistently, and they can afford to eat three meals a day. These are the authors I tend to work with. Maybe money is tight, but their financial concerns are focused more on investing in retirement, saving for a down payment on a home, or being able to feel a little more breathing room for when unexpected expenses arise.

So, when I talk about money in this section, I'm not referring to situations where you simply do not have enough money to afford your essentials. I'm talking about once you get up above that line and are slipping into that more, more, more mindset.

Two people could feel motivated to earn $1,000,000 for their family, but the desire behind having that much money may be completely different from one person to the next. Would having $1,000,000 feel like the security they're craving? Or would it simply give them a rush of power? And when they hit that goal, would they be satisfied, or would they only crave more?

When discussing motivation, it's important we draw a distinction between the energy of aspiration and the energy of *craving*. Most of us probably understand the difference instinctively, or at least we have a general sense of the connotations. However, I hear a *lot* of industry leaders, in the name of "motivation," preach about how we should dream bigger, bigger, bigger and *never* put a cap on how much money we want to make! Don't limit your financial dreams! You can always make more!

Okay, sure. But at what cost to everything else? At what cost to your basic need for rest? At what cost to your true quality of life?

While I'm all for working through upper-limit problems, the wild-eyed calls to "dream bigger!" usually carry *major* craving energy that we'd do well to watch out for. The person encouraging you to shoot for the financial stars has likely *not* done their work of deconstructing what they let money tell them about themselves—their freedom, worth, goodness, power, etc. You don't need a billion dollars in the bank to be happy. You don't even need a million.*

Research on the correlation between money and happiness suggests that if you make a million dollars, great! Good for you! But there is other work to be done on your inner world before the peace, joy, and satisfaction you were seeking will show up on your doorstep with a hot dinner to share.

Let's say we set a big, audacious financial goal and then hit it. What happens to our motivation? Does it disappear?

---

* Ahuvia, Aaron. "If money doesn't make us happy, why do we act as if it does?." *Journal of economic psychology* 29, no. 4 (2008): 491-507.

Many of us will set dollar amounts so high that we spare ourselves the potentially jarring experience of ever attaining that goal and realizing that we missed the point, and, more upsettingly, that we missed out on meaningful moments in life to get there.

This is why I talk about money motivations. Our assumptions around money and happiness are usually way off. That way you think you'll feel about yourself when you hit $1,000,000 or $10,000,000? You won't feel it if you don't practice feeling it about yourself along the way.

WHAT ARE YOU HOPING TO FEEL?

Let's return to the example of making your first million from book sales. And if you've already made a million off book sales, pick a higher number that you're shooting for.

When we motivate ourselves with a financial goal like this, what we're actually doing is expecting that when we hit that goal, we will feel a certain way.

This could be an emotion like relief or joy. Maybe we think that we'll feel proud of ourselves in a way we haven't been able to access before. Perhaps we expect it to feel like crossing the finish line of a marathon. You did it! You succeeded! You are a successful author!

(As someone who's waited by the Austin Marathon finish line, I can tell you that most of the expressions I've seen of people crossing that line are, frankly, ones I never hope to make.)

In short, without realizing it consciously, we're expecting to suddenly feel certain things about ourselves that we didn't before.

The problem is that emotional patterns don't work that way. You don't start feeling completely different about yourself in a day. New emotional pathways must be cultivated. If you have not intentionally developed and reinforced your pathways for the emotion of joy, you are unlikely to suddenly feel it fully for the first time in a situation that might objectively be considered joyful. The emotions that we don't currently have strong access to must be developed like muscles. This includes the way we feel about ourselves.

If you fear-motivate yourself throughout your career with the idea that you're not good enough *yet*, it's unlikely that you will hit an arbitrary monetary or publication benchmark and magically develop the ability to feel like you are, finally, good enough. The *I'm not good enough* patterns are the ones you've cultivated. They're the seeds you've watered, and they don't grow the coveted *I'm enough* blooms.

We must pay attention to the ideas about ourselves that we use as motivation. If we're motivating ourselves with thoughts like *I'm weak* or *I'm a failure* or *everything I produce is embarrassing garbage*, we simply will not wake up one day to check our sales dashboard, find that we've that $1,000,000 mark, and feel things like *I can do anything*, *I'm a success*, and *everything I produce is genius*.

Our brains may try to get us there. We may even do something like say, "Yay! I finally made it! I'm a real author now!" Or maybe we take our partner out to dinner to cele-brate. Or maybe we post about it online in one of those faux-inspirational "I did it and so can you" posts.

All of that is different from *feeling* it. In fact, the more strongly we feel positively about ourselves leading up to hitting that goal, the less likely we'll feel the need to post about it to others in a *performance* of our worth, strength, goodness, etc.

A simple but effective pattern-shifting exercise that I do with my clients is to ask them what they expect to feel when they reached their big external goal (usually a mone-tary- or sales-based one, but sometimes it's the number of books published). Then I ask them how they are cultivating that feeling about themselves and the world *today?*

The answer I receive is usually "I'm not," to which I will respond, "Then you won't feel it when you hit that goal either."

There's a deep fear underlying this pattern of restricting ourselves from the positive feelings until we hit our goal. The fear is that if we allow ourselves to feel successful or relieved or joyful *today*, then we're less likely to complete the tasks that we believe will help us reach that larger goal later on.

We're using deprivation of these positive emotions as moti-vation: "I only get to feel that way once I have reached my goal, therefore I need to do everything I can to reach that goal."

This is a simply brilliant formula for building a miserable life! And what's more than that, it's not going to fuel you creatively through the ups and downs of being a writer.

Think about it: could a thousand days of toil ever be worth a single day of gratification?

(Sevens: "ABSOLUTELY NOT.")

And the reality is that this pattern of behavior does not result in what we hope it will result in. Feelings like self-love, satisfaction, compassion, pride in oneself, and self-acceptance are not things that exist outside of us that we may one day stumble upon.

THE BIG SHIFT

When we stop depriving ourselves of those things that we seek, imagining that they will magically appear once we make our first million/billion/quintillion, or once we make the NYT Bestseller List, or once we've published one hundred books, we will undoubtedly feel our motivation *shift*.

We may find ourselves feeling less motivated to do certain tasks that we used to do regularly. Answering emails from every single reader might feel like a grind. Or writing four thousand words a day, five days a week, to publish a million words a year suddenly becomes about as easy as climbing Everest without a guide.

That's not a bad thing.

And louder for the people in the back: *That's not a bad thing!*

In the words of the universe's most informative guide: DON'T PANIC!

Many of the tasks that we put on our to-do list are only there to make us *feel* productive or *feel* like we think an author should. We've told ourselves lies like "Every successful author does this thing, and therefore I must too."

Responding to every reader email might've been something you were doing because you'd built your sense of worth on every single person you encounter liking you. When you cultivate a sense of worth independent of what others think of you, your fear-based motivation to respond to every single email, regardless of how idiotic, rude, or emotionally draining it might be, will naturally diminish. Congratulations! You just got a little bit of your time and energy back! May you use it with intention.

And maybe you were writing that many words each day because there was a voice in your head telling you: "Real writers don't wait for inspiration. They push through. Don't be a wimp." When you address the need to prove something to that voice (does it sound a little bit like a particular authority figure from your childhood? Just curious), your fear-based motivation will diminish, and writing with that militaristic discipline will likely feel less appealing. You may not be able to write as much each day, and there may be days when you don't write, but guess what? You will feel okay with it. I know that might be hard to imagine right now, but that's because there's still work to do. Future you will be okay with writing less and, say, taking a vacation with their family. Or spending less time writing to "feel like a writer" and giving more time to learning effective and automated marketing and advertising skills, earning the same amount of money with less effort. Woohoo!

When we begin to prioritize the everyday experience, our attention will necessarily shift. The fear motivation will take a step back, and it can take some time for the spell to lift before a healthier and more sustainable motivation steps up. It may not feel as intense, either, but it will be rich and robust, and come from within.

I want you to be ready for that shift and expect it, because at first, it might feel like demotivation, and those unhealthy narratives in your head might still be hanging on for dear life, jumping at you from time to time with the negativity. When that happens, you're likely to backslide to the fear motivations because they're the most familiar.

When you feel that temptation is the best time to remind yourself that you are already the thing you seek. (More on that in the section on resilience.)

And besides, once we take a break from the fear-based motivation, it's almost impossible for it to work as effectively on us as it once did. As we change and grow into more love, acceptance, and peace in who we are, the fears that used to motivate us will no longer be as effective. When the Two connects to deep self-love, for instance, the fear of not being worthy of love slips away. The lengths to which the Two once went to "earn" love will begin to appear too silly and fruitless to continue.

I would argue that this is a positive turn of events. If you believe that feeling good about yourself and your work every day *cannot* lead to a bright future, then I implore you to ask yourself *where* you learned that belief. Sure, never saving a dollar, never delaying gratification, and spending hours scrolling on your phone are unlikely to build a meaningful life long term, but I think you'll find that those behaviors also do not make you feel genuinely healthy on a daily basis. They, too, are distractions from a deep fear.

Feeling good about yourself does not mean living irresponsibly, and it certainly does not mean feeling superior to other people. In fact, when you have a positive but not inflated self-image, you are likely to find that you easily make those healthy choices that you've been trying to guilt yourself into making all this time. Doing so may seem suddenly obvious: fuel your body with what it needs, celebrate it through movement, set boundaries on your time, stop saying yes when you mean no, reach out to your friends when you think about them, cry when you're sad, and dance around when you're happy.

Feeling positively about yourself includes recognizing that you are human, and while you may fuck some shit up from time to time, there's a part of you that deeply wants to bring a meaningful story to the world, and where others only think about it, you are doing it. There are a million reasons *not* to write a book, but you're being brave and doing it anyway. I hope you can be proud of yourself for that today and not wait until the book is finished before you acknowledge your courageous action.

CONCEPT IN ACTION:
An Enthusiastic Writer (7) chases a feeling

When I asked Anna how many books she had in progress, she listed off five in various stages of completion. "And how many have you published?" I asked her. "Four," she told me. "Across two series."

No small achievement, but it did strike me as notable that she had more books in progress than she had published novels. That's unusual to see.

The reason she had scheduled an appointment with me was because she had two preorder deadlines coming up quick on books that were nowhere near where she would've liked them to be at this stage. Which two of the five WIPs? I couldn't tell you. I was having trouble keeping up with all her projects.

Anna was stressed, borderline frantic. She was an Enneagram 7, the Enthusiast, so I could see that she was spiraling down her levels of development and moving into her stress type.

"I screwed up so bad," she said. "I don't know why I always do this. It's so stupid and I never learn." The Inner Critic, who's most notably associated with the One, was showing its ugly head in Anna's self-castigation. I know the voice of the Inner Critic well, so when she speaks through anyone else's mouth, I still recognize her. (Or sometimes him. Sometimes them. Our inner critic can sound like different former authority figures in different contexts.)

Under prolonged stress, a Seven will begin to take on some of the flavor of their stress type, the One. This is not a healthy version of One. What this usually looks like is the Inner Critic making an appearance. The Inner Critic is the "adult" disciplinarian inside of us (essentially the superego), but it isn't bringing the love and compassion that we would hope an adult might, though the intended function of it is to protect us from some sort of pain.

When a Seven falls into the pattern of starting projects that seem pleasurable but bailing once it stops being a fun experience and starts being painful, they can find themselves in a situation like Anna, were they're essentially flopped down on the floor with half-finished projects spread out all around them. They're waiting for an adult to come in and clean it up, to fix this mess they've made. Somewhere along the line, the Seven has learned that the best adult for the job is the Taskmaster. The Taskmaster is the Seven's inner critic who comes, usually too late, to cobble together closure on some of the works in progress. Starting meaningful projects is pleasurable, but finishing them is where satisfaction really kicks in *because* there was pain associated with the process. But when a Seven doesn't build their tolerance for that pain, they never break through to the true satisfaction they're seeking (their core desire).

Unfortunately, the Taskmaster, while pretending to be well intentioned, seems to believe that criticism and self-admonishment are the ultimate inspiration for productivity. And you know what? They *can* be motivating. But only for some people, sometimes. And being the receiver of the Inner Critic's advice is not a pleasant experience at all.

It's also never the *only* way to motivate oneself—in fact, it's usually the most harmful way to go about it.

Anna's Taskmaster was easy enough to spot. It was the Taskmaster, after all, who set those preorder deadlines in an attempt to bully Anna out of her usual patterns of distraction.

Fun fact: bullying people out of patterns (even yourself) doesn't work well.

Anna, like many of the Sevens I work with, explained to me about her ADHD diagnosis and how because of that, coupled with the horrible things her Taskmaster had been saying to her, her self-esteem was at an all-time low and her confidence in her ability to finish what she started was finally hitting rock bottom.

Before I approached the subject of what to do about the preorder deadlines, I asked Anna why she was trying to do so many projects at once.

"I've been at this for so long, and I hardly have anything to show for it," she told me. "I really want something to show for it finally."

"And how many published books exactly would feel like 'something to show for it'?"

It was clear that she hadn't put a number to that yet. Our nebulous, numberless goals are often the things that haunt us when we startle awake at three in the morning. Making them specific is the first step to assessing whether they're realistic and why we chose that number.

"Ten books," she said. "I think I would feel differently if I had ten books published."

"You have five in progress and four already published, so once you finish everything that's in progress you only have one more book to write until you feel accomplished, according to your definition. But let's talk more about what 'feeling accomplished' would really feel like."

I had Anna close her eyes and asked her to describe what she expected it would feel like when she had ten books to her name.

"I think it would feel like a relief. No one can say that someone who has ten books out isn't a real author. I think if I had ten books published, I could stop beating myself up about it when I go for a while between publishing books like I am now."

Ah. That was at the real heart of the matter, then. She wanted permission to start treating herself a little better, and she'd attached an arbitrary accomplishment to the permission.

She was right that having ten books to her name would be no small feat, but when she said her goal aloud, it was clear that what she actually desired was relief from self-criticism.

This was great news. While I was sure she would eventually get to that arbitrary marker of ten books (so long as her Taskmaster didn't take all the fun out of it for her and make her quit before that achievement), the real issue she faced was one she could begin solving right then. The antidote to her crisis was a new emotional pattern—self-compassion—

which would rescue her from the very thing that was keeping her locked in a cycle.

The fundamental pain of Sevens may not always be diagnosed as ADHD, and it may not always present that way, but for most of the Sevens I worked with, they've settled for a pattern of self-abuse rather than addressing the deeper problem of their low tolerance to discomfort and hair-trigger FOMO. When a person's pain/discomfort tolerance is as low as that of many Sevens, even the slightest pain will shoot one's attention in the direction of the nearest exit. This makes it incredibly hard to focus on a project, especially one as rife with emotional discomfort as writing a book. The start of the project might feel fun and exciting, but hit that messy middle, and their attention just can't seem to stay in one place.

The cycle for an Enneagram 7 writer often looks like this: get very excited about a project and start writing it. Usually the Seven stays excited about it until that fifty or sixty percent point hits, and writing becomes more of a slog. The Seven then begins creating more pleasurable distractions, which eventually activates the Taskmaster. At first, the Taskmaster is subtler, and the Seven has, over time, become dependent on the Taskmaster as the responsible adult voice in their life. As long as the Taskmaster isn't the *overwhelming* voice in their head, the Seven will often keep moving on to new projects that seem fun and shiny and promise an escape from the discomfort of getting through the messy middle of their existing WIPs (or whichever part of the process the Seven struggles with the most). So, rather than developing sustaining practices that increase the Seven's pain tolerance and focus over time, the Seven may prefer to continue throwing their party until the Taskmaster comes banging on the door. Sr. Officer Taskmaster arrives to break up the party, lecture the host, and sometimes slap on some charges just for the hell of it.

When a Seven was still in their school years, this process may have been subtler and more externalized, as there were actual adults around to do the job of criticizing, chastising, and corralling. But unless the Seven built a solid foundation of easy daily practices to help them focus their attention and build up a tolerance for the necessary unpleasantness of being an adult who has to pay bills and feed themselves three-ish times a day, the Seven is likely to see a fierce Inner Critic develop the first few years outside of their family of origin. This Inner Critic/Taskmaster takes the place of the adults who used to play the role and acts as a guardrail against complete disorder and unfinished projects.

My conversation with Anna then shifted toward that feeling of relief she expected to experience at the ten-book benchmark. If there was a way that she could accomplish that relief from self-criticism on a daily basis (without going wildly into no-rules territory), it could help focus her attention on the projects that were the most purposeful for her, along with counterbalancing some of the necessary pain associated with the difficult parts of writing. Not only would this help eliminate the need for the Taskmaster to show up and ridicule her into shape when things got out of hand, but she would be more likely to experience a true expression of the type's desire: being satisfied.

This would by no means be an instant fix, since almost none of this work is. If we're lucky, we may experience an epiphany now and again that so instantly becomes integrated within us that we don't go back to the way things were. But we shouldn't hold our breath for that. Things like self-compassion and wresting back our attention from our core fear involve daily practices that support them, and those practices work just a little bit better each week. They're not overnight sensations.

Anna and I then discussed how misguided the Taskmaster was and started to look at the ways that this vicious cycle between the irresponsible child and the overly critical disciplinarian versions of her was not only painful, but unhelpful for accomplishing what she wanted to accomplish. We came up with an easy practice for her to begin working on, one aimed at disrupting the cycle before it picked up pace. That looked like deep belly breathing and naming a specific focus of attention each morning before she began writing, based on what she found meaningful.

And because I knew she wasn't currently in a place to sort through her various projects to prioritize on her own, we worked together to decide which one should get her focus first, based on 1) what was meaningful to her, and 2) which project would likely be the most profitable, since we live in a world that works on money.

For the other project that already had a preorder deadline set, we talked about how it was not likely realistic, based on her past performance (the best indicator of future performance), to get both of her books done in time for the preorder. Then we discussed possible steps to reach out to the retailers and essentially beg for a favor to cancel one of the preorders without canceling both. (I've had success with this myself, and if you're not a serial offender, customer service is usually reasonable.)

Sometimes we get in over our heads so far that we need someone else to talk us through it and steer us toward the most practical decision for our priorities. I'm always happy to do that, and it's important to remember that it's no failing on your part if you need this degree of help. Life is very complicated and too much for anyone to take on by themselves. I have people I can call on who will hold my hand in this way when things feel too big for me. I hope we can all rally that support for ourselves.

Anna emailed me a month later to report that she had much more clarity and felt more in control of her projects. She'd even managed to get that one preorder done on time. She'd been noticing all of the ways her Taskmaster showed up, and while she had by no means mastered all of her unhealthy patterns to become a big, glowing ball of light, she was getting better at separating out the voice of her inner critic from her own thoughts so that she could spot it sooner and use its appearance as an indicator that she was under stress and it was time to make some hard decisions.

This may look small, but accomplishing even this much is what I consider an astounding success.

HOW DO YOU GET WHAT YOU WANT? (AND WHAT DO YOU WANT?)

We've talked a little bit about how each type has a core fear and a core desire, but there are also these things called "triads" that share certain characteristics.

There are all kinds of triads in the Enneagram, and it's all very interesting and could make someone who goes a little too hard into the idea of sacred geometry exceedingly happy, but we're only going to look at two specific triad categories right now.

What you are about to learn may be the biggest a-ha moment you have about how you're been marketing your books... and why it may not be working *or* may be working but is not sustainable.

We do this with two concepts: the childhood need and the approach you take to get what you want.

Sometimes it's essential to travel back in time when you're doing this work, to connect to the child who lives inside you and whose simplistic perception of the world laid the groundwork for the adult you are today.

The foundation of our worldview is built before we even know what clouds are made of. Prior to learning the basics of gravity and how to read, we've already begun solidifying ideas about our place in the world and the role others play in our lives.

News flash: a lot of those beliefs do not hold up against even the most basic questioning. They are overly simplistic and built on faulty assumptions. When one of my nieces was four, she refused to believe that I was too busy with work to come visit. Her reason for calling me a liar, which she still does frequently and with the utmost conviction, was that she'd always seen her dad leave for work and her mom stay home, and Uncle John had to miss events because of his job but Aunt Claire almost always showed up. From that, she'd concluded that "girls don't have jobs." Gut-wrenching feminist fail aside, this sweeping conclusion made sense for someone her age trying to piece together how the world works and, by extension, her place in it as a girl. Of course, it was from extremely limited and incomplete data, and so it was just plain wrong. Kids say the darndest things, as it were, and that's okay! But it's also a good reason not to let them own businesses or run for office.

It's also why inner child work (learning to communicate with the younger version of you to adjust the fundamentals of your worldview) is crucial to seeing certain patterns in ourselves and interrupting their hold on our lives.

The sort of beliefs we develop as a child become the framework for how we build the rest of our worldview. These beliefs can be isolating and detrimental, cutting us off from ourselves and others.

They may look like:

- I'm responsible for how others feel
- I can't rely on anyone to help me
- The real me is not good enough
- I'm only safe when I'm alone
- I must earn love by pleasing others

- I'm not important
- My feelings are a burden to others

And the tragic list goes on.

If we had a happy childhood where our basic needs were met without stipulation, we weren't expected to earn attention and security, and we were allowed to function autonomously once we began to pull away from our caretaker, we will have more positive beliefs that help us carry on as well-adjusted adults, like:

- When I need help, others show up for me
- Connecting with others is safe and pleasant
- I am worthy of love
- The world is full of wonderful possibilities
- I'm allowed to experience the full range of emotions

It's unlikely that any of us can look at our mosaic of foundational beliefs and only see positive ones that connect us to ourselves and others or only see negative ones that separate us from ourselves and others. We have some of each. Some even directly conflict!

It's our responsibility as adults to take the Marie Kondo approach to those beliefs, digging them out from the bottom of the belief pile, holding them up, and assessing them one by one. Instead of asking if they spark joy, though, we can ask, "What does clinging to this belief as true keep me from seeing?" and "What healthy connection is this belief keeping out of my reach?"

Side note: when engaging in this inner-child work, you will inevitably discover that some of the harmful beliefs can be attributed to something your parents taught you, whether intentionally or not. It's important to be open to that attribution and not immediately throw up walls of "They were doing the best they could!" or "But they're great people!" Take a breath, friend. They are not listening to your thoughts. You will not get in trouble for thinking something unflattering about them. Instead, notice how you've taken it on yourself to defend them against even basic accountability for being imperfect; that impulse might show you another belief you developed as a child that is keeping you from moving forward. Our parents don't have to be bad people to have passed along unhealthy messages to us; they only need to be imperfect like the rest of us. And if you have *no* trouble blaming your parents for how they shaped your initial worldview, then this is your chance to heal those wounds, grow into an adult, and move on. You might even be able to get along with them better afterward, even if they've already passed away. (Sometimes the deceased parents are the hardest to get along with.)

And now back to your regularly scheduled Enneagram programming.

THE TRIADS OF CHILDHOOD NEEDS

You might already know from reading *Reclaim Your Author Career* about the Head/Heart/Body triads. They break down thus:

Types 2-3-4 are the Heart Center

Types 5-6-7 are the Head Center
Types 8-9-1 are the Body Center

But there are other distinctions within these groupings, and that's what we get to look at now.

Each triad focuses on a single longing, a strong need they had as children that usually went unmet. The degree to which these needs went unmet is generally related to how much of a hold these needs still have over us as adults.

Don Richard Riso and Russ Hudson explore these needs in their book *The Wisdom of the Enneagram*, going into much more psychological detail than I will here. To keep it short, the needs go:

Types 2-3-4 want attention
Types 5-6-7 want security
Types 8-9-1 want autonomy

Attention and security are generally self-explanatory, but to clarify about autonomy, it looks an awful lot like control. More specifically, it's wanting to control the external environment while fighting against the external environment controlling us.

Each type within a triad relates to this desire differently from the other two types, which we'll talk about in a second, but the overlying desire is the same.

These wants are so pervasive in our lives that we are almost guaranteed not to notice them until they're pointed out. But most likely, you've constructed your entire life, for better or worse, to facilitate your pursuit of this need.

This is not to say that a Five *doesn't* want attention from the right people at the right time or that a Four *doesn't* want autonomy in certain situations, but when you look at the blueprint of the Five's life, you will not see it built around seeking attention, and when you look at the blueprint of the Four's life, you will not see it built around establishing autonomy.

We all have basic needs of attention, security, and autonomy. Your need for the two outside of your triad might be small, but if it's not being met, then you might feel your attention being drawn more toward seeking those things for a time. That doesn't mean you've switched types; it just means you're not a monolith.

Before I move on to describing the second half of this equation—how we approach getting what we want—I encourage you to take a few minutes and think about all the ways you've structured your life around meeting your childhood need. We often build entire careers and family structures around it, sometimes to extremes that don't necessarily benefit us.

The 8/9/1 that goes overboard with autonomy may feel lonely and stuck on an island, and they may burn out from trying to exert too much control over the chaotic external environment.

The 2/3/4 that goes overboard seeking attention may feel empty or end up attracting more negative attention than they can handle, and they may forget to differentiate the types of attention that fill them up.

The 5/6/7 that goes overboard with security may feel frantic from the impossible task of seeking one hundred percent security, and they could miss out on deep relationships by protecting themselves too fiercely.

This is why examining these patterns and how they show up in our author career can give us big clues as to where we've overdone it in our search for that childhood desire to the detriment of what we'd like to accomplish. Pulling back, even a little bit, can be a big step toward achieving different results.

HOW DO YOU GET WHAT YOU WANT?

There are three approaches for getting those childhood needs met: assertive, compliant, and withdrawing.

But these don't fall along the typical triadic lines. Instead, each triad has a single type within it that takes one of the three approaches:

> Types 1-2-6 are compliant
> Types 3-7-8 are assertive
> Types 4-5-9 are withdrawing

This means that no two types share the same childhood desire *and* approach to getting that need met, which creates some fascinating possibilities (and is another way to help sort out which type you might be, interestingly enough).

The compliant/assertive/withdrawn distinctions are known as the Hornevian groups (named after Karen Horney), and I'll explain a little bit more about those because they're not as self-explanatory as the attention/security/autonomy triads.

Compliant types, sometimes called "dutiful" types, "move toward" others to get their needs met. They believe in *earning* their needs, so they use service and being responsible to those around them as a strategy for getting what they want. Ones, Twos, and Sixes: how might you have incorporated this stance into the function and ethos of your writing business?

Problems arise when the 1/2/6 doesn't believe they are being adequately rewarded for their efforts, that others are not reciprocating like they should. This can cause a crisis for the 1/2/6, and the impulse is simply to be even *more* dutiful and serve *harder*. Accelerating our patterns rarely works out well, though.

Assertive types "move against" others to get their needs met. They don't trust that anyone will meet their needs if given a choice, so they demand their needs are met. Threes, Sevens, and Eights: how might you have incorporated this active "take what is yours" stance into the strategy of your writing business?

Problems arise when the 3/7/8 comes up against circumstances that no amount of demanding can overcome. This approach that has generally served them isn't delivering, and that can send the assertive type into overdrive, trying futilely to force it until they run out of steam and crash and burn, usually in an unintentionally eye-catching way.

Withdrawn types "move away from" others to get their needs met. They don't trust that others will ever meet their needs and build inner spaces where they can retreat to meet their own needs. Fours, Fives, and Nines: how might your stance of withdrawing into yourself have kept you from confronting very real obstacles in your writing business?

Problems arise when the 4/5/9 run into situations where they cannot meet their own needs and withdraw even farther into themselves rather than reaching out. Some desires can only be filled through interpersonal connections, and the 4/5/9 misses out on those even more the further they withdraw into themselves and become unreachable to others.

WHEN OUR WANTS INTERSECT WITH OUR STRATEGIES FOR GETTING THEM MET

Here's where it gets fun. When you combine these two pieces of the puzzle, you see a belief emerge in each type that has likely been steering the ship of our writing business whether we realized it or not.

Type 2: Attention + compliant = "**Serving others** will **earn** me the **attention** I desire."

Type 3: Attention + assertive = "**Making myself impossible to ignore** will **guarantee** me the **attention** I desire."

Type 4: Attention + withdrawn = "**Focusing on myself** will **ensure** I receive the **attention** I desire."

Type 5: Security + withdrawn = "**Creating distance from others** will **ensure security**."

Type 6: Security + compliant = "**Being dutiful** to others will **earn** me **security**."

Type 7: Security + assertive = "**Chasing opportunities** will **guarantee** me the **security** I desire."

Type 8: Autonomy + assertive = "**Exerting my will** over everything will **guarantee** me the **autonomy** I desire."

Type 9: Autonomy + withdrawn = "**Retreating into myself** will **ensure** my **autonomy**."

Type 1: Autonomy + compliant = "**Serving others responsibly** will **earn** me the **autonomy** I desire."

I don't know about you, but when I learned about my type's combo, the first words out of my mouth were, "Well, shit."

You may also realize, when reading those descriptions, that it's easy to mistype as something else in your triad or as something within your Hornevian grouping.

Can't decide if you're a Seven or an Eight? That's probably because both types are assertive and spend their lives being told they're "too much." Eights are known for their boldness, but that can look a lot like the novelty seeking of the Seven at times, especially if the Seven has a strong Eight wing. But looking at those childhood needs, we have a differentiator. Does this person care more about autonomy or security? Do they spend more energy exerting control over their environment in a "a strong offense is a strong defense" sort of way, or are they driven by the scarcity mindset of the Seven, who believes the present moment does not have enough to go around and must seek satisfaction in the elsewhere?

The cool thing is that in bringing our attention to these underlying beliefs and how they may be wreaking havoc on our writing business, we can almost immediately remedy the situation.

The assertive types can experiment with pulling back and trusting that the universe will still meet their need.

The compliant types can be more mindful of where they're doing too much for others without the returns they'd hoped for.

The withdrawing types can take a step forward and practice looking to others to have their need met.

Noticing these subconscious patterns is, in short, liberating. It frees us from being servants to them rather than crafting our patterns to serve us. When we unshackle ourselves from the patterns we didn't sign up for, we immediately have a world of new options ahead of us. And to get new results, we must experiment with new patterns.

CONCEPT IN ACTION:
An Authentic Writer (4) who can't stand marketing

"I hate marketing," said Darius. "It's so gross to me."

"What kind of marketing have you tried?" I asked.

"I post about my books on Instagram, and it doesn't get any engagement. I think I'm just done with it. No one wants to read my stuff."

In case you're wondering, yes, I did go look up Darius's Instagram account. On it, he had posted a few pictures of him with his books, but those images were hidden among a heap of other unrelated ones. All of his posts had very long captions. I tried to find an emotional throughline, some kind of coherence, but couldn't put my finger on any.

"This is why I should go the trad publishing route. I won't have to do my own marketing then."

If you're wondering how he went from "nobody wants to read my books" to "I bet a traditional publisher would want to sell my books that nobody wants to read," don't work too hard to make those things make sense together. The logical contradiction was a clue to me that he was not particularly attached to the realities of either of those statements and that there was some other emotional undercurrent going on. Emotions are, by definition, not rational, and that's okay. They don't need to be because they serve a different purpose in our lives.

I wasn't surprised, considering the Enneagram 4's relationship with fantasy, that Darius could easily switch to an imagined reality where a traditional publisher happens upon his manuscript, recognizes it for the genius that it is, and immediately decides to throw some of the corporation's marketing budget toward it. But that is not how the traditional publishing world works, especially not for the kind of niche books that Fours like Darius tend to write.

Before we begin to judge Darius for his magical thinking, let's remember that *most* of us would appreciate being plucked out of obscurity and elevated with no extra work of our own. You write the book of your heart and some other entity bankrolls and manages the advertising to make it a bestseller? Sign me up!

But that system doesn't exist in reality. When we hear stories about it, they're flukes, and we're likely missing important information. There is no reliable mechanism that does that, though when Fours are struggling to move copies of their books, the fantasy may feel incredibly real.

For Darius, the pain point that was hanging him up in his marketing attempts was the Four's pattern of wanting attention but withdrawing into themselves to get that attention (this can range from meaningful introspection to pure navel gazing). Marketing is the process of trying to get the attention of *others*, which is not as natural for the Four. The ineffective way Darius was approaching it with a few posts on Instagram was destined to fail. That's just not how social media works.

But not only did it have no impact on his book sales, but to a Four, making an attempt to be seen and not feeling the attention from others can feel like a very personal rejection.

To depersonalize this for Darius so we could get his thinking Center of Intelligence online, I talked about some of the realities of marketing and social media; namely, how it's pay to play on almost every site at this point.[*]

For the sensitive Four, things can feel very personal when they simply are not. The Instagram algorithm, for instance, is absolutely ambivalent to your brilliance. The only thing it cares about is money.

Once we talked through some of the realities of the game we play called "marketing," and Darius took his lack of success thus far less personally, he was open to new ideas.

One of those ideas, which I recommend to almost every Four that I work with, is to turn to someone who is *not* a Four to help you with the packaging. The obvious go-to is someone in the industry who you trust who is also a Three. The Three's childhood desire is also attention, but the Three has the gift of knowing what other people want. The Four's attention is much more focused on what the Four wants, and therefore the same skills are not developed. This results in the Four picking covers that may be artistic but aren't particularly effective at conveying what the book is about and who it's for. Threes tend to see their products through other people's eyes and can see where it's hitting or not.

---

[*]   And by the time you read this, it may be pay to play on every single site, or maybe a new social media site has rocketed to the top of the charts and has good organic discovery right now along with good conversion to book sales, but that won't last; it never does. One of the best indicators I've found that a social media site has stopped being effective for organic sales is that the authors who were having success with organic sales are now trying to sell courses about how to sell books on that site.

So that was the first place I started with Darius. He really needed new covers if he wanted these books to stand a chance of selling. But more importantly than having the books sell, he needed to experience some positive attention from his marketing efforts if he wasn't going to give up immediately. Appropriate covers will do that.

There was a deeper pattern that I wanted to bring to his attention, though, and that was how his unmet childhood need of attention intersected with his Hornevian grouping of being withdrawn. Subconsciously, and I mean *deep* down, Fours hope that pulling back will lead to being discovered *despite* attempting not to be.

I know it can be painful for an Enneagram Four to see this spelled out so plainly, but there's really no shame in it. It's coming from a much younger version of you, and your responsibility as an adult is only to acknowledge that it's there and begin to make different decisions.

Once Darius saw that he'd been holding on to this hope of being discovered and thereby rescued from the feelings of pain and rejection in marketing his own work, he saw how this pattern of *protecting himself from the anguish of not getting the attention he needed by withdrawing to give himself the attention he needed* permeated just about every facet of his life. Friendships, relationships, you name it.

I warned him that it can be grating for people who have the pattern of *withdrawing* to get their needs met to be around the people whose pattern is being *assertive* to get their needs met, hence why he found some of the savviest marketers off-putting. It wasn't that they are fundamentally off-putting, it's that it was salt in his wound of not getting the attention that he craved that they were willing to go out and get that need met, sometimes shamelessly.

We discussed some marketing tactics that would be more comfortable for him and wouldn't trigger his feelings of rejection. And now that he was taking the disappointing results of his ineffective previous marketing efforts less personally, we had more options to choose from.

We didn't put an end to Darius's tendency to withdraw in the areas where he most craved attention. For one, there's no better or worse approach to getting what we want—it's just a matter of looking at the situation and asking if we're happy with the results of what we've been trying or if we want to experiment with something new. Seeing the pattern was a major step for him, though, and I could tell he would continue noticing all the ways, big and small, it had shaped his writing career. From there, the adult part of him would be back in the driver's seat, better able to diagnose where his efforts were leading to disappointment and to try something new.

SECTION 4: TROUBLESHOOTING YOUR BLOCKS

COMMON BLOCKS BY TYPE

There's a strange rumor that surfaces in the writing community every few years that writer's block doesn't exist. To me, that's like saying robberies don't exist because you personally have never been robbed. Just as you can know with some certainty that robberies exist by listening to the victims, you can tell that writer's block is real by hearing authors describe it.

There are many other kinds of blocks that we face in this business, though, and these tend to be so subtle that we don't always know we're running up against them. Blocks on marketing, collaboration, networking, reader interactions, and all the rest. If it's a thing that one could do as an author, it's a thing we can get blocked on.

Thankfully, once you've identified your core fear, there's a collection of somewhat predictable patterns that arise from it, and familiarizing ourselves of those narrows down the possibilities of what's behind the block.

There are a few main culprits underlying most blocks—emotions, thoughts/beliefs, and health issues being the main ones.

Emotions can block us when they're calling for our attention but going unaddressed, or when we're trying to hold on to them rather than letting them move on. When you start having feelings *about* your feelings—feeling ashamed or guilty for simply experiencing a particular emotion that you've dubbed unflattering or off-limits, for instance—you've entered the kind of thick mud that will suck the shoes off your feet when you try to take the next step.

Thoughts and beliefs can also weigh us down to the point where we can't carry on. If you don't believe that the next step in the process will work, if you've ruled it out before even trying it, then good luck getting yourself to waste your one precious life doing it with any sort of gusto. If you hold beliefs like "people are selfish," or "nobody cares what I have to say," then it makes perfect sense that you have a block on communicating regularly with your readers, for instance.

Health issues are so frequently overlooked as a cause for blocks, but as we've seen more and more people recently discover that brain fog is a very real thing, we're starting to accept how much our physical health affects everything in our career. If you can't sit comfortably, what are the odds that you'll be able to sit for an hour to get your writing done? If you suffer from chronic fatigue or are in the throes of menopause, you might be overlooking how tired you are all the time, or not accounting for what times of day you have the most energy so that you can write during those times. It's quite something how easily we'll dismiss our health concerns when looking for why we're not getting the work done. You wouldn't believe the way I've heard countless authors dismiss their physical pain and disabilities like they *should* just be able to deal with it. "I can't seem to focus when I sit down to write." Oh, you mean while you're recovering from *back surgery*? What a medical mystery. Someone call Dr. House.

Seriously, though, ask yourself if you've been dismissing pain or low energy this way. Most people do. We forget that we age, get sick, have medical complications, and our body chemistry changes over time, and then we measure ourselves by the physical standards of our youthful self. There are certainly things within our power to make ourselves feel physically better or worse, but that twenty-something version of you who could balance a full-time job, college classes, partying, and intense physical workouts on four hours of sleep is dead. RIP.

Sometimes the block is temporary and will go away on its own (once you stop feeling so angry about a specific situation, or once your body starts feeling better). And sometimes you must make changes for the insufferable block to crawl back to the depths of hell from whence it came.

Either way, it can help our level of suffering to be able to diagnose the block and determine whether it's likely to disappear on its own or if we need to be proactive.

Is the solution to struggling with the block ever to stop trying to fight it? To give in? To temporarily surrender?

Sometimes, yes.

When my dog passed from cancer in fall of 2022, I was deep in the middle of creating a bunch of rewards for my *Reclaim Your Author Career* Kickstarter backers. It was not difficult to diagnose *why* I was struggling to focus and be productive between the sobbing fits. But *identifying the block* and *allowing it to exist there* without fighting it are two separate skills.

So, I had a decision to make. Did I try to push through while I was grieving (likely to the detriment of my health and the quality of the work I produced), or did I *allow* the block of my grief to exist between me and my work until the grief wasn't so extreme?

I'm glad to say I chose the latter option, and when I emailed my backers with an update that things might be delivered later than normal because of my situation, I received nothing but support—exactly what a person needs while they're grieving. Although hitting pause on work didn't relieve me of my grief, it instantly eliminated my unnecessary suffering related to the block. Once I felt slightly more myself, I got back to work, and the block was no longer an issue.

Sometimes we must let the block be. Forcing through is not always a great solution (you hear that, Eights?).

As Viktor Frankl discusses in his book *Man's Search for Meaning*, we suffer when we don't understand *why* the things that are happening are happening. Understanding alone, then, can be enough to ease some of our suffering. This is why creating meaning through our author career is so important, and why we can find ourselves so stuck and worn down when we lose touch with that sense of purpose. Often, this is where a block gets its foot in the door.

So let me try to ease some of your suffering by examining how to create meaning and fight blocks for each of the Enneagram types.

Type 1, The Principled Writer

At their core, Ones' desire is to be good, moral, and balanced. Their fear is that they are bad, corrupt, or imbalanced. Fairness is also important to this type, which connects back to the need for balance and righteousness and extends to a deep dedication to justice in its various forms and a fair application of the rules.

If you're a One, you likely connect everything you do to a deeper purpose of making yourself and/or the world around you a better place. That's what Ones do. It's why they're called "the Reformers." The One's ability to find the flaws and injustices of the world, to sniff out hypocrisy and corruption in themselves and others, is their strength. Their ability to envision ways forward toward something more just, equitable, and righteous (note: not self-righteous) is the gift Ones can share with the world.

How do you use this information to motivate yourself as a writer?

The trick is simple: write books that you believe will make the world a better place by existing and attracting readers. Writing to trend in some genre you don't care about with stock characters who go through the motions will not be enough to get you out of your warm bed in the morning. It will not be enough to keep you writing when the inner critic whispers lies to you.

Write stories that activate those healthy parts of yourself. Write stories that require imperfect characters to stand up for what they believe in. Show your readers, through the art of fiction, how we can fix the things that are broken in the world, in others, and in ourselves. Inspire others to love and accept themselves, imperfections and all. You are a fixer and healer by nature. Notice how your heart responds to the idea of what you just read, and know that only a heart full of goodness would react that way to it.

When you start to feel less motivated, it's usually because you've lost sight of the purpose and impact of the work you're creating. You might start thinking, *Nothing in the world would be any different if I never published another book, so why bother?*

Exactly! Nothing would be any different, and the way things are isn't working. But your voice, your stories, can nudge the world toward something better. You can't do all of it all on your own, but you can do your part of it. That's all you need to do because one-ninth of the population is a Reformer like you, so you're not in this alone.

I have a sticky note on my computer that says, *What the fuck else are you going to do with your LIFE?!* In typical One fashion, I approach myself with a little tough love and pitch-black humor, but the message reminds me of my sense of purpose, and that's why it's there where I see it every day.

Pay attention to where your mind goes when you're writing. Are you having trouble getting to the next scene because you've slipped into harsh self-judgment? Are you working on projects because you feel like you *should* or because you're passionate about them?

There's really nothing like watching a One who's developed their gifts of wisdom and discretion pick up a cause and fight for it. Nelson Mandela is an example of this. As far as fictional characters go, you have Bruce Wayne and Hermione Granger as Ones. Batman fights corruption (especially this new version, which Ones should definitely check out), and Hermione fights for house elf rights (and constantly follows her conscience in tricky matters of the wizarding world, much to the detriment of Malfoy's nose).

If you find yourself facing a block and unable to write the next word or execute your marketing strategy, see if any of the following beliefs might be running on a loop in your head:

- *"Nobody cares if I publish this or not."*
- *"Why am I writing made-up stories when there are so many problems in the world that need fixing?"*
- *"This book is garbage and I'm just going to embarrass myself."*
- *"I can't believe I agreed to this project. How dare someone ask this much of me."*
- *"I can't move on to the next scene until this one is fixed/perfect."*
- *"Nothing I do is going to make any difference in this screwed-up world anyway."*

All of these statements are false. You may not believe me, but try entertaining the idea of how your life would feel if you *stopped* reinforcing these beliefs. (Spoiler: much lighter and more joyful.)

Your inner critic—that harsh voice that parades as you but may sound a little like your parent or a childhood teacher or coach—is trying to protect you from your worst nightmare of being bad or corrupt. Unfortunately, it's going about it in the least helpful way possible. When those unhelpful and negative thoughts arise in your mind, try saying, "Thank you for trying to protect me, but I don't need your protection and I don't need that belief anymore."

If you're a One who's struggling with motivation:

- Take a moment to reconnect to your purpose for writing about what you want to change for the better in this world.
- Get your karate hands up when you realize you're operating on a sense of personal obligation rather than passion, and either drop that project like it's hot or find a way it can support your goals of making the world a better place.
- Watch out when you become overly critical of others. It causes you to be equally critical of yourself, and that is detrimental to creative work.
- Learn to laugh at yourself. You're not perfect and never will be. Might as well have a chuckle at it.
- If you find yourself telling lots of stories that paint you as the hero or the good guy, it might mean that you're feeling more like a villain and need to stop and reassess. Great insight can be found in those

moments, and you can stitch them into your next book!

- Build relationships with other people who share your passion for specific causes, so you remember you don't have to do it all on your own.
- Schedule frequent time for rest. You're an intense person, and when you commit yourself to something, you go hard. You can't do that forever. Rest is an essential part of your work if you want it to continue long term.

Type 2, The Helpful Writer

At their core, a Two's desire is to be loved. Their fear is that they'll be unworthy of love. Caring for and service to others are central to this type, who can enjoy fulfilling, lifelong friendships... as well as plenty of one-sided relationships if they're not careful.

The Twos I know are almost too sweet for this world. They have so much love to give that not showing it to others through acts of service can be physically and emotionally painful for them. They're natural nurturers, which makes them exceptional at anticipating the needs of others. But if they don't learn a few raw truths about the nature of help vs. enabling and interdependency vs. codependency, the world will use them up. And as you can imagine, it's hard to get the words down when you're all used up.

If you're a Two, it's important to attach everything you do to a deeper motivation of nurturing the world, *and that includes yourself equally*. We hear the words "self-care" thrown around in somewhat obnoxious ways all the time, but it's a necessary ritual for Twos to build into their daily routine. I'm not talking bubble baths and manicures (though feel free to treat yourself to those, too). I'm talking about setting boundaries around your writing time. I'm talking about learning to ask for and accept help. While caring for *others* comes naturally for a Two, these forms of *self-care* do not.

How do you use this information to motivate yourself as a writer?

The trick is simple: write books that provide nurturance for you and your readers. Twos often end up writing romance for this reason. The promise of an HEA gives readers who need some TLC a safe place to find it. But any genre can have a happy ending, so you can find Twos writing in all of them. (If I ever discover a Two writing bleak endings, I will stage an intervention.)

Write stories that heal others while you heal yourself. Write stories where the conflict is resolved through your protagonist's self-love. Show your readers, through the art of fiction, how we can build healthy relationships where love flows equally both ways and leave toxic relationships that take more than they give. Inspire others to love themselves the same way they love the world. You are a healer by nature. Write stories that serve your soul, and those stories will serve the souls of your readers as well.

Writing a book is a long process. There are weeks, months, or years between when we write the first word and when others see our product and can benefit from it in the way we intended.

This means that those quick fixes our brain often craves—instant gratification for our core desires and numbing to soothe our core fear—are not always baked into the book-writing process. (If we're smart about it and self-aware, though, we can build those in.)

If you're a Two, you may know in your heart that your book will provide the nurturance to your readers that you hope for, but between the first word and hitting publish, what are you supposed to do, hold all your love inside?

No way. Especially when there are all kinds of people you can help on a daily basis! Woohoo!

So, you wake up at six a.m. to pack lunches for your kids and have breakfast ready for them. Then it's time to sit and write for two hours.

But then your wife overslept and can't find her keys and the printer isn't working but she needs to print out something before she can go to the big meeting at work in half an hour! Helper to the rescue!

Finally, you sit down with an hour and fifteen minutes left in your writing time. Better than nothing. But your sister just texted you saying that she had a big fight with her husband last night. Poor thing. You give her a call. When that's done, you sit down to write and only have fifteen minutes left.

Well, shoot. That's hardly any time at all before you head over to the women's prison to volunteer. Probably better to leave fifteen minutes early in case you hit traffic.

Suddenly, no writing.

Is this a familiar story?

I would never tell a Two not to care for the people they love. But when giving becomes a matter of instant gratification for our core desire (to be worthy of love) and a balm for our core fear (to be unlovable), then it rules our schedule and kills our ability to create meaningful projects that require more time investment before the payoff.

Don't come at me with pitchforks, but maybe your kids can order lunch at school. Maybe they can make their own breakfast. Your wife got herself into this mess and she's a grownup. Let her fix it for herself (she'll feel better about having done it solo). And while your sister might need a shoulder to cry on, she can wait until you have available time, or she can speak with a therapist. None of those options makes you selfish or unloving, although I've heard Twos describe ignoring a request for help from others as "scarier than death." It's standard boundary setting, and you *can* work up a tolerance for it through incremental practice. People may respond poorly at first as you break the pattern of being constantly available and at their service, but if they genuinely love you, they'll adjust, and you're helping them in the end by asking them to solve their own minor problems.

There's really nothing like watching a Two who's developed their gifts of love and caring express all of that through their creativity. Dolly Parton is an example of this. She made a name through the soulful songs that could only be created by someone with the ability to feel love so truly and deeply. But she also didn't let all the men around her take advantage of her and bleed her dry. As a result, she's amassed enough financial resources to have plenty to give without 1) leaving nothing for herself, or 2) expecting others to reciprocate. The people she allows in her life love her fiercely and freely because of the love she's given without expectation of receiving.

Same for Stevie Wonder, another Two. As far as fictional characters go, you have the loyal servant Samwise Gamgee, whose love for his friend Frodo inspires love back (okay, shippers, I see you). And then you have Molly Weasley, whose love for her many children takes all sort of shapes, from knitting them every article of clothing they own to uttering the only instance of "bitch" in the entire series. The love of the Two can be fierce when it needs to be.

If you're struggling to put the words down or market your book, see if any of these scripts are running on a loop in your head:

- *"I should be helping [whoever], not selfishly writing a book."*
- *"No one wanted my last book, so why spend all this time on another?"*
- *"Oh, I can't write this. What will [random person] think about it?"*
- *"My family needs me more."*
- *"Is this book actually going to help anyone?"*
- *"I haven't earned my writing time."*
- *"I can write after I've completed X, Y, Z."*
- *"I'll write again once [whoever] is in a better situation and doesn't need my assistance."*
- *"How can I write when there's so much pain in the world and no one's doing anything about it?"*

Creativity is a human requirement like exercise or a healthy diet. If you've chosen writing as your passion (or it's chosen you), then it is not selfish to meet your basic human need. It is also not selfish to meet it before you meet the needs of others. After all, the only person who can meet your creative needs is *you*.

If you're a Two who's struggling with motivation:

- Remember what your purpose for writing is and the caring world you want to create for your reader.
- Find ways to connect with readers frequently (daily, even) throughout the writing process so you don't have to wait months for any meaningful feedback.
- Express your needs and boundaries to readers. They care about you more than you know, and you probably have a lot of Two readers who would benefit from seeing that modeled.
- Learn to recognize when a relationship with another adult has fallen into a pattern of you giving more than you're receiving and address it. (Maybe they'll leave, or maybe they'll change their behavior. Their response is outside of your control, but advocating for yourself is not.)
- If you start to feel like a martyr, ask yourself who you're trying to rescue and whether you've been helping or enabling, then set aside time ASAP to care for your own needs.
- Build relationships with other authors who will support you when it comes time to set and enforce

difficult boundaries around your writing time.
- Schedule frequent time for self-care like exercise and sports, journaling, psychotherapy, preparing healthy meals for yourself, naps, and time with self-sufficient friends who make you feel unconditionally loved.

Type 3, The Productive Writer

At their core, Threes' desire is to have value. Their fear is that they're valueless. The concept of value is central to what makes Threes tick (and tick and tick and tick until the other types are like, "Give it a rest, already!").

Indie publishing is chock-full of what many people would label "successful" Threes (at least based on the information the Three presents to us). Any speaking gig or gathering where the stipulation for entry is raw sales numbers, you'll find Achievers, some of whom are absolutely miserable but have no idea about that yet.

That's because Threes are built to thrive in whatever structure you drop them in. They are incredibly resourceful by nature. Whereas Twos can sense what others need from them, Threes have an unmatched ability to sense what others *want*. And then they have the work ethic to make it happen—assuming the reward moves them closer to their (often nebulous) definition of "success."

And speaking of that definition, an Achiever's definition of success, as a default, is whatever their family, culture, or society defines it as. Growth for this type looks like reevaluating that definition to match their personal desires rather than their desire to impress and seek external recognition.

It's rare for me to meet a Three who does not exhibit classic workaholic tendencies. Maybe they aren't a workaholic now, thanks to Enneagram work or other therapeutic practices, but they definitely were at some point. Other types can certainly fall into workaholism, if that's what they believe will soothe their core fear or fulfill their core desire (for instance, if a One is raised to equate a relentless work ethic with being good, or an Eight is raised to believe that resting shows weakness), but it's almost a given with Threes. And because of that, their lack of motivation, even as they near the edge of burnout, can show no outward signs.

One of the Achiever's favorite responses to being maxed out and running on fumes is to take on more projects. Their willingness to look good at the cost of feeling good can take them far in the realm of external validation. So far, in fact, that they can completely self-alienate from their personal desires. Ask an average-health Three what they want, and their first response will be to tell you what you or society wants them to want.

Their hard work and determination are impressive. But to watch them put it behind a project they don't truly care about and are only doing for the sake of external validation is a real tragedy.

How do you use this information to motivate yourself as a writer?

If you're a Three, you must pause and determine what books you *want* to write. Threes are notorious for trend-hopping, and y'all are quite good at it. You can make bank doing it. But you can make bank in *any* genre if you stick with it, so why not start by asking what kind of stories you'd like to write and build out from there? I have no doubt you'll find a way to make the money you need from it. (And you'll need to make exactly $0 before you'll be happy, rather than $NeverEnough.)

Write stories for the young Achievers who don't yet know their value doesn't depend on their parents' approval or their good grades. Write stories of inspiring figures who persevere and find a way to overcome all odds. Write the kind of stories that make you glow from the inside out.

If you're a Three who's struggling to put the words down, or you're still meeting your daily word count but feeling uninspired by the stories, see if any of these are running on loop in your head:

- *"Is this what the readers want?"*
- *"Could I be making more money writing [hot genre]?"*
- *"Get through this book and two more, and then you can write something you enjoy."*
- *"I just want this to be done."*
- *"Is this how [more successful author] would do it?"*
- *"How does this scene make me look?"*
- *"Is this story too sappy?"*
- *"Did I do all the tropes right?"*
- *"Does this follow the formula exactly?"*

- *"It doesn't matter if this scene makes sense. My readers won't care."*

The above statements show an emotional disconnect from the deeper purpose of storytelling, and sometimes even a contempt for the people you're so desperate to impress. It's sort of hard to let the emotions flow into your characters when you're not giving them space to breathe in yourself.

If you're a Three who's struggling with motivation:

- Keep asking what you want to write until you come up with an answer, then write that (you can still include popular tropes, but only the ones you like).
- Learn to create bite-size benchmarks, and when you hit them, *celebrate*. Give yourself the acknowledgement and praise you're chasing without making a show to others about it. Do it! You'll feel instantly more successful!
- Stop moving the goalposts. This is not the only way to motivate yourself, even if it's the only way you've ever known. As you become more inner-directed with a clear vision of your dreams, every day will feel worthy of recognition.
- Learn to spot when you're in job-interview mode. You are not a product to be pitched. Instead, take a step back and remember that people are lucky to be around you, and if you have to sell them hard on you, they're not in alignment with your dreams.

- There is such a thing as healthy competition, but you run the risk of misaligning your dreams for the sake of winning the competition. If you find yourself feeling bitter toward your competition, that's a sure sign that it's time to remind yourself of your inherent value independent of what others bring to the table.
- Build honest and trusting relationships with other authors who you can share your authentic feelings and fears with.
- Learn to rest. This doesn't necessarily mean staying in bed all day or lying on a beach. This can be a hard workout, learning a new language or instrument, joining an improv troupe. Your "rest" might look like other people's "active," but that's okay. The point is to hit pause on your publishing brain.

Type 4, The Authentic Writer

At their core, Fours' desire is to have significance. Their fear is that they're insignificant. In this context, significance doesn't necessarily come on a large scale. They don't necessarily need to be famous, though some may crave fame, but they long to feel their own significance in the cosmic landscape. The concepts of significance, authenticity, and personal identity are central to what compels or repels Fours.

Indie publishing can be a perilous landscape for Fours, who are so full of this raw urge to create the beautiful as well as the intentionally ugly that asking for money for such a natural act can feel dirty. Humans are made to create and express, so how would capitalism do anything but cheapen the experience?

"Marketability" is also considered a taboo subject by many Fours, who often believe that the confines of genre or page length or even the most basic accepted rules of grammar and punctuation are at odds with true creativity.

But this rejection of delivering something others can comprehend can butt up against their need for significance. If you want to be a significant creative force in the publishing world (or the world at large), you can't do that if no one reads your stuff. And people will not read your stuff if it's incomprehensible, the cover doesn't give a clear indication of what's written inside, the blurb is a mess, and your words do not follow the expected and accepted rules for your language of choice.

Only once you hit a certain threshold of comprehensibility can you realistically get the book into people's hands. Yes! Your work could expand and shape hearts and minds! But only if people know about it. And for people to know about it, you must tell them. You know, marketing. It's not a dirty word, I promise.

If a Four has a strong enough Three wing, they might not eschew marketing as strongly, and certainly not every Four presents as a tortured artist.

But every Four will struggle with envy. Envy is the feeling other people are getting the praise or life you deserve without earning it, and you're earning it but are not getting it. Envy can create a fantasy version of the world where everything is stacked against you, and it murders motivation. It says, *Why even try? It's hopeless.*

How do you use this information to motivate yourself as a writer?

The trick is simple: remember that nobody can write the stories you have to tell but you, and those stories are important to human consciousness. When you find yourself getting hung up on asking the big questions about your significance in the grand scheme, it's important to view that as raw motivational power. You can let it fester into negative, nihilistic thoughts like *Does it even matter if I write this?* or you can remind yourself that these kinds of questions and considerations are shared by everyone, and you're the best person to explore them because they are so central to who you are. You were built to write stories that explore identity and our place in the world. This is your gift, and that insatiable longing you feel will never let up unless you plumb these depths. Sorry, but creativity is your only way through and out of the thickest of your emotions.

Structure can also be your friend. If you feel unmotivated, it might be that you are unable to wrangle your emotions into something tangible. Give yourself constraints, be that what length of work you're going to produce, what voice you'll write in, what tone you'll aim for, or what theme you'll write to. Have you ever told five-year-olds to entertain themselves without any boundaries or instructions? Of course not. That's a bad idea. They will immediately apply permanent marker to your favorite keepsakes. We give the unrefined creative energy of little kids rules and supervision, and that's when they can most fruitfully enjoy themselves. Too many rules and restrictions will make things much less fun, but as a Four, you're in little danger of giving yourself too many constraints. But some are helpful. You must build channels for your creativity to flow through rather than flooding the entire plain.

Write stories about outcasts, oddballs, and pariahs. Write an antihero. Write from the perspective of an alien landing on a new planet. And write it all for the younger you who clung so dearly to works of art like that.

Your ability to sit with the full range of emotions without flinching is a gift you can give to others through your words. People need to see the characters they like and respect run the gambit of messiness. It gives the reader permission to feel. Though you might view your flood of emotions as a weakness, I can tell you that in this emotionally stifled world, it's a gift you can model for others.

I'll admit, I'm a little jealous of the work that Fours can produce once they find that motivation and set their mind to it. It's the kind of art that stops you in your tracks, that moves you, that creates powerful emotions even in the Enneagram types most disconnected from their emotional centers. The Four is so powerful that even simply having it as your wing (wing = a type on either side of the dominant type that can be used to reinforce the aims of the dominant type) can turn a Three with a Four wing (Taylor Swift) or a Five with a Four wing (Stephen King) into a powerful creator whose art thrusts us into particular moods whether we like it or not.

It's easy to spot an Individualist writer when you read them because their work transports you, and the mood and emotions of it stick to you like a film for hours, days, or even years after. Edgar Allan Poe—the quintessential Four—writes about this, describing it as a "singular effect" that he aims for in each of his pieces. Not sure what I'm talking about? Go read "The Fall of the House of Usher" and you'll understand. When I started reading *Interview with the Vampire* by Anne Rice (a Four) a few years ago, I put the book down after the first page, said, "Oh shit, this is going to be *that* kind of book," made myself some tea, discarded the bra, and snuggled under a heap of blankets to prepare for the moody onslaught I could already tell I was going to thoroughly enjoy for hours on end.

Individualist artists love to play with themes of identity, too. Virginia Woolf does it brazenly in *Orlando*, and Prince did it for the span of his entire musical career. Those types of public explorations can challenge the reader or audience to analyze their own identity, which may have calcified over time, with a fresh and critical eye.

If you're a Four who's struggling to put the words down or the words you're writing feel aimless or like "meaningless garbage," see if any of these are running on a loop in your head:

- *"Is this unoriginal trash?"*
- *"Someone's already written this."*
- *"There are no original ideas left in this world."*
- *"I loathe writing."*
- *"Anyone who writes faster than I do is turning out garbage."*
- *"If I write any faster, I'll turn out crap like everyone else."*

- *"No one will ever understand my art."*
- *"It doesn't make a difference to anyone if I write this or not."*
- *"Readers only like pulp nowadays, like the stuff [bestselling author] writes."*
- *"Books have to fit every genre trope for anyone to read them, and I don't write tropes."*
- *"Nobody reads anymore."*

I hate to be the bearer of bad news, but every one of these beliefs is faultier than the Texas power grid. Each of them is your ego or personal identity trying to spare itself possible injury. It doesn't care about YOU. It doesn't care if you ever create anything meaningful. All it cares about it risk aversion. You can say, "Thank you, ego. I know you're trying to protect me, but I have something important to share with the world."

If you're a Four who's struggling with motivation:

- Honestly, what else are you going to do with your life and all that longing? Express it or it'll eat you up.
- Create a few more rules on form or process, then let loose with the creativity.
- Remember that the path to feeling less isolated is communication, and the first step to communication is expression. Withholding your ideas out of fear of being misunderstood is the fastest way to keep people from being able to understand you.

- If you're feeling alone and misunderstood, practice deep listening to others. You may be low on inspiration because your own inner world is the only place you're attempting to draw from.
- Learn to spot envy in yourself and use that as a signal that someone has something you want. Then plan action that will move you more toward that thing, grabbing the power to achieve your dreams out of the hands of the universe, restoring it to you.
- When you find yourself ruminating, fantasizing, or spending too much time in your own imagination, go out and engage your senses in the present. This is where you'll find so much inspiration that not writing may feel impossible.
- Build relationships with other authors, even if you feel like the oddball in them. If you don't, your tendency toward fantasy will fill in the gaps of what you think you know about the community, and if that envy gets involved, it won't be a positive view.
- Try framing "I'm misunderstood" as "I have a unique perspective people can't get anywhere else." Don't mentally dramatize others rejecting you before you even give them a chance to love and appreciate you.

Type 5, The Rational Writer

At their core, Fives' desire is to be competent. Their fear is that they're incompetent. The concepts of knowledge, learning, and self-sufficiency are central to the way the Five relates to the world.

The relationship between knowledge and learning is a complex one, and it's in these details that Fives can entrap themselves. Knowledge is valuable. The desire to learn is important. But believing one must *know* to be competent is a quick way to stop learning in its tracks.

It's not so much the desire to know but the need to *already know* that begins to pull Fives into the dangerous pattern of isolation and withdrawal that severs their connection from the world and from themselves. And this stems from the fear that if they do not already know, they are not yet competent.

Additionally, Fives worry a whole awful lot about their resources, particularly their internal battery. They can view social connections as energy drains, overlooking how many relationships can fuel us rather than simply draining us. They worry that if they allow others to deplete their battery, they won't have enough left to take care of their own basic needs, and so they tend to erect a lot of barriers between them and the outside world to protect them from this.

And, yes, those same barriers meant to protect them also cut them off from the natural flow of interpersonal energy. Now it's all up to them to generate what they need.

This detachment severs connection not just to others, but to parts of ourselves. For Fives, it can take the form of compartmentalization. Head and heart function separately from one another, and Investigators tend to neglect the latter entirely. Even parts of a person's life and history can be severed through compartmentalization—happy memories, trauma, past relationships, etc.

And why would that stifle creativity? To create something new, to innovate, one must lay out all the tools and resources one has access to and find new connections. By compartmentalizing, a Five is diminishing their items to choose from and may end up stuck in the realm of dusty old ideas that lack the richness of emotion.

How do you use this information to motivate yourself as a writer?

Unfortunately, you're going to have to practice the art of trust and embrace experimentation.

First, work on trusting yourself. You don't have to know things to write about them. The beauty of fiction is that it's a playground for us to experiment with and explore new ideas we haven't completely fleshed out. And in writing those down and publishing them, we share what knowledge we've gained in the process and encourage others to develop the ideas even further. Trust that your emotions have something important to contribute as well, and experiment with listening to your gut, even though it doesn't seem rational.

Trust others. You may not possess all the pieces and tools you need to experience the breakthrough you've been seeking. The good news is that you don't have to. Trust that other people will bring fresh perspective to the ideas you've been developing, and maybe by sharing with them, rather than keeping ideas in your mental incubator until they seem complete enough, someone else will offer just the missing piece you've been seeking. If greater understanding is the goal, it doesn't matter whose ego gets to claim that final piece of the puzzle.

Trust the universe. This one is the hardest for Fives. But a lack of trust in the universe/humanity leads straight to a scarcity mindset, and this is where we hold on to more than we need out of fear that our needs won't be met otherwise. Our sympathetic nervous system runs on overdrive when we live our lives this way (this means lots of fight/flight/freeze/fawn), and it leads to—surprise!—us running on empty and at a lack later on (as well as various health issues). So, for the sake of your nervous system, run a little experiment: see if everything falls apart if you loosen your grip on your time and energy. Go *connect* with the world instead of observing it from afar. You may find that the connection gives more energy than it takes.

You have a mind, yes (and it's a good one!), but you also have a body and emotions. Give those a spin. Will you feel tired afterward? Yes! But that could be because your emotions and body have been underworked and need to get back in shape. Sleep can fix that problem for you, so the tiredness is only temporary.

The Enneagram Spectrum of Personality Styles says something so profound about the Five that I'm just going to share the quote directly: "being known, seen, and revealed (transparent) is just as vital as knowing, seeing, and revealing.*"

---

* From https://enneagramspectrum.com/enneagram-styles/#style5

If you've spent a lot of time alone and feel the motivation waning, there's an easy fix: go let the world know you.

Fives who've stopped compartmentalizing can be incredibly compelling communicators. The works of Ursula K. Le Guin, Agatha Christie, Stephen King, and Eckhart Tolle are examples of Fives' writing that engages intellectually, emotionally, and instinctually. And Gary Larson, creator of *The Far Side* comics, shows us the Five's gift of boiling down a concept into one clever or pithy phrase or idea.

So, if you're struggling to put the words down or feel like you're using the same tired ideas over and over again, see if any of these are running on a loop in your head:

- *"This will go over their heads anyway."*
- *"I know everything there is on this subject, so it's boring to me now."*
- *"I need to learn even more before I can start writing."*
- *"They don't deserve this effort from me."*
- *"I can't write the next scene until I know exactly how it will turn out."*
- *"If I don't publish faster, I won't be able to pay my bills."*
- *"I don't trust my editor to keep me from looking foolish."*
- *"The success of this is all up to me."*
- *"This is getting too sappy; I'll look like an idiot if I publish it."*
- *"I can't start writing until I finish reading a few more books on this topic."*

These stifling ideas can usually be tamed by treating your stories as part of a learning process. Maybe it's time to switch from the desire to already know to the desire to learn more through experimentation.

Take your need to know out of the hands of your ego and hold it up as a valiant pursuit, something you dedicate yourself to act toward each day. And remember that the kinds of knowledge that can only be attained through your heart and body are equally as important to seeing the big picture as the knowledge attained through your head.

If you're a Five who's struggling with motivation:

- Reframe your identity from a knowledgeable person to a seeker of knowledge.
- Ask yourself how you can *share* what knowledge you've gained with those around you on a daily basis. (If there's no one around you, then leave the house and find people.)
- Learn about emotions. Gifting yourself with emotional vocabulary is the first step to accessing those things you've wasted so much energy keeping at bay. Having something like an emotion wheel visible in your writing space can go a long way. (You can print one out or buy one on Etsy.)
- Notice what thoughts lead to what emotions, as well as what emotions lead to what thoughts.
- Keep an eye out for scarcity mindset, and incorporate daily practices that remind you of the natural flow of energy in the universe (meditation, stimulating conversation, time with good friends, walks in nature, etc.).

- Ask for help. The reason this is so hard is that somewhere along the way you learned that self-sufficient and competent people didn't need help. But that notion has been disproven time and time again. No one has ever done it all on their own. *Collaboration* is required for the fullest pursuit of knowledge and understanding, not isolation.
- Build relationships with other authors, and relax into the exchange of information. Clear boundaries can eliminate the need for isolation, so practice those, but don't be afraid to share what you know and ask what others know.

Type 6, The Faithful Writer

At their core, Sixes' desire is to be supported and to have guidance. Their fear is that they're unsupported and lacking guidance. The concepts of courage and faith are central to the way the Six relates to the world.

Of all the types, Sixes have the most fraught relationship with authority. Because they are fear-focused (they're in the "fear" triad of the Enneagram, and their unique Passion is also "fear"), they crave an authority figure to guide and protect them. But because they are fear-focused, they also don't necessarily trust authority figures, who by their very nature have the power to harm the Six and get away with it. You can see how much of a pickle this creates.

The crux of this problem is that the Six is looking externally for authority in these situations, and this results from their rejection of their Inner Authority. But as Loyalists move to healthier levels of development, they befriend their

Inner Authority and begin to trust that all the clarity they need can be found within themselves. In short, they learn to trust their instincts rather than endlessly doubt them.

In the meantime, though, Loyalists can struggle with indecision as all the possible threats to their best-laid plans appear obvious to them at all times.

The trouble with talking about Sixes is that this fear at the core of the type presents in two starkly different ways: phobic or counterphobic.

Most people know of the fight/flight/freeze/flop/fawn responses to a threat. Fight is to attack the threat, flight is to run away, freeze is being caught in indecision and not acting, flop is to submit to the threat, and fawn is an attempt to ingratiate oneself to the threat. These are all possible responses of a Six, but the first one—fight—is the typical counterphobic response we might see.

Contrary to what our society might tell us, the counterphobic fear response *isn't* more courageous or admirable than any of the others. That's because it's still a reaction to fear rather than a response made by their Inner Authority. The counterphobic response still lacks a faith that the universe is, generally speaking, on one's side. Nevertheless, this counterphobic response tends to get more praise from society, even though it is usually a reckless reaction rather than a reasonable response.

The phobic response catches much more flack. It can look like retreat, like indecision, and like behind-the-scenes manipulations of others to increase one's own safety through social standing.

It's not uncommon, though, for a Six who is usually phobic to reach a breaking point. They can no longer stand the endless voices in their head pointing out all the ways things could go wrong, and they no longer have the energy to stay small and invisible. In this case, that energy that's been repressed can explode in a reckless counterphobic act, which in our industry usually looks like publishing a book before it's ready and before there's a plan in place for its success.

But don't worry, because it's not all bad news for a Loyalist. Once you embrace your Inner Authority, your leadership and courage can't help but show—after all, *there's no courage without fear*.

How do you use this information to motivate yourself as a writer?

Have faith. Loosen the reins a little bit, at least in the creation process. There is no threat in a shitty or bold first draft. There is no threat in revisions. There's very little potential danger in publishing, too.

I'm not telling you to close your eyes and jump off a cliff, hoping a giant eagle will catch you before you hit the ground, of course. Faith takes practice, and it takes baby steps, so you must start practicing your baby steps.

You'd do well to incorporate as many practices as you can into your daily routine that lower your heart rate and tone your vagus nerve. This is because fear, that thing you do so well, activates your sympathetic nervous system, and once that's triggered, everything in life is harder and burns more fuel. Your aim at the start of each day might be to relax your sympathetic nervous system and engage your parasympathetic nervous system with things like deep breathing, singing, stretching, or a quiet walk through nature. Doing this will free up much-needed mental bandwidth to make smarter decisions by accessing your inner clarity. Make enough of these small, smart decisions, and you might just begin to believe the universe is working with you rather than against you!

If you're an independent author, you can't keep looking outward for an authority to tell you exactly how to market your books. Your readers are the only gatekeepers, and no matter what you write, there will be readers for it. The only thing that can stop you is your anxiety. But when you *choose* courage instead, when you accept that you'll always feel a little afraid but choose to do it anyway because your inner guidance tells you to, you're unstoppable.

Stop waiting until there's no fear to take the action. Practice acting despite the fear.

Perhaps there is no better example of trusting one's Inner Authority above that of the external world (i.e. society) than Mark Twain, a strong example of a Six who ridiculed various forms of external authority. Writing down the iconoclastic ideas that he did and publishing them in the time when he did took repeated acts of courage, but as if often the case with the boldest written words, those ideas changed hearts and minds. I would guess it's the reason schools keep assigning *Adventures of Huckleberry Finn* despite the egregious racial slurs and stereotypes; in the context of the time, the story took serious *cojones* to publish.

Need another example of the sheer guts that a Six can access when they've chosen to trust themselves? How about Malcolm X? His writings challenge the authority structures of our society and will continue to for generations to come, I suspect. Sixes *can* be brave. And because they have the most fear, they also have access to the most courage. If you're a Six, you were built to be braver than most.

If you're a Six struggling to put the words down, see if any of these are running on a loop in your head:

- *"I don't know what should happen next."*
- *"I need to read one more plotting book before I'm ready."*
- *"I can't write that! They'd crucify me!"*
- *"I should play it safe with this scene."*
- *"I should wait to write the next scene until I talk with my writing coach."*
- *"No matter what I write, this book is going to flop."*
- *"What if I [normal writing action] and then [catastrophe happens]?"*
- *"I just need more time to consider all the worst-case scenarios, then I can avoid them."*
- *"I need feedback from a few more people before I can be sure this is the correct approach."*
- *"How can I write when the world is on fire?"*
- *"#$(*@()&*#&$@"* <— *The fuzzy brain scramble of anxiety*

These stifling thoughts will begin to fade when you remember that there is no sure thing in this world, no matter what you do, and that you always have the choice to do the brave thing anyway. No matter how anxious you are, remember that there is someone out there who needs to see your courageous example. You could change the trajectory of their life by acting despite your fear. When your deep wisdom and Inner Authority speak to you, it's time to set fear aside and do as they say. No matter the consequences, you won't regret it.

If you're a Six who's struggling with motivation:

- Develop meditative practices that activate your parasympathetic nervous system and connect you to your inner authority. I'm not telling you to "clear your mind" because I know you'll yell at me for suggesting it. Instead, try other meditative practices like journaling, a walk in nature, tarot, yoga, or anything else that activates your Body Center so your Head Center doesn't have to do all the heavy lifting. Do these things prior to your writing time.
- Unlike real life, writing allows for revisions. That makes it a perfect low-stakes arena to practice trusting your instincts. See where they lead you, and if that's somewhere different from the last book about story structure you read, that is A-OK! Keep going. Keep experimenting. Keep playing.
- Summon to mind the child you used to be. At some point, they learned not to trust themselves and to listen to an untrustworthy authority instead. Show courage for that child who was too vulnerable to show it at the time, and remember that there are all kinds of people who learned this

same thing and will have their world changed by your brave example.

- Connect to a purpose bigger than yourself. Bad news: you won't live forever, no matter how safely you live. But through courage and trusting yourself, you can be remembered and felt for generations by making the world a safer and braver place.
- There is no right or safe way to write a book. If you want to play it safe, you should stop writing immediately. Yeah, never again. It's the only way. What's that you say? Your head would explode? Perfect. Then accept that writing is risky, but you can't not do it. Start from there, and remind yourself of this when you have to. (Put it on a sticky note on your computer, if you must!)
- Write stories that will change lives. Make the stakes for not writing higher than those for writing. Danger for the sake of it is a pathological disfunction, but danger for a greater purpose is called "courage." And you have lots of it in there.
- Re-evaluate your definition of betrayal. Almost all betrayal is a matter of perception. If you're expecting others to betray *themselves* to stay true to you, then you're expecting too much and creating a self-fulfilling prophecy that everyone will eventually betray you.
- Re-evaluate your definition of loyalty. If others expect you to betray your creative vision and your Inner Authority to stay loyal to them (this includes editors, coaches, beta readers, cowriters, and advance readers), then they may not be the

right person to collaborate with. Don't keep
deferring to them; let them go.

- Build relationships with other authors. As you do,
  continue to choose the brave thing by offering
  your collaborators the benefit of the doubt rather
  than slipping immediately into suspicion when
  conflict arises. Show up for them the way you
  wish everyone in the world showed up for each
  other.

Type 7, The Enthusiastic Writer

At their core, Sevens' desire is to be satisfied. Their fear is
to be dissatisfied and deprived or stuck in pain. The
concepts of opportunity and enjoyment are central to the
way the Seven relates to the world.

Sevens bring a great optimism to the world because they
see the possibility in everything. Whereas other types may
view things through a lens of threat or caution, Sevens, with
their rose-colored glasses, see the world in terms of pleasure
(and are so pain averse that it causes them to have a blind
spot for it in the world). They see what is to be gained,
gained, gained.

But it's a thin line between running toward things and
running away from things, and while the Seven appears to
be focused on the positive, the first sign of potential pain
can send them running... though they will usually frame it
to themselves and others as "I'm not running away, there
was just something even more amazing somewhere else."

You might see how this can trip up Sevens in their writing. Though the talk style of the Seven is literally "storytelling," part of the appeal is the instant gratification of telling that story to another person and getting immediate feedback. This is not a mechanism naturally built into the process of writing a book, and the delayed gratification can prove frustrating, like deprivation, and send a Seven seeking that gratification away from the keyboard.

While not every Seven is an extrovert (a common misconception of the type), every Seven craves frequent positive feedback. If you're an introvert, this could be from an online community or in a small-group or one-on-one setting. If you're an extrovert, this might look like book signings, panels, and live online events. And if your WIP is proving tricky or frustrating, expect a lot more of these events to magically appear on that schedule.

It's not all avoidant behavior for Sevens, though. When they can channel their enthusiasm into a single project and bring that project to completion, the excitement is contagious.

How do you use this information to motivate yourself as a writer?

It's important to think of both focus and pain tolerance—two things Sevens can struggle with—as muscles. Some activities strengthen them, and some cause inflammation that weakens your performance.

Take focus, for example. If you haven't read a book in a year, it's unlikely that you'll read the whole thing in a sitting without wandering off to do something else, no matter how good the story is. I used to tell my students that they had to work up to thirty minutes of reading at a time like they would have to work up to bench-pressing four hundred pounds. I told them to use a timer and start with five minutes at a time. Once they started getting annoyed by the timer interrupting their focus, they could move onto ten minutes, and so forth. (I also let them pick out whichever books they wanted to read, because ain't nothing worse than reading books you don't enjoy. PSA: DNF it if you don't enjoy it.)

The same theory applies to your writing. If you've only written five hundred words a day three times a week for the last year, you're not going to suddenly have the stamina to switch to three thousand words a day seven days a week. Sorry. Focus isn't a matter of "willpower" like some will tell you.

The same concept goes for pain tolerance, and in the case of the Seven, we're usually talking about emotional pain more than physical pain. You can never get acquainted with the richness of the moment if you never practice sitting in the discomfort of your FOMO rather than immediately trying to soothe it.

And as with working out and building muscle, there's a psychological component to all of this. You must become aware of (i.e. notice) when your focus is slipping. That's a sign you're disconnecting from the story, and that moment of disconnection is your first clue about what's up.

Ask yourself: is this a particularly painful scene to write? Am I struggling to know what to write next? Do I legitimately need a break or to wrap for the day? OR do I need to pause, take a few deep breaths, remember how satisfying this scene will be for the reader, and then carry on enjoying that experience?

In short, learn to recognize that first twinge of dissatisfaction and hit pause long enough to explore it. That way, you're responding rather than reacting.

If you're a Seven struggling to put the words down, see if any of these are running on a loop in your head:

- *"This is boring."*
- *"I need to find weekend plans."*
- *"Ugh, this story is getting too heavy."*
- *"This isn't fun anymore."*
- *"My other book idea is more promising. I should start on that one instead."*
- *"Where should I go for dinner tonight?"*
- *"I'd rather be [literally any other activity]."*
- *"Writing should be fun and easy, and this isn't."*
- *"What am I going to do on my upcoming vacation?"*
- *"I wonder what so-and-so is up to."*
- *"I should take a picture of myself working and post it to social media."*
- *"Maybe I'll be in the mood for writing later, but for now, I want to grab brunch somewhere."*

Each of these thoughts pulls you away from the present experience of writing and draws your attention toward escape and stimulation. But each of those things can be found without getting out of your chair if you shift your focus back to your story.

I'm not trying to deprive you here. Instead, I'm showing you that the wealth you seek is already inside of you. It's not to be found in bougie pancakes and bottomless mimosas (okay, sometimes it is). Reroute those neural pleasure pathways. Work the muscles of delayed gratification. Cut out the unhealthy behaviors that dull the strength of your focus.

If you're a Seven who's struggling with motivation:

- Sorry, but you gotta cut back on the social media. Fast from it completely for two days if you can. Then use an app like Freedom to limit when you can access those sites. The instant dopamine hits available through social media (especially TikTok) are bad for everyone, but are especially toxic for your type. And the FOMO generated by apps like Instagram will drag you down your development levels faster than you can say "hashtag."
- Treat focus like a muscle. Eliminate distractions in your writing environment as best you can and use a timer to work in sprints. Start small if you have to with five- or ten-minute sprints for a few weeks. When those start to feel too short or the timer goes off without your noticing it, move to longer increments. But just like with physical exercise, it's not a constant step forward. Don't be discouraged if lack of sleep, life circumstance, hormones, or illness make it harder for you to focus today than the week before.
- Take a couple of minutes to visualize the scene you're about to create, focusing on the most

exciting moments in it that you can't wait to write. Even the dark night of the soul will have something that you can't wait to try out, so give yourself a moment to locate it. If you find you can't locate anything exciting about the next scene, maybe you need to spice it up!

- It's okay to work on multiple series at a time. It's probably ideal for you, honestly. But try to limit yourself to two or three, and ask yourself if you're switching between them because you're running from something unpleasant in one or because it makes sense for you to take a break and work on the other.

- Pleasure isn't the path to satisfaction, but enjoyment is. Enjoyment is deep engagement with the present, and you'll find that the present has everything you need to feel contented if you dig deep enough in it.

- Absolutely do hands-on research for your novels, and use your enjoyable experiences to enhance your stories. Is your protagonist at a trendy diner on a first date? Schedule time to visit a trendy diner, and as you eat your meal there, sink into the experience and commit every sensation to memory. Go ahead, close your eyes, separate out each flavor, texture, shape, color, and scent. Not only will you create an enjoyable experience when you do your "research," but you'll reactivate that memory in your writing. The same goes for travel. Build it into your process if you enjoy it, because life's too short to only write! (Bonus tip: don't forget to save your receipts for tax time.)

- Pay attention to the moments when you feel JOMO (joy of missing out). This might be skipping a night out with friends to stay home and read a book on the couch with your dog snoozing at your feet. It might look like leaving the gathering early so you can feel rested and ready to write the next morning. JOMO is a product of connecting to yourself in the present; FOMO is the opposite.

- Build relationships with other authors who enjoy the same things as you do outside of writing. If you're really into sailing, plan a beach retreat with those authors that combines writing with the activity you love. And be sure to schedule dedicated writing hours for everyone, so you can easily focus without wondering if you're missing out on conversations.

Type 8, The Bold Writer

At their core, Eights' desire is to be independent and strong. Their fear is to be harmed and controlled by others. The concepts of power and vulnerability are central to the way the Eight relates to the world.

This fear/desire combo makes Eights natural-born leaders, which is good, since y'all don't enjoy following anyway. The world needs leaders like you, with your keen eye for power structures that are invisible to many others and your bent toward justice.

You're not afraid of a fight, which is admirable, so long as there's a legitimate fight to have and you're pretty sure you can win. And when that's not the case, you don't usually let that stop you from trying, do you?

If you're an Eight, you've probably been called "difficult" or "stubborn" or "argumentative" a few times in your life. When it comes time to argue for justice or to stand up for the little guy, you're just the person for the job, but how is the other ninety percent of your life treating you? Is it the peaceful rest you need? Are you a pro at trusting that, in the words of your fellow Eight Martin Luther King, Jr., "the arc of the moral universe is long, but it bends toward justice"?

This need for justice and your inner call for strength in the face of tyranny is much needed in the literary world, and that's something you will naturally inspire in your readers. Your stories can't help but be about standing up for the little guy, showing tremendous power and determination when the odds are stacked against victory, and brave leaders inspiring the same kind of drive in those they lead.

Since power is so central to this type, it's crucial that we discuss its various forms. In plain terms, an *unhealthy* Eight seeks power over others, and a *healthy* Eight aims to empower themselves and those around them. Meanwhile, an average Eight is in the process of losing their grip on their own sense of empowerment and seeking that need for power from external sources rather than reaching internally for it.

The choices an Eight makes about how to proceed in these average levels very much determine if they become a hero or a villain, the protector or the predator. Because while all types have the potential to function in unhealthy ways, when someone with a natural fixation on power becomes unhealthy, it creates an especially frightening situation for those around them.

How do you use this information to motivate yourself as a writer?

Get real with yourself on this one thing: your impulse to exert power over others is a direct result of not feeling empowered in that moment. Reconnect with your inner power, and you'll find you have less of a desire to exert it over others... and more of a desire to help others find their own inner power.

If you're feeling unmotivated, it may be that you're expending all your energy trying to control external things and people rather than turning that energy inward to focus on the only thing you ever have a chance of controlling: yourself.

Or maybe you're sad. Maybe there's some soft human emotion you genuinely need to deal with and surrender to that you're not allowing in because you've attached the label "weak" to it. This emotional stifling can lead to anger being your only acceptable outlet, and anger burns hot and can wear out even an Eight over time. But if you try letting that "weak" emotion in, you won't be so emotionally constipated, and on the other side of it, you'll be stronger having mastered the skill of feeling a wide range of emotions.

Creative Eights embody this example of surrender. It may surprise you to learn that Toni Morrison was an Eight, as was Paul Newman. It probably won't surprise you to hear that Ernest Hemingway, Pablo Picasso, and Mae West were Eights as well.

Not everything is a struggle, but some things are. Mae West was fighting against all kinds of body and behavioral expectations for women, and it took every bit of her defiant Eight attitude to keep it up. But better for the rest of us women that she did.

Oskar Schindler, another Eight, embodies the benevolent strength of the Eight when the time comes to defend those who need it. And Serena Williams shows us how an Eight can soar to greatness despite the established barriers of racism and sexism in her chosen arena. Her creativity is undeniable on the tennis court, as is her passion and power. And by doing what she's done and in the unapologetic way she has, she's inspired a whole generation of girls, especially Black girls, to try out a sport that was, until recently, almost entirely the domain of white men. Talk about challenging power structures.

If you're struggling to put the words down, see if any of these are running on a loop in your head:

- *"This is too easy."*
- *"I should be able to overcome this challenge on my own."*
- *"I shouldn't be tired yet."*
- *"I'll write... after I destroy this person on the internet."*
- *"I can't write because my nine-to-five boss is such a prick and won't stop bugging me."*

- *"If my editor is going to question me like this, I should just find another editor."*
- *"I've dug deep before, so if that isn't working this time, it's because I'm not trying hard enough."*
- *"No pain, no gain. Work is supposed to hurt."*
- *"This is too much [violence/sex/language] for the readers. But I also don't want to let them dictate what I write."*

Each of these thoughts rejects the signals your emotions are trying to send you and concocts external challenges where there aren't any, pulling your focus away from what you can control and toward what you can't control but will try to anyway.

Writing doesn't have to be a struggle from start to finish. It can be a soft place for your tender side to land. You don't have to fight against your environment all the time. You can take breaks (and must) without being "weak." I'm telling you right now, a story where none of the main characters show vulnerability without being painted as weak will be a hard one to read and enjoy. You need to let the vast range of human emotions (yes, even the softer ones) flow through you to your characters, or else you could exhaust your readers.

One of the most challenging emotions for an Eight to show is tenderness, but when you do tap into that well, it's a display of the purest form of power—the strength to be kind when one could easily be otherwise.

Because the Eight's corresponding defense mechanism is *denial*, there are also a lot of things that the Eight isn't seeing about themselves. Anything that relates to their vulnerabilities will fly completely off the radar as a possible cause of writing or marketing blocks. Eights, especially those with a Nine wing, will dismiss certain challenges as unimportant if those challenges get even close to touching on the Eight's vulnerable parts.

So, if you're an Eight who's struggling with motivation:

- Use your writing to practice the art of surrender. Let your characters be who they are and stop trying to control them so closely. If the scene doesn't want to bend to your will, see where it leads you, trusting that you're still the one in control, because... you are.
- When something feels like a struggle, ask yourself if it needs to be. It's not weak to make the process of publishing easier on yourself, just like it's not valiant or brave to make it harder than it needs to be.
- Remind yourself of who your work will inspire simply because it came from someone as empowered as you. Empowerment is not a zero-sum game. There is an unlimited amount of it to go around, and you help it multiply just by showing up in your creative work as an empowered person.
- If your writing feels dull, maybe you're not examining invisible power structures enough. Maybe you're relying too heavily on tired examples of power and need to dig deeper and take a more nuanced approach. You know better

than anyone that explicit power and implicit power are not always the same.

- Work with an Enneagram-trained coach on your pattern of denial. You can't see what you can't see, but someone who understands the patterns of the Eight can show you what you're missing. And when they show you, *fucking listen*. Your type is the most "my truth is the only truth that matters" type of them all, and it's keeping you from any growth and probably causing to you harm others without realizing it. If you want to be a protector rather than a predator, you must learn to spot the predator patterns in yourself through overcoming this pattern of denial.

- Create an emotions-based practice. What I mean is some special time and space where you check in with yourself and ask what you're feeling. And then you need to feel it, even though doing so might make you feel out of control. Your type is firmly planted in the Anger triad, which puts you in jeopardy of having every emotion feel like anger. Unpack that and sort out the individual emotions so that you can keep moving forward.

- People will try to exert power over you. If you're always reacting to this, they've won. But if you begin to recognize your body's sensations whenever this happens, you'll learn to pause and remind yourself that you are the only one who can give your power away. This exercise will empower you and keep you focused on your story rather than throwing hands at every hater who comes your way.

- Build a network of authors you like, and don't feel like you always need to lead. If you find yourself only networking with authors you believe are behind you in their career, it's time to reel in your need to be in the power-up position. Network with people you believe know more than you do and who don't need you to lead them. Then, you know, learn from them. There will come a time when they need your gifts in return, and you can provide them then. No need to force it.

Type 9, The Harmonious Writer

At their core, Nines' desire is to feel whole and harmonious. Their fear is to be separated or cut off from the rest of the world. The concepts of peace and unity are central to the way the Nines relate to the world.

I'm married to a Nine, and the naturally calming energy they bring is what first caught my interest. It's one of the many things I continue to love about him. But it's also at the core of every moment when he makes my eye twitch with annoyance. That's because the peaceful energy can stagnate into inaction and neglect. It can also turn to ambivalence, which is a passive-aggressive way of making everyone else take on responsibility for major decisions.

The irony is that Nines believe that by not expressing a strong opinion, they are avoiding conflict. And maybe that's true in the short term, but it doesn't work out in the long run.

That conflict aversion is at the heart of Nines' suffering. It's their big lesson to learn that not all conflict weakens bonds and creates disunity. Sometimes conflict is the only path to the harmony Nines so desperately seek. (Don't we all have fun ways of keeping ourselves from what we need?)

A sure-fire way to avoid conflict with someone else is to merge with them, abandoning your own wants and needs and replacing them with theirs. It's also how Nines end up never completing their book, losing sight of themselves, and generally feeling like a ghost floating around an old, abandoned manor.

But never fear, Nines, because you have this one amazing thing going for you: you are at one with the universe, especially when you claim and express your wants and needs. And you're the best suited for the tough conflicts of life because you can see things from the other side's perspective and find a solution that works for everyone. Only through those types of solutions can true harmony—not a false and precarious one—be achieved.

How do you use this information to motivate yourself as a writer?

The key is to remember that unity is a matter of addition, not subtraction. You don't create harmony between two people by erasing one of the people. That's not harmony; it's self-forgetting. For harmony to exist, everyone must show up as whole as possible. The universe is a complete system, and it was born out of more conflict than our human brains can imagine. But that heat gives birth to new stars and galaxies, and without it, there would be nothingness, not wholeness.

Your ability to resolve conflict is why you need to be writing, completing, and publishing your books. You can put your characters in the most perilous situation and show the reader that hope is never lost, that the solution requires everyone showing up and offering their unique gifts, and that no matter how dark that dark night of the soul, confronting the issues head-on it is the only path to personal and social harmony.

Nines are natural storytellers because you see the complexity and richness of a situation. Your talk style is "epic saga" as a result. Further proof of that can be found in some notable Nines like George Lucas, Walt Disney, and Jim Henson. Talk about creating complete and believable fictional universes.

Joseph Campbell, the first person to popularize the idea of the Hero's Journey, is another interesting example of the Nine finding commonality in humanity.

If you're a Nine struggling to put the words down, see if any of these are running on a loop in your head:

- *"Does anyone even care about this series?"*
- *"If I never wrote again, it wouldn't be a big deal."*
- *"There's no rush. I can finish that chapter when I feel like it later."*
- *"I want to include diversity, but I'm not going to do it right and everyone's going to get mad at me."*
- *"I should drop this and write about a safer topic."*
- *"Where is this story even going?"*
- *"This isn't really the genre I want to write, but it'll make [whoever] happy."*

- *"I don't know what any of these characters want."*
- *"This is more effort than it's worth."*
- *"What's the point? The world won't end if I don't finish this."*

Each of these thoughts diminishes the importance of your voice or sells your contribution short. Sure, maybe you should run your book by a sensitivity reader to make sure it doesn't offend them... but their word isn't law (and as we know from the principles of the Enneagram, when a person turns their attention toward finding something specific, they're bound to see it everywhere). You could find two sensitivity readers who disagree or something being offensive, and then what? You'll have to make the final call anyway. Own your voice. It's just as important as everyone else's.

Your words build bridges. They help opposing tribes see the other side of the argument. They heal wounds caused by separation. To say your stories don't matter is, plain and simple, an egregious abdication of responsibility. No other type can do what you do the way you do it, and no other Nine has the personal experience you have that shapes your unique voice. Keeping it to yourself for fear of conflict is selfish. Will your books change the world? Maybe not. But they'll change some people's world, and those ripples add up.

If you're a Nine who's struggling with motivation:

- Find a Nine role model who inspires you—
  George Lucas, Abraham Lincoln, Gloria Steinem,
  Audrey Hepburn, Barack Obama—and keep a

picture of them on your desk or near you when you write. Let it be a reminder that they had the same self-doubts that you did and thought it was worth adding their voice anyway. And look at their contributions!

- Set yourself a writing challenge: how much chaos and conflict can you create in your story that you then resolve? Exercise your gift of peacemaking—I promise it'll feel great.

- Ask yourself what in your life you're saying yes to when you mean no, then see if you can rectify one of those situations. This will deepen your connection to yourself, and you can use that energy for your writing.

- Think about what stories you needed to read when you were younger—what do you wish someone had told you and encouraged in you? And then write those stories. (It doesn't have to be children's books or YA, either. The inner children of adult readers need to hear your wisdom, too.)

- Learn to recognize your body's gut reaction of *hell yes* and *fuck no*. Get back in touch with these sensations through journaling and through paying attention to yourself when you make decisions; pay attention to the feelings in your body. This will also help you write characters who are more in touch with what they want.

- Remember that slow and steady is a perfectly good approach. Slow and *unsteady* is how you will lose steam (or "rust out"), though. Fast and steady is how you will likely run out of steam. If you feel yourself slipping into the frantic fear energy of your stress number (Six), take a step back and look at the bigger picture. Extend the timeline. Your work doesn't have to be urgent to be important, but you do need to keep at it if you want to publish it.

- Hit pause on listening to others' suggestions for your work. You have enough voices in your head as it is without the input of everyone else. The answer you're looking for is already in your gut. Take a moment to listen, then forge onward.

- Maintain a regular movement practice. This doesn't have to be intense, but physical exercise is crucial to combating unhealthy lethargy, un-numbing yourself, and inspiring the kind of action you must take to reach your healthier levels of development. When you feel the sleepiness and apathy start to set in, evaluate your life critically. Are you lacking sleep, or would you benefit from elevating that heart rate and getting your blood pumping?

- Build a network of authors who value your voice and will remind you why it's needed. External accountability might not make you write when you don't feel like it, but it might help you keep track of how long it's been since you've written (time gets away from us when we numb), and that keeps weeks and months from slipping by unnoticed between writing sessions.

Phew, that was a lot. Sorry, not sorry if that was painfully accurate for you. Hopefully your brain is on overload just a bit, but in the best way. Now is a good time to step away, get a cuppa tea or whatever you find soothing, and do something fun and easy. Maybe it's lying out in a hammock listening to the birds. Maybe it's catching up on whatever your favorite entertainment is. Maybe it's dancing to the new album by your favorite artist. All of these can be restful, depending on your type.

Not sure how you best rest? You're not alone on that, but don't worry; we'll talk more about this in the next chapter.

BLOCK: YOU NEED REST

If none of your type's suggestions from the previous chapter works for you, then there's a good chance that the solution to your block is simple: you need rest.

It's one thing to say that and a completely other thing to do it, though.

Rest, as we know, can be one of the hardest things in the world to do.

When we hear the word "rest," we may think of something like lying on the couch in front of the TV or sitting on the beach and watching the waves roll in. While those things might feel restful to you, they are not always the most effective ways to rest, and many folks recoil at the idea of so little getting done.

We must become more specific when we talk about rest. What is the intended purpose of it? What might it look like for you? How do you want to feel on the other side of it?

Certain types—Ones, Threes, Sevens, and Eights especially—are unlikely to feel particularly "at rest" doing nothing at all, especially if they're used to going a hundred miles per hour all the time. If that's the case for you (whatever your type), then doing nothing is not restful, and you don't need to force it on yourself. There are other options, which we'll talk about in this section. (You might cringe at these, too, but they're effective.)

The reason we need rest is that we are human, not that we are weak or faulty. If we didn't need down times and moments throughout our day, week, and year where we change gears and renew our energy, we would be the only animal on Earth with that distinction.

When we deny our need for rest and attempt to push through when our heart, head, and body are tired, we end up *completely* depleted later on. If you have a clear purpose in your author career, the idea of being completely depleted and unable to keep going will bother you, and I won't dissuade you from that feeling.

> **To build a sustainable career, we must prioritize rest the same way we prioritize our work.**

That's easier said than done, of course. We've all worked on our dedicated days off because we thought, *It'll just be a second.* Then it's rarely a second. Or maybe it is a second, but then your head can't stop spinning on work-related thoughts for hours afterward, meaning your heart and body might have had a day off, but your head did not. The next day, however, we expect our head to feel rested. When it isn't, we can take that to mean that "rest" doesn't work. But... we didn't rest that part of ourselves.

I published eleven books in 2018. To some, that sounds like a lot, and to others, it sounds like a slow year. No point in comparing yourself either way, because it wasn't done from a healthy place for me. I burned out. I neglected to take time off because I was grinding to reach my goals. By the end of the year, every day felt like mental torture. I'd dedicated so much time to writing that I hadn't watered the seeds of anything else in my life, which meant that even on the weekends, I ended up working because "I don't have anything else to do."

Because I am a genius, I deduced that if I couldn't write books anymore, I would have a difficult time being an author. Something had to change. It started with taking a week off at the end of every quarter, and two weeks over the holidays at the end of December. I stuck to it for the first two quarters of 2019, and by my third-quarter break, the painful memories (and lessons) of that burnout were fading, and I decided to spend what was supposed to be my week off writing the first book of a new series I was excited about.

You can probably guess how much I regretted missing that break. By November, I was out of gas and still had a month and a half to go. But it was worth learning the lesson again, solidifying it this time.

The next year, 2020, gauging that I might need a little extra rest to pull through, I decided to take all of December off and *two* weeks in March. I'm glad I did. And because of, *ya know*, I got to spend a lot of time at home reading during my breaks, which is restful for me.

I experimented with working only four days a week last year, on top of my quarterly breaks and taking the *entire* month of December off, and not only did that feel better than ever, but I ended 2023 with gas left in the tank for the holidays and rolled into January with a clear mind, a plan, and confidence that I had exactly what I needed in my toolbox to pull it off.

I describe these stages and how long it took me to cultivate to a rest regimen that works for me so that you don't expect yourself to feel comfortable doing it right away. Anything that feels unfamiliar will be difficult to integrate into your life. It takes time. It takes trial and error. It takes learning the same damn lesson over and over again until the lesson hurts so bad that it sticks.

And for those who are wondering or the Threes who need convincing, I get much *more* done over the course of a year when I allow myself proper rest. I keep records. My income has only increased since I incorporated more rest. Now, that may not be the healthiest reason to do it, but if it is the reason *for now* that convinces you to try it, I'm fine with that.

You may be wondering why people don't rest, when many of us dream about an easy and restful life so frequently.

To those who've built their self-respect on their output and exertion, rest poses an existential threat.

I was one of those people back in 2018, and it kicked my ass in the end. Our flawed beliefs always do. To me, resting felt irresponsible, and I had very little expectation of anything "work-related" being fun, even the career I'd dreamed about since I was a kid. If it was fun here and there, that was a bonus, but that was by no means necessary for me.

Allow me to point out that I didn't burn out *optionally*. It's not that it got to a point where it was so laborious to write that I decided not to. I, a champion white-knuckler, *could not* will my body and mind to write books anymore. Forcing myself to "just get it done" was my specialty. Maybe it's yours, too. Or maybe it was, but it's not working as well anymore. It always stops working entirely in the end.

I once had a woman who I respect very much look me dead in the eyes and tell me, "You need to learn how to say, 'I won't,' before you have to say, 'I can't.'" At the time, the idea that I had that option seemed revolutionary. *You're telling me I don't have to take on everything that needs to be done until it breaks me?* If you, like me, have ever fantasized about being committed as an in-patient at a mental health facility so that you *finally* feel free to let a few things slide, then you might want to think about saying "I won't" a little sooner, too.

Taking weekends off and occasional vacations is great, and a huge step for many. But it's not realistic for everyone's complex schedule all the time. If you're one of those people, then before your stress and burnout causes you to write me off completely, allow me to offer another approach to rest that can help us develop sustainability.

Building regular and appropriate rest into our daily schedule is one way we can say, "I won't," before we say, "I can't." It might take some experimenting to find what rest feels like for you and how much you need, *and* it's also okay if you need a lot right now. In fact, with "a lot" being totally subjective, it's likely that whatever amount you need will feel like "a lot" to you.

Don't worry. You may not need as much later on. Life changes, our needs change, and so the best thing we can do for sustainability is to keep checking in with ourselves (learning how to do that effectively, of course) to see what needs to be adjusted.

The truth about writing is that taking a day off does not directly impact our sales. If you feel like it does, like every day off is lost money, then you are probably stuck in a fear-based cycle. Maybe you can't take *specific* days off because you have a podcast appearance scheduled or you're running a promo, but most things can be automated in advance. Even if you can't take today off, you can take *a* day off in the near future without any noticeable dip in your income. I promise you. I took a whole month off once and it turned out to be my highest-grossing month, thanks to automated ads and emails. The connection between your hours of toil and your income is not as direct or 1:1 as our minds may have us believe.

One of the myths about rest is that it is akin to stagnation. Unless you're struggling with a *physical* illness or injury, where bed rest and low exertion are required, rest is likely to be an action. For most writing-related exhaustion, it's almost guaranteed to be so. That's because it's our heads and hearts that we use up in the writing process, and so it's those that need the rest and recovery. Our body may be crying out for movement and exertion, though.

Thankfully, activating one of our three centers (Head/Heart/Body) gives the other centers a break, which is why physical exertion can be restful to our heart and mind.

The most effective approach to rest is to work it into your daily routine. Humans require rest every day, throughout the day. Maybe you have small children who shriek when you try to have quiet time, or you have an elderly parent living with you who needs care, or you're simply under a few writing deadlines. You might view these things as reasons why you can't rest every day, but I would argue that the constant stressors are only more reasons why you must rest every day. I'm not talking about taking an hour at a time for rest multiple times a day (though if that's what you need right now and you can swing it, be my guest). Rest can come in bite-size pieces, and that's often the only way we can work it into our busy lives. A minute of effective rest every hour is better than no effective rest throughout your day. You might be shocked by how much a single minute of effective rest can reground you, fill your well, and sustain you.

When we begin to think of rest as an activity, we realize that it can look like a lot of things.

Here are some ideas that could take sixty-plus minutes and may be employed more infrequently:

- Finishing a house project that has been dragging on
- Going for a hike
- Attending a protest march
- Taking a class for something that feels frivolous
- Volunteering
- Dinner with good friends

Here are some things that may only take thirty to sixty minutes:

- Going for a walk or jog
- Tidying a room in your home or your office
- Practicing an instrument
- Chatting with a stranger at a café
- Yoga
- Trying out a new recipe

Here are some restful ideas that may take less than thirty minutes:

- Cuddle your pet, partner, or child (assuming they let you)
- Chase your dog around until they get the zoomies
- Set out a blanket or chair and look up at the sky
- Make plans with friends for later on
- Do some deep stretching of the muscles that usually tighten up
- Water your plants

- Have a dance party in your living room

And here are some options that take less than a minute:

- Close your eyes and repeat your mantra (more on this Section 7)
- Stretch out your neck and shoulders as you remind your body that it's safe
- Complete three sets of box breathing (more on this in Section 7)
- Jot down all the tasks floating around in your head so you can stop mentally juggling them
- Place your hands on your heart and check on what emotions you're feeling
- Lean deeply into gratitude for something in your life
- Comfort and encourage yourself the way you would a good friend or a child
- Drink some water, bringing your attention to how good it feels to simply drink water (I usually end this one by saying, "Gah, I fuckin' love water," because that's my truth.)

Or maybe you *do* just need a good old-fashioned nap. That's okay, too.

Not all of the options listed above will be restful to you. And some of these suggestions might, in fact, be more of the same patterns you usually follow and are therefore draining.

For instance, a Seven-Enthusiast might be spending too much time with friends to avoid an unpleasant feeling, in which case adding more time with friends to their schedule probably isn't what they need to feel rested. Or a One-Reformer might be tidying their space with thoughts like *Look at what a slob you are. How can you let things get this disgusting?* Those kinds of judgmental thoughts are probably more of the same for a One and are therefore not going to be restful. (The cleaning could be done with more compassionate self-talk and feel like rest, of course.)

However, if a Three-Activator hits pause on their work to meet up for drinks with old friends who know them deeply, that could certainly be restful because it's an interruption to their regularly scheduled patterns. And if a Nine-Peace-maker awakens to the mess in their home and takes action to tidy their space as a gift to themselves, they may feel incredibly energized on the other side of it.

Your mission, should you choose to accept it, is to discover what activities feel restful to you.

On top of our head, heart, and body needing rest after use, there are particular patterns each type is prone to that can wear us out extra quick. Rest often looks like benching these patterns for a bit. If that includes drinking a mai tai on the beach, so be it, but it doesn't have to be that extravagant, and we can give ourselves rest even during our normal work hours. Our tired ol' patterns tire us out, so the first step for rest can be to interrupt those draining patterns.

Here's how we wear ourselves out by type... and how to stop.

Ones: Drop something that you're doing out of a

sense of personal obligation and replace it with
something that brings you joy.

Twos: Set and enforce a boundary around your
energy, and ask for help where you need it.

Threes: Hit pause on seeking approval from
others and take a moment to privately celebrate
how far you've come.

Fours: Simplify something you've made overly
complicated.

Fives: Share yourself and your ideas with people
you love.

Sixes: Have a laugh with people you trust.

Sevens: Pass on pleasure and go deep on something—a book, a topic, an emotional conversation.

Eights: Pause to feel compassion for yourself or
others, and let the sensation of it settle in your
body.

Nines: Take focused action on something you've
delayed taking action on.

These suggestions may look like nothing, but they will hit
at the heart of your exhaustion. If you haven't been practicing aligned rest on regular basis, which most people have
not, give it a try. Make it a part of your daily routine, and
you will be absolutely shocked by how much different your
life looks, and how much energy you feel, in even a month's
time.

CONCEPT IN ACTION:
A Bold Writer (8) trying to do it all

When I asked Tammy what was going on in her writing business, it was a good ten minutes before I was able to get a word in. According to her, her virtual assistant was lazy, her editor had disappeared on her, her husband wasn't picking up the slack at home, and she was pretty sure Amazon had a grudge against her, because her ads had stopped working as effectively a month before.

Everything was working against her, but she told me she was used to that. For some reason, though, this time felt especially hard, and I could read between the lines that she was afraid she didn't have what it took to keep going. She was recently diagnosed with high cholesterol and was in the throes of perimenopause with frustrating brain fog and poor sleep. Oh, and her stupid doctor kept nagging her to sit at the computer less and go for walks. She was supposed to change her diet and eat out less, but she didn't have time to make those changes with her business going down the crapper, and she sure couldn't count on her husband to step up and do it.

There was a lot going on with Tammy. But despite how many disparate problems she described, I suspected there were really one or maybe two underlying patterns at the heart of it all.

As we age and our energy levels decrease, eventually we will hit a point where the patterns we've been relying on no longer work. They require too much energy to maintain.

This is especially true for Enneagram 8s, whose patterns tend to be highly energized and all-or-nothing.

Tammy had reached a point that many of us reach, where we've so had it with the world that everything bugs the crap out of us. If you've ever had poison ivy, this state feels like that, where even a gentle breeze brushing over the rash irritates it so much that you either want to fight the wind or crumble into a fetal position.

What I was hearing beneath Tammy's irritation was an exhausted person saying, "I'm so tired of feeling like I have to do everything myself." It's a very human and relatable feeling for many of us, but especially an Eight. Whether Tammy truly had to do everything on her own or whether she had fallen into a pattern of believing she was an island was still up for debate. I felt hopeful about her prospects for growth and release, though, since she had shown the necessary vulnerability of booking an appointment with me.

I started with Tammy by telling her that it sounded like she had a lot on her plate, because she did. We have a tendency to underestimate how much energy health issues sap from us, so if anyone reading this is going through that—which is most of us, because life is a super-fun dying process—take a moment and give yourself credit for how much you're getting done despite the overwhelming weight of health concerns.

Eights can smell a bullshitter from a mile away, so I wasn't trying to flatter her when I told her that I thought she was dealing with a lot. She legit was. I asked her to tell me a little bit more about the situations she was having with her virtual assistant and her wayward editor. With regards to her virtual assistant, the problem seemed to boil down to Tammy feeling like he lacked initiative. She had to tell him every single thing to do, and she felt like he should have already anticipated the tasks without her telling him.

There are certainly some folks who have not learned to take initiative in any aspect of their life, but in my experience, those people are few and far between. More often, when someone is relying on their boss to tell them every single thing to do, it's a result of that person not feeling *empowered* to take initiative. They may be afraid that if they take initiative but don't do exactly what their boss would have done, they may be facing some wrath.

I suspected this might be the case with Tammy's assistant, because there are a few common patterns that we see emerge with Eights in leadership roles. Sometimes the Eight's desire to feel powerful leaves very little room for the people around them to express their own power without a conflict arising. Eights don't generally mind a clash of wills, and often enjoy it, but other types are not as big on it and may opt out altogether, even if that means remaining small. It would be silly to blame Eights entirely for this, because we all have things that we do outside of our awareness that affect other people negatively, and other adults *also* have a decision about how to respond to what we're putting off. Regardless, the big, powerful (and sometimes scary) energy of the Eight comes through strong and clear in their leadership style.

Another pattern of the Eight that tends to discourage people who work under them from taking initiative is the Eight's honest and direct, frequently blunt, communication style. Eights tend to speak in commands, orders, and declarations. When someone who works for them does something they don't like, only an Eight who has done extensive and intentional work on their communication style will respond with gentleness or tact. The Eight usually isn't trying to be cruel, but what they view as clear and concise communication, another person may take as a dressing-down.

I broached the subject of communication styles between Tammy and her VA, and ways that she could express to him that she values his initiative. I stressed to her that when he inevitably takes initiative on something and she's not a fan of his decision, it would be a pivotal moment in their working relationship. It might be worth letting what she perceives as an error in judgment go if she wasn't sure that she could give constructive feedback without him shutting down and returning to his less proactive tendencies to protect himself. She pushed back against this idea, which was fine. I would expect no less from a stressed-out Eight. Eventually, she agreed to it as an experiment.

Next, we addressed the situation with her editor. The editor had multiple family crises happening around her and had more or less communicated that before dropping off the face of the Earth. It can be difficult for Eights to watch people not push through every single challenge they face to get the job done, since Eights ask that of themselves, whether fairly or not, for most of their lives.

I offered compassion for Tammy's tough situation, because, yeah, when your editor bails, even for good reasons, it fucking sucks. Once I'd commiserated with her on that point, Tammy was able to access some compassion for the editor, too. It didn't solve her problem, but I could tell from her mannerisms that she was feeling much more open to new solutions.

There's a misconception that Eights lack compassion, but I don't buy that. An Eight can struggle to *access* compassion for others, but it's almost always their compassion for themselves that they lose touch with first. If they can reconnect with it, they're much more likely to reconnect with it for others as well.

By the time we made it to the problem of her husband's lack of picking up the slack where she needed it, we had already dug in at the underlying patterns so much that Tammy didn't need me to tell her what was going on. "He probably assumes I don't want any help. I usually don't."

And there it was. The common thread that ran through all her frustrations. For most of her life, she was extremely proficient at doing everything herself. If something was a challenge, she shifted into high gear and powered her way through. Offers of help felt like attempts to usurp her power or question her independence. I could tell she had developed a lot of skills to help her do so much on her own and was probably more successful at it than ninety-nine percent of the population.

But with all she had going on with her health, there was no longer a higher gear to shift into, and so the pattern of *forcefulness*, what we call the "Wake-up Call" for Eights, was no longer working. Forcefulness was her go-to tool, but it wasn't the tool for *this* job. The skill she now needed to practice, much to her dismay and denial, was that of vulnerability. She needed to accept that she couldn't do it all herself anymore.

I had no clue if her husband would step up and help out, but she wouldn't know either until she asked. It wasn't fair to him to assume he *wouldn't* without giving him a chance. Admittedly, Eights can sometimes end up surrounded by relationships where the other person is completely oblivious to the fact that they need help, and if the other person were to offer the Eight help, they would probably refuse it simply to reaffirm their own belief that they can be entirely independent of other people and that they're strong. These patterns can take a long time to reestablish, but it's worth the effort.

Only a few things had been decided by the end of our call —steps to take with the VA, asking for help from her husband, and looking for another editor—but the big shift was that Tammy seemed relaxed, confident, and much less angry. That alone put her in a much better place to take on the challenges she had ahead of her, and I had no doubt she would be successful in those challenges.

BLOCK: LACK OF CERTAINTY AND CONFIDENCE

Many people—and by extension authors—can struggle with confidence. How do you feel confident that the decisions you're making for your career are the right ones?

Confidence felt rather foreign to me when I started writing as a profession back in 2015. Plenty of people around me seemed vastly more confident, and of those people, a few actually knew what they were talking about. Many, however, did not.

How could someone like me tell the difference? Which of these confident people could I trust to have solid information?

Flash forward to today, and I consider myself a confident author. Making big, tough decisions doesn't make me anxious ahead of time or leave me in a hangover afterward. Naturally, it got me wondering, what changed?

Was it that I know this industry better than I once did? That's probably part of it. But that doesn't explain why the social anxiety that used to cripple me in groups of people I didn't know doesn't show its ugly head like it used to. And it certainly doesn't explain why I say "I don't know" now more than I ever have in my life.

If confidence is cultivated through factual knowledge, then shouldn't I be saying "I don't know" *less* often than before?

According to my girl Merriam-Webster, "confident" is defined in two ways:

1. Feeling or showing confidence in oneself; self-assured
2. Feeling or showing certainty about something

This seems to be the important distinction. English speakers ought to have done ourselves a huge favor by coming up with two separate words for these definitions rather than assigning the single word two meanings.

Over the years, as I gained more experience in this industry, what was happening was that my confidence in the results of any given decision *went down*. I learned to stop believing that if I did X then Y would happen. If I do X then it might increase the likelihood of Y happening, sure. If I write a book (X), I increase the likelihood of selling more books (Y). But there's no guarantee that I will even sell one. All kinds of things could happen. However, I like my odds of selling copies if I write the book, so I'm going to go for it.

Meanwhile, my confidence *has* increased in terms of the other definition of the word: I've gained confidence in my ability to handle whatever unpredictable situation comes my way.

It's not a given that through experience we gain confidence in our ability to handle what comes our way. There are plenty of experienced authors who feel great levels of anxiety that their next book will be the one that flops or leads to a public pile-on. Plenty.

Experience alone will not build our confidence in ourselves. There are additional processes to follow before that can happen. (More on those in a bit.)

Seeking certainty in an outcome is one of the most insidious blocks authors face. If we're waiting to feel certain about how things will work out as a result of our action *before* we take the action, we will be waiting forever. There is no such thing as certainty in an outcome.

This is why, so many times when I'm talking to authors, the question that needs to be asked is not simply "How could you be more certain?" but rather "What more information would you like to have before you make this decision?" followed by "Is it reasonable to expect that you can gather that information ahead of the decision?"

When we're waiting for a guarantee, we wait forever. We're not usually conscious of what information we feel is missing that would give us that beautiful glow of certainty. Instead, magical thinking sets in: *I'll see a sign, then I'll know!*

What if the sign never drops down from the heavens? (Or what if it does and you don't like it?) What if you could *never* be confident that any of the pathways would work out exactly the way you want?

These are uncomfortable questions to ask, and many authors are trapped in an uncertainty cycle at this very moment as a result.

"Should I sell direct?"

"Do I need to start a new pen name?"

"Should I query an agent?"

"What book should I write next?"

These are all important questions that might be best made after a bit of consideration. So, consider them. Talk it over with friends. Consult a coach. Meditate or pray on it.

But do yourself a favor and stop expecting to feel certainty before you take action. The information you're hoping for to feel confident in the outcome *does not exist*. The impulse of wanting certainty is a yearning of our subconscious mind to control things that are out of our control, and when we attempt to do that, we waste time and energy galore.

Return your attention to what you can control: you.

We are never in control of outcomes, but we can become confident in our ability to respond wisely to them.

Instead of focusing your attention on certainty seeking, then, the wisest thing you can do with your attention and experience in this industry is use it to develop a toolkit that allows you to handle when things inevitably go sideways.

Confidence in one's ability to handle whatever shitstorm blows in can only be built upon a foundation of trust of oneself. In case you're wondering, this is not an overnight process. And yes, this is why I most commonly see Fives and Sixes (or folks with those wings) stuck in a pattern of certainty seeking.

Anyone can learn to build trust with themselves, though, just like we can learn to build it with others and with the universe.

Almost fifteen years ago now, I met my dog Penny. She was seven weeks old, and apparently hellbent on getting herself killed. She was the first dog that was ever mine, and I was determined to train her to stay at my heel off-leash. Basset hounds don't do that, you say? Fie! Maybe the border collie half of her would win out and she'd be trainable. (In case you're wondering, no, border collie and Basset hound was not an intentional mix. I was literally paid to take her.)

The problem I faced was how do I train her to be off-leash while also making sure she doesn't take off into traffic? How do I build that trust between us?

The answer to this ageless question is *a little bit at a time and in the right setting.*

Letting her off-leash in my apartment courtyard where the worst she could do is dig a little hole in the dirt? Perfect.

Letting her off-leash by the street where people regularly sped while texting on their phones? Not ideal.

Eventually, though, I did want her to be able to run next to me in less secure environments. So, how did I graduate from the courtyard to a trail or a sidewalk?

I was terrified of seeing her hit by a car (more precisely, I was terrified of the grief, trauma, and guilt I would feel as a result), so how did I move forward without risk?

The answer is that *I couldn't.* I couldn't get to where I wanted to be without risk.

Building trust is necessarily a risky process. There no way to build it otherwise. It's developed like a muscle, through strain and repetition.

For that reason, the dog-training process had some close calls that involved me throwing myself in front of moving vehicles, knowing they would see me easier than a low-rider hound mix. It involved her getting bowled over by bigger dogs from time to time. I suffered a few minor heart attacks along the way, and I developed the ability to sit with my anxiety for longer periods as we took necessary risks.

By the time she was a year old, she was jogging around the block with me, staying by my side on the leash (because laws) but with slack in it. When we went to off-leash parks, I took the leash completely off, and I learned what her orbit length was—how far she would trot ahead before waiting for me to catch up, and how far she would lag behind before she would take the chance to dart off in a different direction.

I learned what I could trust her with, but I also learned what risk I was willing to accept to allow her to have a fun and happy life.

There were some situations where we never built trust. Near a road she's not familiar with? Leash time. Places where the squirrels would lure her across a busy road? Leashed.

While I occasionally felt envy for the dogs who stayed by their owner's ankles no matter what, it wasn't important that Penny should be trustworthy off-leash in every environment; rather, it was important that I felt confident in my understanding of which approach with her leash was appropriate for any given situation. I built trust with her, but I also built trust in my ability to read a situation and make the right decision to keep her out of unnecessary danger.

This is how the trust necessary for confidence is built. It's cultivated through action, graduated risk, and repetition.

Not sure if you should publish that book? Take the risk. Learn what it's like to be you in that situation. Did you survive? Could you survive again? What did it feel like? Was it unpleasant? Was it thrilling?

A fear of taking action is almost always rooted in a fear of feeling a certain way about ourselves that stirs up unpleasant emotions. (I say "almost always" because there are times when your physical safety or even life is on the line, which is a whole different situation.)

> **When we're stuck in uncertainty, how we feel about ourselves is a useful sore spot to poke at for answers.**

Have you felt like a failure before? What did you do in that situation to get through it? Would you feel exactly the same if it happened again, or have you learned more about yourself and the world so that it wouldn't be an exact déjà vu?

Have you felt foolish before? What happened next? Did it ultimately make you wiser? Is living a silent and invisible life worth not risking it again?

Have you felt like a bad person before? What criticism followed? Was it from other people or from you? Could you still be a good person after all?

I could go on here, but I think you get the picture.

Our fear of how we will feel about ourselves and the emotions we'll experience as a result are the #1 force keeping us stuck in an uncertainty cycle.

By and large, when I talk with authors about the decisions they're facing, they already know the next best step. Their gut has usually been hollering it at them. But they're holding out hope that they can find a way to do it that carries *no risk* of harming their self-image.

Thankfully, the way we see ourselves is within our control. We don't have to believe every negative thought we have about ourselves, and we're healthier when we don't. There's no point to it. Most negative self-talk is our ego's misguided attempt at protecting itself. Not you. Itself. When we work on our Enneagram liberation, we dismantle this defensive pattern.

If you want to be a confident writer, practice separating yourself from the anxiety of *What if this doesn't work out? How will I keep going?*

It's a voice, a habit, but it's not truth.

The truth is that you *can* be okay regardless of the outcome.

The truth is that nothing worth living for was created through inaction.

The truth is that the story is only over when you decide it's over.

All of this can be hard to hear, but if this is the block you're facing in your career, you need to look at it straight on. Stop pretending if you wait long enough an option will appear with a no-risk guarantee to your writing dreams.

Maybe, just maybe, it's time to make the call. Maybe there isn't and has never been a "right choice."

Grab a stress ball, shake out your hands, throw back a shot of bourbon—whatever you need to do—and then write that email. Hit publish. Start the opening chapter. Whatever you've been deliberating on for so long, ask yourself if it's time to stop forming a hypothesis and start running the experiment.

Practice existing, exploring, and thriving within the uncertainty.

Don't wait to feel brave, because bravery is not a feeling. Bravery is action we take when while we're still afraid.

CONCEPT IN ACTION:
The Faithful Writer (6) seeks certainty

Alex had spent the last two years of his career cowriting with a better-known author. The situation was that Alex would write the books, and the other author would sign off on them and stick his name on the covers to help move copies. The partnership had worked well for Alex for the last two years, and he was incredibly grateful to have had the opportunity.

But he was starting to wonder if he could have success on his own. Once the question emerged in his consciousness, it only grew, and he could no longer ignore it. He needed to know what he was capable of, and he was also wary of continuing to build his brand on his cowriter's land.

The reason he came to see me was because he had a new idea for a series, and he was thinking about making it his solo debut. He described the concept to me, and I thought it was genius. I could already see all of the ways it would hit pleasure buttons of his target audience. Once he finished describing the series to me in depth, since he'd plotted out most of the first few books already, I found myself a little bit confused.

"What is it that you want my help with?" I asked.

"Do you think it's a good enough series?"

"I think the premise is fantastic. I could see a lot of people really enjoying it, and it sounds like you have a firm grasp of the protagonist and theme that will make for a strong, cohesive story."

"But what's wrong with it?" he asked. "Where do you think I'll run into problems with it?"

"From what you just described, and based on the stage you're in, nothing jumps out to me as a problem."

I wasn't just being lazy or ignorant here. I was an editor for a long time and worked on and read hundreds of manuscripts. I've written quite a few books myself, and have been helping authors align their stories for years. I genuinely thought he had nailed it with the premise and the beats he described to me. At no point had my sensors alerted me to a possible issue. It's extremely rare that this is the case, too. I can usually spot a few elements that don't quite click with the others and offer a few suggestions on how to adjust. But nothing needed adjusting that I could see.

Alex was not accepting that as an answer.

So, I asked, "You got a hundred percent on the test—why are you upset?"

"I want to make sure that I'm doing this right before I commit to it."

Because I already knew from working with Alex that he was an Enneagram 6, the phrase "doing this right" carried a different implication than if I'd heard it from an Enneagram 1, say. He wasn't thinking in terms of right and wrong; he was thinking in terms of avoiding catastrophe later on.

I suspected that the major transition of leaving the more experienced cowriter, who he presumed would let him know if this story had gone completely off track, to venturing out on his own and relying on his understanding of story left him feeling destabilized and unsupported. And while he'd had the inkling that he might be able to do this on his own, he hadn't fully tapped into his own Inner Authority. He was struggling to trust his gut, so his head was picking up the slack and spinning circles. His gut had put together one hell of a story plot, in my professional opinion. He just wouldn't hear it.

I decided to bring up what was at the heart of this matter. "Let's say you go ahead and start writing this book as you have it planned. What's the worst-case scenario?"

Somewhat predictably, he didn't need long to think about that. "I could get stuck midway through, not know how to finish it, and never get it done."

"If you get stuck midway through, what's a step you could take to get unstuck?" and because we could all use a hint from time to time, I pointed at myself after asking the question.

He laughed. "I could book a call with you."

One disaster averted.

"What else?" I asked. "What else could go terribly wrong?"

You might think me sadistic asking a Six to describe to me everything that could go wrong, but this process can be useful. It forces us to name that fear that's just been hovering like a shadow in the back of our mind. By discussing it with someone else, the Six can feel supported as they address whatever the issue is and is usually in a much better state to look at it and come up with a workable solution.

"The book could bomb, and then I would have wasted all this time and be completely out of money because I wasn't writing books with my cowriter."

"Okay, let's say you publish the trilogy and the sales just aren't happening. Your bank accounts at zero. What could you try?"

Together we came up with a whole list of possibilities, and over the course of that discussion I learned that he had been in a position of having no money to his name before.

"And you have money now?" I asked.

He did.

"Then you already have evidence that you can go from zero money to some money. If you did it before, you can do it again."

One of the things I've noticed about the Sixes in my life is that they're absolute bosses in a crisis. Maybe not the minor crises, but for the big stuff, their gut takes over and they appear to know just what to do. If you're a Six, see if this rings true for you as well.

For instance, one of my closest friends is a Six, and when he had a gun pointed in his face during a road rage incident (long story), he suddenly knew how to strip the gun from the guy's hands, and did so before he even knew what he was doing. Did he then drive the rest of the way to work and spend his entire shift vomiting from nerves? Sure, but in the moment he somehow knew exactly what to do. He's also survived knife fights, a group sword melee, multiple assaults, and someone shooting at him while he drove (he's a counterphobic Six who can't keep his mouth shut, so he likely escalated most of that).

Most authors, Enneagram 6 or not, will not end up with a gun pointed in their face. At least, I hope not. But the doubts that tend to absorb the most attention of Sixes surround worst-case scenarios. We can never have certainty about the outcome of our decisions, but we can develop confidence in our ability to handle a crisis effectively. And that's what I was helping Alex to realize. The crisis he was imagining—being without money—was one he had already handled effectively. Therefore, if I was the betting type, I would put my money on his being able to handle it again. Once he saw it laid out that way, he agreed. He was good in a crisis—possibly the bigger the crisis the better he was—so rather than focusing his attention on what could happen, he felt much more comfortable focusing it on writing his manuscript. The future didn't require his anxiety and attention.

Alex came to me searching for certainty, but what he left with was even better. He left with a seed of confidence that he would know what to do when the moment came.

BLOCK: NEED FOR CONTROL

How much control do you have over your career?

This is an important question for authors to consider, because not only does our subconscious brain assume we are in control of everything, but society feeds us a boot-strapping narrative that says the circumstances of an individual's life are a direct result of their choices.

That narrative can easily curdle into the idea that people who are broke or ill brought it on themselves in some way, and that the people who are wealthy and healthy have simply made better decisions in life. We've all met monetarily successful people who are notorious for poor life choices and struggling people who seem to have tragedy follow them around regardless of the choices they make, so it doesn't take much conscious prodding to realize that the equation of "rich=good decisions, poor=bad decisions" is not only grossly oversimplified, but also grade-A horseshit.

And yet we still frequently fall into this pattern of thinking when it comes to our author career. We look at others and assume that if they're selling a lot of books, they've made all the right choices (and maybe we would do well to make those same choices). Then we look at those who have been writing forever without a breakout success and assume they're doing something wrong.

Of course, thanks to the concept of the fundamental attribution error, when many of us look at our own career, we are usually able to assume all our success is attributable to our smart decisions, but all our failure is a result of bad luck and unfortunate circumstances.

That belief can hold up for a while, but eventually, an author struggling to find success as they define it will start to wonder, *Maybe there's something wrong with me.*

In short, our ideas about what is and is not in our control in this industry can be flat-out bonkers.

When our underlying thought patterns have no coherence in this way, we end up wasting a lot of energy trying to control what we cannot control and abdicating control over what we do have some say over. Very few things in life will leave you feeling stuck and drain you faster than trying to control things that aren't in your control. So, in this section, we're going to spend a little time sorting that out.

Let's look at a list of author-y things to begin sorting out what is and what is not in our control.

CANNOT CONTROL
How readers will react to my book
Whether a reader bothers to read my blurb
What the market does
What types of covers are trending
What genres are selling well
How effective a given marketing tactic is
What other writers in my genre are doing
The results of the advice I take
How much money I earn from this business
The ROI on each dollar spent

CAN CONTROL
The time I schedule for writing
The time I schedule for blurbs

The time I spend on market research
Who I hire to design my covers
What genre of story I write
What books I read about marketing
What fiction books I read in my genre
Whose advice I take
How much money I invest in my business
Where I spend my money in my business

So, this is not a revolutionary list, is it? But it's amazing how often we'll let ourselves get down because things on the "Cannot Control" side aren't going our way. You can only control what you do. If what you do is not getting you the results you want, you must do something else.

This is where most people get stuck.

The Enneagram framework is designed to remind us of what we can and cannot control and shows us not only a path to walk to integrate that knowledge, but a way to accept that reality without becoming frustrated.

It turns out that the true form of our core desire can only be found in the one place where have any control at all: ourselves. This is very good news, because it means that we can develop our ability to access what we desire at any time, day or night. All we need to do is remember that it's there, not outside of us.

Curious what I mean? Let's look at it by type:

> **Ones**: You can't achieve perfection through your actions and appearance in the outside world; the moment is already exactly as it should be, whether

you judge it to be good or bad. The only thing that fluctuates is your ability to perceive how you are perfect in your imperfections.

Twos: You can't *earn* the unconditional love you crave. The concept that it would be earned through selfless acts makes it conditional by definition. You are already worthy of unconditional love without doing a thing. The only thing that fluctuates is your ability to perceive your worthiness of love.

Threes: Your innate value is not something to be attained through performing for and impressing others; you have inherent value without doing a thing. The only thing that fluctuates is your ability to perceive your value.

Fours: You don't need to construct significance for yourself through insisting you're special or forcing eccentricity; you are already significant and irreplaceable. The only thing that fluctuates is your ability to perceive your significance in this world.

Fives: You can't amass enough knowledge and resources to do everything on your own; the world around you is full of resources meant to be shared. The only thing that fluctuates is your ability to perceive the easy flow of give-and-take around you.

Sixes: You can't forge enough beneficial alliances or catastrophize enough to protect yourself from all danger; you already have an Inner Authority who can guide you when a crisis arises. The only thing that fluctuates is your ability to trust and hear that Inner Authority when it speaks.

Sevens: You can't pleasure-seek your way to satisfaction; all the richness of life you need exists in this moment. The only thing that fluctuates is your ability to perceive that richness.

Eights: You can't force or intimidate your way to power; all the power you need already exists inside of yourself. The only thing that fluctuates is your ability to perceive your inherent power.

Nines: There is no amount of avoiding conflicts that leads to lasting peace and harmony; you remain connected to everything else in every moment, even heated conflict. The only thing that fluctuates is your ability to perceive that disharmony is also part of the wholeness of the universe.

Once we begin to wrap our heads around the concept of our type, we are treated to a huge relief: we don't have to do anything or exert any control over the outside world to suddenly feel that we already have our core desire. And in the moments where we really *feel* that truth, we give up the tiresome search outside of ourselves, accept what we can't control, and know that we'll be okay, come what may.

This is the gift we unwrap when we learn to make ourselves feel like home.

If you achieve this state, I encourage you to enjoy it while you can, because we will inevitably be pulled back into our old and established patterns by the drama of everyday life.

Unfortunately, growth is not a linear path. We may be able to perceive our truth around our partner, but then we get around, say, our parents, and kick our old patterns into overdrive (I've heard visits with one's parents described as the "final boss" of growth work).

Now that we've looked at the truths of our types, and how the truth doesn't fluctuate but our ability to perceive it does, let's look at what happens as that ability to perceive diminishes to the point where we can't see it at all.

This is where authors get stuck. When we forget that the thing we're looking for can only be found in its truest sense inside of us, we start looking for it outside of us, which simply does. not. fucking. work.

The result is that we end up playing stupid games, and all we can hope to win from those are stupid prizes.

Each type has a different game it likes to play, and while it may be the best at that particular game, it has already lost the moment it starts playing.

I know you're curious, but I also know you're probably not ready to see your type's stupid games and stupid prizes laid out. It's going to feel personal, and it's so unflattering that there's a chance you will immediately throw up a wall to protect your ego and say, "That's not me." Here we go anyway:

Ones' stupid games: Trying to be flawless. Keeping impossibly high standards to live above reproach.

Ones' stupid prizes: Stress, workaholism, inviting criticism, perfectionism, depression, headaches, digestive issues.

Twos' stupid games: Being needed by as many people as possible. Acting selflessly and never asking for help from others to be the "most wanted" person around.

Twos' stupid prizes: Codependency, resentment, martyrdom, being surrounded by energy vampires, exhaustion.

Threes' stupid games: Being the best at everything they do. Winning the approval and admiration of a nebulous audience.

Threes' stupid prizes: Workaholism, severe feelings of inadequacy, feeling like a constant failure, massive impostor syndrome, cutthroat behavior, having no idea you actually want out of life, obsession with physical appearance.

Fours' stupid games: Seeking significance through being incomprehensible. Asserting specialness to avoid looking ordinary.

Fours' stupid prizes: Being consistently misunderstood, insatiable longing, identity issues, depression, loneliness, emotional instability, feeling broken.

Fives' stupid games: Seeking complete independence from society through collecting (hoarding) resources.

Absorbing endless knowledge to feel competent but rarely sharing it to avoid appearing foolish.

Fives' stupid prizes: Social isolation, ignorance of practical world, loss of empathy for others, emptiness, various health issues resulting from neglect of physical needs, emotional suppression.

Sixes' stupid games: Being a die-hard follower of industry experts. Constantly testing your relationships with others to ensure they have your back and won't betray you.

Sixes' stupid prizes: Severe anxiety, betrayal (both feeling it and doing it), abuse by authority, paranoia, trans-actional relationships, rapidly narrowing pool of longtime friends.

Sevens' stupid games: Being the most interesting person in the room by experiencing as much of the world as humanly possible. Pleasure seeking to avoid pain.

Sevens' stupid prizes: Lacking depth, avoidant personality, superficial relationships, FOMO galore, constant dissatisfaction with the moment, panic when options seem limited, reckless behavior and endangerment to self.

Eights' stupid games: Being the strongest and most powerful person in any situation. Overcompensating for any perceived weakness.

Eights' stupid prizes: You scare people, surrounded by sycophants, everyone seems weak, lack of true intimacy with others, no one offers you help, target on your back, vengeful urges and behaviors, self-sabotage, victim complex.

Nines' stupid games: Keeping the peace by never rocking the boat. Being the most liked person in the room by accommodating others and saying yes when you mean no.

Nines' stupid prizes: Procrastination, becoming disconnected from others through disconnection from self, enmeshment, identity struggles, passive-aggression, chronic pain, lethargy, dissociation.

Phew. You okay there? Take a deep breath. Maybe one more. Okay.

This is why it's so important to remember what you can and can't control in life and in publishing. We don't want to play the stupid game of our type. We don't want to win those stupid prizes.

Instead, we want to control what we can control and enjoy the benefits of a happy, balanced, and fulfilling author career. When we remember that we already are the thing we seek to be and the only thing that changes is our ability to perceive that, we no longer need to set ridiculous goals to motivate ourselves, because we're always fulfilling our core desire and therefore succeeding every single day.

CONCEPT IN ACTION:
A Productive Writer (3) wins her stupid game

Jessica came to me with a big problem: her romance books were making her six figures a year. Of profit.

That itself wasn't the problem, but it was certainly an important component of it. The problem was that Jessica didn't like, and had never liked, writing romance.

I asked her why she started in that genre, and she said she had gone to a writing conference years ago and saw how many romance writers were making the kind of money off their books that she could only dream of. She thought, *I could do this,* and then she went and did it.

She studied the top sellers, learned what tropes were hot and how to write them, became friends with other romance authors who wrote similar books to hers and would promote her releases, and found the thrill of the chase exhilarating. She spent a year and a half churning out books, learning the ropes of marketing, watching her social media followers skyrocket, and burning the candle at both ends.

For the first year, she didn't mind working that hard seven days a week. There was nothing else she would've rather been doing. But in the last six months, whatever energy and motivation her pursuit was giving her had begun drying up. She now found herself sitting on a mountain of books she didn't care that much about, talking to readers whose interests she couldn't relate to, and ignoring all of the book ideas that spoke to her but didn't fall into her niche.

Oh, and she'd used her money to buy a house, which she now had a hefty mortgage on. As her income grew, so did her living expenses. For this reason, walking away from her romance books was not an option in her mind. But the thought of writing another one made her sick to her stomach.

She had played the stupid game of chasing stats and dollars and now she was trying to figure out what to do with the stupid prizes of feeling financially trapped and falling out of love with writing.

"I've watched every episode of *Supernatural* in the last two months," she lamented.

I didn't know watching fifteen seasons of TV was even possible in that short amount of time, but in true Ennea-gram 3 form, she had found a way to get it done.

Through getting sucked in to the games of the Three, she had disconnected from her natural energy flow, and had overdone it *big time*, grinding her down until she slipped into her stress type of the Nine. Enter: checking out in front of fifteen seasons of *Supernatural*. She had probably been working on autopilot for months before she hit the wall, as is commonly the case with Threes. They are, in my experience, the hardest type to spot potential burnout in prior to it actually happening, because even a disconnected Three on autopilot can often produce more books in a year than many do in a lifetime. The stories likely feel formulaic and somewhat empty, because that's the best autopilot can produce, but books like that from a known author can still manage to sell, and so the Three keeps playing that game until they absolutely can't anymore and end up on a couch with a CW show playing endlessly. (CW shows feel so good when you're burned out, don't they?)

I'll admit, Jessica's situation is not a coaching situation I love to be in, because there's no easy fix, and the process of solving it is going to be *painful*. Many people will simply refuse to take my advice because of that. They hold out hope that there is a much easier and less painful way out, but that's not the reality once they're so far in. It's why I spend so much time trying to warn people to look for the signs that they're playing stupid games with stupid prizes, because it's so unfortunate to find yourself as deep in the trap as Jessica was.

While the idealist in me may want to tell the person to stop writing the books they hate right away and pivot to something they love, money be damned, money doesn't be damned, and bills come due. No creditor wants to hear that your Enneagram coach told you to follow your dreams and that's why you're three months late on your car payment.

I had to lay it out for Jessica as plainly as I could. She was in a tough spot, and the way out would not be quick. It would also not be painless. Because until she looked at her issues around self-worth and examined her relationship to her innate value, she would not be able to make the kinds of decisions that would get her out of this situation *and* keep her from falling right back in it.

She needed to lower her monthly living expenses to give herself some breathing room from the book production pace she was on. However, since her spending habits were a result of trying to convince herself and others that she was a success, until she redefined for herself what it meant to be valuable and integrated that new truth so that she actually *felt* the truth of it, she would have a really fucking hard time spending less money.

Our spending habits reflect our core fears, so when our spending gets out of control, that's a sign that it's time to address our core fear in a much more honest way than we have been to that point. Only through doing that work will we address the patterns underlying the overspending (or underspending, if you lean miserly). You may have a particular day where you're at your wits' end and frantically cancel all of your subscriptions, and while that's not nothing, if you haven't addressed the underlying pattern leading you to subscribe to so many services, you will simply end up with the same or a greater number of subscriptions before long.

The spending patterns look different by type, but in Jessica's case, it was about presenting herself as monetarily successful. She equated her value to how much money she made, and how many nice things she could buy and post about on Instagram, and the only way she knew to access her value was through the attention others gave her for her purchases.

I soon discovered that her business expenses reflected the same pattern, which was to be expected. If she saw a cover she liked, she would buy it on the spot, regardless of whether she knew which book it might go with in the future. She certainly had enough money to do this, but if she ever hoped to pull back on the romance books, she needed to get way more serious about building a cushion in her finances ahead of a pivot to a new genre. Of course, until she could find ways to tap into her infinite and innate worth, she would struggle writing in a genre where she wasn't getting as much attention right off the bat.

While there was no way this was a problem we were going to fix in a single session, I considered it a success when Jessica told me about how she'd wanted to write epic fantasy as a kid, after reading Lord of the Rings. That admission showed me that she was still connected to the authentic writer inside of her, and as long as she could stay connected to that part of her *in some way*, she would be able to differentiate when a business option was alluring to her because it promised attention and praise from others or because it might fulfill her on a deeper and more authentic level.

Since the outcome of her situation hinged so entirely on her ability to connect to her innate value and worth, we discussed a few simple practices that she could incorporate to start her day, and multiple times throughout her day, that would reconnect her to that authentic self and allow her to make decisions that moved her marginally closer to what *she* wanted, rather than what she thought others wanted her to want. We looked at some basic re-parenting visualizations to remind her that she was the only voice for the child inside her who wanted to write epic fantasy, and we talked about options for downsizing the big expenses in her budget and what a relief her husband (a very stressed-out Six) would feel if they had a larger nest egg.

I could see deep emotions welling up when we connected her to the love she had for her inner child and her husband, and that gave me hope that she'd reconnected to an anchor more solid than the vaporous appeal of praise from strangers. She valued the child who was taught so many wrong things about how to earn love and worth, and her husband had made her feel worthy and valued long before she was making the big bucks.

It may seem like there was very little publishing-related conversation in our coaching call, and you're right. But tactics and strategy weren't the issue. And until Jessica saw the patterns that got her into this mess, she wouldn't be able to start choosing different ones to get her out of it.

BLOCK: OVER-LABELING

One of the creative ways that authors get themselves stuck in a rut is by unconsciously narrowing their options through over-labeling. Our Enneagram type works like a filter. It allows information that is relevant in and filters out what does not seem relevant. This helps us function in a world full of information. The issues arise from the relevancy criteria, because our default is almost always based on our core fear.

Once a piece of information makes it through, having been deemed relevant by our filter, our subconscious sorts it along one of a finite number of continuums that our type uses. That continuum can become a problem for us because not everything fits nicely onto it.

That's a lot of theory and vagueness, so let's look at an example. One of the common continuums for an Enneagram 2 is *selfish<—>loving*. In practice, this might look like the Two assessing his marketing tactics based on where they fall along that continuum. How loving would it be to do this thing? Would it be even a little bit selfish? If so, the Two will look for any other option before trying it, because it is intolerable for a Two to think of themselves as selfish. That's the last thing they want to feel about themselves.

Whether or not it makes sense to sort things for your business along the *selfish<—>loving* continuum is irrelevant to the Two because 1) they probably don't realize they're even doing it, and 2) this is how they've always done it.

This is what I mean by "over-labeling." Once a person has attached an unfavorable label to a process or tactic, they've eliminated that option from their vision. It can certainly be beneficial to narrow your options occasionally for the sake of getting something done, but each of us tend to be over-sensitive to what we consider the negative side of our type's continuums.

For example, what the Two might consider too far toward the "selfish" side of the continuum for comfort, every other type might not consider selfish at all. Enforcing boundaries around writing time, for example, even if other people ask for your help during it. For a Two, saying no to preserve their writing time is almost guaranteed to be automatically sorted on the selfish side of their continuum, so they'll struggle with it. Meanwhile, attaching this label to it will leave other types scratching their head and asking, "How do you get any writing done, then?"

The other types are sorting things along different continuums, so they'll have their own sensitivities to work through, but objectively speaking, not every action that could be taken in your author business should be labeled *selfish* or *caring*.

If the labeling of writing-related tactics as *selfish* gets too out of control for a Two, the symptoms may look like: pricing their books too low, giving away too many free copies, and even never writing the next book because there are always more "caring" things they could be doing for other people than sitting and writing another chapter.

When I spot that over-labeling is tripping up one of my clients of *any* type, what I like to do is talk about the continuums that other types are working with. Sometimes it can help us to see that other people are functioning in completely different ways and are still what we would consider good, caring, intelligent, responsible, fun, and so forth people.

In other words, it helps to remember that you have options, and that you need not be ruled by the continuums of your type.

If you're not a Two, you're likely wondering at this point what the continuum associated with your type looks like, so I'll show you an example of each. As you read yours, I challenge you to ask yourself where you are attaching your labels to things where it doesn't quite make sense for them to be. Where might *removing* these labels from certain marketing tactics and strategies or from your writing process open up fresh options to get fresh results?*

Each of the following example continuums is followed by two italicized examples of the thoughts where the labels are attached. You may not see the word itself used there, so look for the general sentiment.

One: Wrong<—>Right
Asking for reviews is wrong.
Am I using the right tropes for this genre?

---

* The following continuums are borrowed from or inspired by those used by Dr. Jerome Wagner. His are based on George Kelly's dichotomy corollary, which states, "a person's construction system is composed of a finite number of dichotomous constructs." Dr. Wagner was the one who introduced me to this concept, and I can't tell you how much mileage it's gotten in me coaching sessions since. You can read more about this theory from Dr. Wagner himself at http://enneagramspectrum.com/446/enneagram-styles-and-the-cognitive-theory-of-george-kelly

Two: Selfish<—>Loving
Not promoting [author]'s book during my launch week is selfish.
Giving this reader a free copy of the next book is the only caring thing to do here.

Three: Failure<—>Success
I'm failing at writing this book.
Successful authors get trad pub deals.

Four: Inauthentic<—>Authentic
Everyone is so fake on social media.
Writing tropes stifles my creative expression.

Five: Foolish<—>Wise
The readers in my genre are idiots.
Smart authors research the hell out of their books.

Six: Dangerous<—>Safe
Publishing this under my real name is dangerous.
Cowriting with someone farther along than me is a safe bet.

Seven: Boring<—>Fun
Writing the messy middle is boring.
I have to be fun for readers to like me.

Eight: Weak<—>Strong
Emotional characters make weak protagonists.
Pushing through on a book when it hurts is a sign of strength.

Nine: Conflict<—>Harmony

Turning down this anthology offer will rock the boat too much.
If my characters curse, I might offend too many readers.

Usually when I point out these continuums in my coaching, I receive one of two reactions. Sometimes a person will look at the continuums and be so entrenched in their own that they don't see how much they are unnecessarily attaching the labels to in every inch of their world. The One doesn't recognize how many times during our coaching call he's used the words "right" and "wrong" to describe his writing and marketing processes. The Six doesn't realize how many options they've shot down a suggestion immediately because it's "too much risk." (Everything carries risk with it, so if you're a Six, think about how that might immobilize your decision making if you're waiting for something that only carries a tolerable amount of risk with it.)

The other common reaction I get from authors when I show them their continuum is "For fuck's sake, Claire!" And sometimes "Why are you attacking me?" which, yes, I love to hear.

The next time you're stuck and unable to see any way around it, pause and ask yourself how this continuum is showing up for you. Are there great options that you've dismissed due to over-labeling? Are you leaning one way or another because of where you sort the present options along this continuum? What if you assessed this decision along the continuum of your growth type or one of your wings instead? What options might appear that you haven't seen before?

If you're stuck, ask a friend of a different type to brainstorm other options with you, and notice where you're immediately assigning labels, then question those labels.

This practice on its own could change the entire trajectory of your career in delightful ways, but your ability to use it does depend on where you are in accepting that your Enneagram lens isn't the only valid view of the world. So, if you feel resistant to the idea of other continuums being equally valid to yours, that can be an indicator that it's time to loosen your grip slightly on your own perspective.

Remember that each of the types plays a crucial role in sustaining a healthy society, none is more important than the others, and you have all nine types inside of you to varying degrees. It's not being untrue to who you are to experiment with other modes of thinking, feeling, and behaving. In fact, those small experiments are the best way to liberate yourself from the deeply entrenched patterns that you've developed throughout your life. As someone who has run these experiments herself and has guided many other people through similar experimentations, I can tell you that it will be okay, and you will be okay. It does take the choice of being brave, but I know that you can do it.

CONCEPT IN ACTION:
A Principled Writer (1) slaps too many labels on things

Michelle was at her wits' end. She was carrying too much on her shoulders, and she'd come to a grinding halt in her manuscript. She'd pulled out all the tricks that she knew to force herself to write the next scene, but every time she sat down to do it, it just wouldn't happen.

"My brain keeps wanting me to do it the wrong way," she said. "I know the hero and heroine aren't supposed to have sex this early in the book, but this scene just doesn't feel right if they don't have sex. It doesn't make any sense for them not to."

"Why can't they have sex this early in the book?" I asked.

"Because they're not supposed to! I need this book to sell, so I have to get everything right with the beats."

It was clear from the conversation that Michelle was not having any fun with this work in progress. She had the typical facial expression of an Enneagram 1 running up against a problem she didn't how to solve—the terse lips, the furrowed brow, the tight voice.

The block Michelle was facing looked like a plot problem on the outside, but deeper down it was something else. She was locked into an over-labeling pattern, sorting everything and its mother onto her WrongRight continuum.

It's a common misconception that being a One means you must be highly moralistic or dogmatically religious. This stereotype is how some people who are Ones have trouble typing themselves as such, because they *don't* adhere to any particular religion. But the ideas of "right" and "wrong" are still deeply ingrained and show up in the filtering system of relevant information. For Ones, there is a right way to do things and the wrong way to do things. Religious or not, they hold a default belief that a right way exists and that it is their responsibility to find that right way and take it. Anything else is wrong and bad.

What Michelle was dealing with was something I've worked on with a lot of Ones (and worked on intensely in myself), which is the belief that there is a right way to write a book. I assure you that there is not. There's also not a wrong way to write a book.

Similarly, there is not a right way to *plot* a book. That's why you can find a near-infinite amount of approaches to plotting. Even romance, which is the genre most commonly associated with a predictable structure, does not have a single right way to plot it. *There is no right way.*

"Let's say you find a way to keep your hero and heroine from having sex in this scene," I said. "How do you think readers would respond to that?"

"They would probably be frustrated or confused by it," she said.

"Do you care more about getting an A-plus on following plotting structure, or pleasing your fans?" This question was intended to get the wheels turning for Michelle and hopefully dislodge her from some of the fixed thinking that was keeping her trapped and unable to continue with her manuscript.

I also pointed out how many times in our conversation she had used the words "right" and "wrong" to describe things that did not, in fact, have an objectively right or objectively wrong way to do them.

Unsurprisingly, she hadn't realized how much these two words occupied her vocabulary, but once she did, she was able to witness her thoughts with clarity. In doing so, she realized that the stress of her life outside of writing was triggering black-and-white thinking in her writing, a pursuit that generally is more enjoyable when not subjected to oversimplifications and harsh judgment.

"If there's no right or wrong way to do it, then how do I decide what to do next?" she asked.

A fair question. I proposed a solution: "If there's no right or wrong way to do it, then what if you decided what to write next based on what would be the most fun for you to write and for your readers to read?"

Her tense body language relaxed immediately. She was smiling now and staring dreamily ahead of her. I didn't even find it weird that she was likely imagining her characters banging in that very moment. Instead, I was thrilled that she was able to let go of her tight grip on the idea that there was a right or wrong way to write. That belief was, after all, the thing that was keeping her from enjoying the wonderful work that we authors get to do.

By the time our call had reached the hour mark, Michelle was ready to leave, but only because she was so excited to sit down and let her hero and heroine have a little fun. If that was the wrong way to write a romance, then she didn't want to be right.

BLOCK: STALE PATTERNS

There's a reason why our growth requires experimenting with other patterns, like I discussed in the section on continuums. The reason is this:

The patterns that got you stuck will not be the patterns that get you unstuck.

I'm a big renaissance faire nerd, and the Texas Renaissance Faire runs from September to November each year. Those are some of the rainiest months in these parts, so when I think of "renfaire," I generally also think of mud. Deep mud. The thick clay of East Texas.

It's a common sight to wake up after a night of camping on the fairgrounds to find multiple vehicles stuck in this mud. If you've ever found yourself in this unfortunate situation, you probably learned rather quickly that the solution to getting unstuck does not include stomping the accelerator. Doing that only causes the tires to sink deeper into the mud, leaving you even more SOL.

The same is true for when we get stuck in the patterns of our type. Our instinct may be to kick those patterns into overdrive or press our foot on that accelerator (after all, that's how to drive a car in other situations), but that doesn't work. It only lands us deeper in the mud.

Let's say you're an Eight and one of the beliefs you hold is that strong people don't need help from others. To prove to yourself and others that you are a strong person, there's a good chance that you have taken on a lot of projects at once and been able to "make it work" where others haven't. Now let's say one of "your people" falls sick and needs caring for. The Eight will likely step up in that situation, because once an Eight has decided that you are one of their people, they will move heaven and earth for you.

But this is a lot to be carrying all on one's own, even for an Eight who has developed a high pain tolerance. The Eight may find themselves overwhelmed and feeling not so strong and powerful.

Ideally, this is where I would have a session with the Eight, because this is a make-or-break moment in their growth. What the Eight is likely to do based on the patterns that they have developed throughout their life is to hit the accelerator on their patterns of forcefulness and not ask for help. But the situation has changed. That worked for them before, or else they wouldn't try it, but the situation has changed: their tires are stuck in the mud.

What the Eight needs instead is to try out a new pattern, and they would do well to look toward their growth type. On the Enneagram diagram, follow the arrow away from Eight and you end up at Two, which means that's their growth type. Specifically, they would want to look at the patterns of a *healthy* Two.

Healthy Twos have learned how to ask for help as well as give it, and they've learned self-compassion by overcoming their pride. The Eight would benefit tremendously in this situation by rejecting the urge to take on more (in an attempt to reinforce their identity as a strong and independent person) and instead reach out for help from other competent people, who would probably be shocked and delighted that the Eight was asking for help.

In effect, the Eight would be asking around at the campsite to see if anyone else had a wooden board they could borrow to wedge under their stuck wheel—a much better solution to get out of the mud.

When we find ourselves stuck and hit the accelerator of using our old patterns as a response, the sick irony is that doing so brings about the thing we are trying desperately to avoid.

The Four fears that their work is not unique or authentic enough, so they hit the accelerator to make it extra complicated and complex, and in doing so they thwart their hopes of it being received well and praised.

The Seven fears deprivation and missing out, and so they hit the accelerator by trying to do *all* of the marketing tactics and bailing on WIPs when they become unpleasant, and in doing so deprive themselves of the satisfaction of completing a project and seeing a marketing tactic all the way through to effectiveness.

These are just some examples of how our attempt to get out of the mud by hitting the accelerator tends to bring us closer to our worst nightmare than to lasting relief.

It can be a useful exercise to step back, look at your writing and marketing, and ask how your efforts to avoid your core fear may have unintentionally brought it about.

CONCEPT IN ACTION:
A Rational Writer (5) hits the accelerator on existing patterns

JB loved his alone time. It was part of the reason why he chose the independent publishing path. But his LitRPG books weren't selling like they used to, and he finally decided it might be worth the effort of talking about it with someone, in this case me.

"I used to be able to publish a book and then it would sell," he lamented to me on our call. "Now it's like shouting into a void."

His frustration made total sense. For someone who is especially concerned that energy out is met by energy in, shouting into a void is a worst-case scenario.

JB then went on to tell me that he's taken every class he can on increasing sales, and by implementing what he's learned (which is such a lovely thing to see someone do, coming from the teaching perspective), he's found himself in an even *less* pleasant situation: almost all his time goes to creating and monitoring ads. He could spend all day tweaking and checking the analytics, so much so that he might never write another book.

"It used to be such a simple process. I want to get it back to that."

The Five's burning desire to simplify the complicated was coming through loud and clear.

I could sense that what JB wanted me to do was recommend the course that would show him how to keep maintaining all the systems he was maintaining, but in a more streamlined way. If only, right? I'd take that course.

The underlying issue was that JB wanted to see the results that generally require a team to produce without bringing on a team. His pattern of isolation (for fear of being depleted) was what had gotten him into this situation. It was a classic case of "be careful what you wish for," because his need to fly solo and unbothered by the interruptions of working with others had gone so far as to allow his work to eat up all his time, so that the few social hobbies he *did* enjoy with his close friends didn't fit anywhere into his days.

You might see an obvious answer here, but I assure you that a person who is trapped in their own patterns will not. The patterns that got JB into this situation—a desire for self-sufficiency and being overprotective of his energy—were not the patterns that would get him out.

Courses can become an Enneagram 5's addiction if the Five is not careful, because each nugget of information they collect satisfies their core desire to feel capable and self-sufficient. The Five might feel like it's a productive use of their time, and it may be *to a point*. But it can become tricky to sort out what is the information you need and will use effectively from what information you are collecting to armor up against the possibility of needing others.

I asked JB how he felt about bringing someone in to handle his ads. He was, unsurprisingly, not immediately thrilled with the idea.

"It's not that you can't run your ads effectively," I said. "You clearly can. By bringing someone in, you're not going to become *dependent* on them. What you'll be doing is freeing up your energy for your fiction again. That's about as simplified as this system gets."

"But how can I be sure the ads person will know what they're doing?"

This is a sound question, but I suspected it came from a place of fear to the idea of letting go of a piece of the puzzle.

I asked, "How do you know *you're* any good at it?"

This question allowed JB to think critically about how he measures success, and thinking critically is not only a comfortable place for the head-centered Five, it's one of their innate gifts. Discussing the heuristics led to two important understandings: 1) he wasn't some sort of ads genius, and his skills were based on courses that lots of people have taken; ergo, it was entirely possible to find someone who was as effective, if not better, at running ads than he was, and 2) we defined specific metrics of success, so that he could bring in someone on a trial basis and feel confident letting them go if they weren't any good.

But what about the possibility of wasted time and money?

Experiments don't always go as hypothesized, but you never have the data you need to draw a conclusion until you run them. JB could get on board with that. Fives do tend to appreciate the universality of the scientific process.

In the end, JB's next step was simple on the surface in that it was clearly defined: start looking for capable help with ads. That didn't mean it would be easy for him to take that plan and put it into action, though. He lacked practice in trusting others and asking for help, both of which are muscles we must build. What he had opted for instead to that point was to do more of what he'd been doing when his sales started to slump: learn more skills.

While it may soothe a Five's core fear to learn new things, a turning point for this type is when they begin to recognize that they don't need to learn things that other people already know. They can simply pay those people for their expertise instead. Sustainable self-sufficiency doesn't look like isolation; it looks like building a network of competent and capable people around you and knowing when it's time to tap into their expertise.

Because I doubted JB would take that first step toward finding someone, I sent an email to my friend who was good with ads and asked if they needed a new client. And then I let JB know I'd be checking in with him in a week, and he'd better have taken some steps toward onboarding someone for his ads. As long as we could get through that first painful step, I knew JB would appreciate the simplification of getting back to his writing so much that the pain of trusting someone else would be worth it.

BLOCK: NEGLECTING YOUR CENTERS

The Enneagram framework defines three Centers of Intelligence. There is the Head Center, associated with thoughts and the intellect, the Heart Center associated with emotions and feelings, and the Body Center (sometimes called the Gut Center) associated with action, intuition, and our physical well-being. It's important to understand that while we define these as three separate centers, each one is constantly influencing the other two and being influenced by the other two. For instance, we may experience an emotion like loneliness in our sternum. And a thought like *I can only ever count on myself* may make our arms feel heavy and generate the emotion of abandonment.

However, while each of us possesses all three of these centers, our conscious connection to them can vary significantly. Some of us struggle to connect to our emotions, some of us struggle to connect to our body and intuition, and some of us struggle to connect to our thoughts.

Each person has a primary center that they access most frequently without even trying. Because this function happens as a default and it's the most comfortable for the person, this primary center is almost always overused, and we would benefit from offloading some of its function to our other two centers. Some, but not all, of us have the additional option of connecting to a secondary center if our primary center is overwhelmed or not giving us a satisfactory answer. This may look like a primarily Body Center person who's unsure if their first instinct is to be trusted tuning into their Head Center for a logical examination of the situation.

And then there is our least-developed center. That one is usually a sticking point for us, and our lack of easy connection to it lies at the heart of most of our struggles. Oh yes, even the writing ones (sometimes especially the writing ones).

However, the good news is that through intentional practice to reconnect with our least-developed center, we experience rapid growth in *all* parts of our lives.

If your Body Center is your least developed, then finding ways to connect to your body through deep breathing, walking meditation, exercise, eating healthy, dancing, listening to your intuition, and taking productive action on your thoughts and feelings will be life-changing almost immediately.

If your Heart Center is your least developed, then developing practices of tuning into your emotions—sitting with them and naming them—throughout the day, telling trusted friends how you feel, seeking therapy, and noticing where your emotions exist within your body will jump-start your growth.

And if your Head Center is the least developed, then practices that expose you to new ideas, establishing space for you to think in peace throughout your day, deep learning about something new, and challenging yourself intellectually are going to open you up to a whole host of new options you hadn't imagined before.

Identifying your primary, secondary, and least-developed center can be incredibly helpful for when you run into blocks in your writing and marketing. Evaluating how our centers are at play in a situation is a useful diagnostic tool for addressing our blocks. It's common that the underlying factor of the writing or marketing block is that one of our centers is trying to do the work of all three. But there's a reason that there are three Centers of Intelligence. Your head alone cannot gather and process all of the information that you need to thrive. Neither can your heart nor your body. You need information and insight from all three.

And yet it's not uncommon for someone to ask their Head Center to deal with emotions or their Body Center to do all the thinking. We may believe we're operating on solid information when we do this, but we aren't. Your heart doesn't speak instinct or reason, your body doesn't speak reason or emotion, and your head doesn't speak emotion or instinct.

In short, if one of your centers is trying to tell you something but you're not paying attention, shit will go south eventually.

Here's why thinking in terms of the Three Centers is so helpful for your author career: let's say I'm working with a client who knows that her least-developed center is her Heart Center. When she tells me that she sits down at the computer each morning, opens her manuscript, and simply cannot get started, I may suggest a practice of closing her eyes and tuning into what emotions she is feeling. Heart information is the most likely kind that she's missing, and so it's likely where the answer she needs to get around the block is hiding.

And if you don't have a strong connection to your Heart Center, you may have no freaking clue what emotions sound or feel like when you start tuning in.

I'm someone whose least-developed center is the Heart Center, so I keep a colorful emotion wheel on the wall next to my computer. Each morning when I sit down to write, I look at the wheel and ask myself which emotion I'm bringing with me to the computer. It's often more than one. Because I have a strong connection to my Body Center, that's how I approach this process: read through each of the emotions until I feel that kick in my chest; that's probably an emotion I'm feeling.

Because I don't have that easy connection to my Heart Center, those emotions can easily exist beneath my level of awareness indefinitely until I make a conscious effort to pause and listen to them or they stop me dead in my tracks. I've found that simply naming what emotions are existing inside of me each morning (or when I get stuck throughout the day) and tuning into what action they are requesting I take (often it's none) keeps them from tripping me up so that I can proceed with what I had planned.

Sometimes, though, they require me to change my plans before they'll allow me to focus on my writing, and I suspect this is why so many of us would rather not even go there. But if we proceed as if our emotions aren't calling to us, we'll have to change our plans sooner or later, and it might be better to adjust accordingly now, before we get too far in.

For instance, I may tune in and discover that I feel *overwhelmed*. That calls me to take action toward asking for help or removing something from my plate. Once I take the action that my emotions are requesting, the writing is almost guaranteed to flow.

Or maybe I tune in and recognize that I'm feeling irritated. It may be difficult to write until I can address that irritation through something like meditation or giving voice to that irritation.

Or maybe I realize that I'm carrying a large amount of grief in my chest that's making it hard for me to breathe. Perhaps I'll have a good cry or reach out to someone who will understand my grief. And maybe, if the grief is too large, the action I need to take is giving myself permission to skip my writing for the day and do something that reminds me of everything I still have in my life despite the loss. Once I process some of that grief, I know that my writing will be richer for it when I'm ready to return.

Our least-developed center still exists within us, regardless of how disconnected we are from it, so what makes it the least developed is our *awareness* of it. It is still doing its job, but if we have not consciously connected with it, then it can thwart our best-laid plans. It becomes a cartoon banana peel that we slip on over and over again.

You'll find that as you deepen your connection to your least-developed center, your primary center gets a break from carrying the heavy load. When we allow it to stick to the job it was designed to do, we see it function much more effectively.

Here's what we can look forward to for our primary center when we work on our least-developed center:

- The person whose primary center is their Head Center moves from unproductive thinking, like chewing on the same problem over and over again without getting anywhere, into productive thinking that offers clarity.
- The person with the primary Heart Center moves from unproductive emotions, as in having feelings *about* their feelings, to productive emotions that pass through without getting trapped or ignored.
- The person whose primary center is their Body Center moves from unproductive action, like remaining busy without a clear purpose to it, to productive action that aligns with their values.

Do you recognize any of this in your career? Do you see where you might be ignoring your least-developed center, leading your primary center to take on too much in areas where it isn't qualified? Do you see how unproductive thoughts, feelings, or actions might be burning fuel you can't afford to lose?

I encourage you to take a moment to consider which of your three centers is your primary, which one is your secondary, and which one is your least developed. This is usually not a difficult process to sort through, as over the years we come to identify as "overly emotional" or "stuck in our head" or "a fire-ready-aim type."

But don't worry, because even if it feels like you have no connection to one of your centers, I promise that you do.

It's there, and it's probably been calling to you, ready to reconcile. With practice, you can learn to hear what it has to say.

Since I know a lot of you are struggling to figure out what center you would benefit from paying more attention to, I'm including a Concept in Action for each center that I hope will be illuminating.

CONCEPT IN ACTION:
A Bold Writer (8) struggles to connect to his Heart Center

Calvin, an Eight, knew what his perfect author career would look like, and he was close to achieving it. There was only one thorn left in his side: readers. He had plenty of them, so that wasn't the problem. The problem was when those readers responded to his emails or sent him unsolicited emails, it drove him nuts. They required so much of what he referred to as "coddling." He was sick of it. He didn't want to hear about their feelings. He wasn't their therapist.

Thankfully, he hadn't yet told any of them where they should shove their feelings, but it was clear he wanted to.

"Which kinds of stories are the most intolerable for you to hear about?" I asked.

"When they complain about how their life is falling apart or how their husband died recently and my books kept them company after that. On and on. Half of the time I just want to shout at them to get their shit together, and the other half, it's like... why are you dumping this on me?"

I agreed that reader emails can be a lot sometimes. "Do you feel like they're forcing you to respond to them?"

"Sort of. What kind of an asshole would I be if I didn't?"

"Their bids for emotional connection with one of their favorite authors feel like an attempt to control you?"

He hadn't thought about it like that, but after he did, he chuckled. He was well aware of the Eight's core fear of being harmed or controlled.

"How often do these emails cause you to feel compassion or even gratitude for the reader reaching out to you?"

Calvin gave me a blank look and asked what I meant.

"Can you name some of the emotions you feel when you receive these emails?"

"Anger, annoyance, sometimes disgust."

Before you judge Calvin, let me assure you that this is a pretty standard range of emotions for people who have a limited connection to their Heart Center. Depending on the type, the emotions may vary, but three is a pretty average number of them that folks can name.

"What would you say," I replied, "if I told you that some authors would read the kinds of emails you describe and feel compassion or sadness for the readers sending them?"

"I would say those authors are naïve."

Remembering what type I was speaking with, I countered, "It kind of sounds like you're scared to be compassionate or sad."

"Oh please. I'm not scared of that."

"Bullshit. You think those emotions are weak, right?"

"Yeah, but I'm not scared of them."

"You are. You're scared of emotions that will make you feel weak. I'm telling you that as an Eight, that's your fear. If you buy this Enneagram stuff at all, then I'm right."

Calvin didn't look happy about this, but I could tell he was thinking about it.

(By the way, the rest of your types don't have to worry about my talking to you this bluntly. I enjoy reaching individuals in the way they need to be reached, and this was special treatment for not only an Eight, but for the relationship I have with Calvin specifically.)

"I'll have to think about that," he said, which was as good as I was going to get for the time being.

So I asked, "What if those people simply admire you? What if they see you as a competent and respectable person, and only want to make a human connection with you? Is it possible that these emails are, at least in part, written by readers who are offering you connection rather than trying to control you?"

After a pause, he said, "Okay, there may be something to that."

"For the people who are genuinely trying to connect with someone they admire, albeit not always in the most self-aware ways, how could you receive that and complete the connection?"

I could see him softening slightly as he came up with some fairly obvious answers, like responding kindly. Then I reminded him of his purpose in writing: to inspire others to be bold and fearless. "How are you rewarding the boldness it takes for them to email an author who they admire?"

That one landed, and he cursed at me, which I'm not upset about.

Once he realized how his anger and annoyance had actually been keeping him from living out his purpose (which we'd discussed on previous calls), he immediately had incentive to consider what I had to say.

"I would bet your Heart Center *does* feel compassion for them when you read these emails," I said, "and it's actually your denial of that emotion that takes so much energy from you."

The defense mechanism of the Eight is *denial*, and Eights expend a lot of energy trying to deny the parts of themselves that they consider "weak."

"Think about how amazing a reader will feel," I continued, "if they get a response from you that's validating and encouraging. Think about how you would feel if you received that sort of email from *your* favorite author."

He threw up his hands in defeat. "Okay, I get it. You're right."

I let off the attack, knowing I'd gotten beneath the defenses and he'd heard the truth in it. He was (and is) a wonderful person, and like most Eights, he was quite sensitive below the armor. He had no desire to hurt his readers' feelings, so his sentiment about the emails was just a product of his core fear being triggered. For the Eight, that looks like anger, so it can appear scary if you're not expecting it. But I was expecting it.

Calvin's issue was never really that readers were emailing him; it was that his disconnection from his Heart Center left him with a narrow range of emotions that he was comfortable with, and anything outside of that range was quickly transmuted into anger, which was much more familiar to him and therefore felt safer.

His homework was simply to notice every time something annoyed, angered, or disgusted him, and, when that happened, pausing a beat to ask if one of those "weaker" emotions was trying to break through and was being reshaped into his go-to emotions.

When I checked in a week later, he told me he'd experimented with connecting to a couple of readers via email and it felt incredibly awkward. But he would be damned if he let his fear of feeling those softer emotions control him. This was a new kind of courage he hadn't explored, and it was not only helping him add more dimension to his fiction, but it was also giving him a new perspective on life.

And those reader emails didn't annoy him so much anymore.

CONCEPT IN ACTION:
A Helpful Writer (2) struggles to connect to her Head Center

Desiree had been stuck on the same scene in her manuscript for the last two months. Sometimes this is a story issue that either needs more time to percolate in the subconscious or the sounding board of another person to brainstorm a solution. And sometimes the block has nothing to do with the story itself.

So, I asked Desiree to describe what happens when she sits down to write the next sentence.

"I can't even bring myself to do that at this point."

I knew from working together previously that the early morning before her kids wake up is usually her writing time, so I asked her what she was doing instead during this time.

"I check my email, Facebook, Instagram, respond to any comments or texts from when I was asleep, and then the kids are up and I start getting them ready for school." Desiree had moved to Hawaii from the East Coast with her husband and kids two and a half months before, so most of her friends and family had a six-hour head start on her each day. By the time she was getting up, it was close to lunch for most of her connections, and her phone had all kinds of social notifications waiting.

I felt for her, because her heart was clearly so starved for connection, which is why moves like these may seem idyllic in theory but turn out to be lonely for at least a little while.

"The last time you were able to sit down at the computer, even if you weren't able to write, what did it feel like?" I asked.

She thought about it. "Like dying? It really felt that unbearable. I felt like screaming. I usually enjoy the silent time, but the silence felt less like peace and more like emptiness."

"And had you already checked your notifications that morning?"

"I'm sure. I do it every morning now. My phone alarm goes off, and when I silence it, I see all the notifications waiting for me, and I go through them."

"Your Heart Center is waking up with a bucket of cold water in its face, it sounds like."

She agreed with that description.

"There's not a whole lot of space for your Head Center to function here," I continued, "which it needs to do if you're going to be able to focus on writing the next sentence."

She didn't have an alarm clock that *wasn't* her phone, so I told her to go grab the cheapest one she could find and try using that in the mornings, keeping her phone somewhere she wouldn't encounter it accidentally before she could sit down at the computer. Not everyone can reasonably keep their phone on silent all night, but because the only people in Hawaii who might need her in an emergency slept in the same house, and her husband kept his phone by the bed, she agreed that it could work.

Her homework, should she choose to accept it, was to not check her phone until after her writing time. At all. The phone was a landmine of Heart Center triggers for her, and she was basically at the whim of whatever emotions people dropped on her doorstep while she was sleeping.

While this homework also meant she had to wait to connect with any of her East Coast friends and family for a while each day, holding the anticipation that there *might* be love and connection waiting for her was actually easier for her Heart Center to do than responding to those messages immediately and then entering a holding pattern as she waited for another hit of connection.

As a Two, Desiree cared a lot about other people, even people she didn't know. Social media could easily hook her in with stories of dogs being rescued, videos of war-torn countries, or even just people being kind to one another. All of the emotions we experience through social media can hook our Heart Center. We experience a hit of emotion from them, but not one as substantial as we get from being in the presence of the people we love, so we can become addicted to these small but ultimately unsatisfying nibbles. I suspected that was the case for Desiree.

I explained to her that putting these boundaries on her Heart Center would allow her Head Center to come through with some focus, and she agreed to try it. I also encouraged her to go meet more people in her new town so she could get the real kind of connection on a regular basis rather than craving whatever morsels she could get through her phone from five thousand miles away.

When I checked back with Desiree a week later to see if she'd gotten any words done on her manuscript (even one word would be a step in the right direction), she told me that she was way past that scene she'd been stuck on. It only took one day of not checking her phone in the morning to sit down at the computer, catch up on the scene, and write straight through it and beyond. She said she felt amazing that day but had admittedly checked her phone first thing a few mornings since, and it derailed her day again.

I told her, "At least you know the process works. You won't be stuck for two months next time. Maybe you'll just be stuck for a week before you remember to follow the process. Then maybe it's only a few days the time after that. It's another tool in your toolbox either way. Back-sliding is normal, so success looks like remembering what works just a little quicker each time. And sometimes it takes longer than the time before, and that's okay, too."

"Damn," she said. "I was enjoying beating myself up about relapsing."

"Sorry," I said, "I'm forcing you to be as loving to yourself as you are other people."

Like I always say, doing this work is hard. Sometimes it even requires us being kind to ourselves.

CONCEPT IN ACTION:
A Rational Writer (5) struggles to connect to her Body Center

Maggie was at a point in her career where she knew she needed to pivot. She had taken her historical romance series out of Kindle Unlimited (and its exclusivity) and had been selling it wide on other retailers for a year. She still wasn't anywhere close to making the royalties that she made when she was in KU, though. To Maggie's credit, she already knew that this was because she hadn't treated each retailer like its own business and had failed to give ample attention to jump-starting sales and finding ways to keep them consistent across all the platforms. She also knew herself well enough, as Fives often do, to feel certain that she wouldn't magically take an interest in learning to master each of these other digital retailers.

The decision she faced was whether she should take her books down on the platforms like Barnes & Noble, Kobo, and Apple, and make them exclusive to KU again, *or* if she should invest effort in creating a direct sales platform and give that her attention for the next year.

Because of Kindle Unlimited terms of exclusivity, she couldn't do both with her e-books.

The reason Maggie came to see me wasn't because she was incapable of doing the research on both options or learning the skills necessary. She came to me because she was struggling with something that she almost never did: she couldn't seem to focus her thinking. Her mind felt scattered, and her focus wasn't as sharp as she was used to. It was making her feel a little crazy.

The inability to focus can feel career-ending for Fives, since they build so much of their lives around their mental capacity and enjoy spending time in their head. So, when you build everything around one Center of Intelligence, and that intelligence is not functioning like it used to, you can find yourself in a real pickle.

The first question I asked Maggie was what sort of movement practices she had in her daily routine. She wasn't sure what I meant.

"Do you go for walks, stretch, dance, do yoga, kickboxing?" I asked.

She did not do any of those things on a daily or even a weekly basis. When she wasn't writing or marketing, she was reading or crocheting.

"I'm not an athletic person. I'm totally uncoordinated, and I prefer to do something quiet at home."

The problem she was running up against was one that I see in a lot of authors. She didn't identify strongly as an active person. She saw movement as "exercise" and exercise as something that other people did. Athletic people. And she did not identify as an "athletic person."

Each of us has our own physical limitations, but physical *movement*, whatever we're capable of, is a non-negotiable for our mental and emotional health. I suspected Maggie's lack of a movement practice was not only part of the problem, but the best point of approach for a solution.

For Fives, it's rare that they have a strong connection to their Heart Center. That's frequently their least-developed center. So, for a Five like Maggie, disconnecting from her Body Center of Intelligence through that neglect left her solely dependent on her Head Center to do the job of all three centers. No wonder it was struggling. It was all out of RAM.

I asked Maggie if she enjoyed going for walks, and she said she did. She rarely made time for it, though.

There are certain problems that can only be processed through movement in our bodies. I know this sounds woo-woo, but our bodies know things that our brain don't. By getting more in touch with our Body Center as we think over options, like Maggie's decision between KU and selling direct, we may feel a clear *yes* or a *no* in our body. But we have to connect to it, and to do that, we need to give it some love. Bodies are literally made to move, otherwise we could just be a brain in a vat. We've evolved such that exercise increases the endorphins and other chemicals like dopamine and serotonin that our brains need for clearer thinking. Endorphins decrease any physical pain we might be feeling in our body and help us regulate our emotions without suppressing them—two things that might be interfering with our ability to think clearly, even if we're not aware that they are.

Appealing to Maggie's intellectual preference for information, we discussed the proven benefits of walking each day. I also asked her to put time on her calendar to suit up and go for a walk, even a short one around the block, once a day for a week. After that week, I would check in with her and see how she felt about her publishing dilemma, and whether she'd settled on a decision.

She emailed me after her walk the following day to tell me that she'd settled on a path and had already begun taking action on it. I asked her to make note of how much a single walk had done for her mind. Imagine what thoughts and insights she might come upon if she walked proactively every day or even just three times a week rather than waiting until she was miserable and stuck in a loop!

SECTION 5: BUILDING AUTHOR RESILIENCE

YOU ARE ALREADY THE THING YOU SEEK TO BE

There's a fundamental concept of the Enneagram that tells us that *the seeking* is where our problems begin. Each type wants to be able to confidently identify in a specific way—good (Ones), lovable (Twos), valuable (Threes), significant (Fours), capable (Fives), supported (Sixes), satisfied (Sevens), strong (Eights), or whole (Nines). The basic truth that the Enneagram describes is that you already *are* all these things.

Yes, even you.

Your type expression arises from which one of these self-identifiers you've lost touch with the most. Because once you lose touch with the fact that you already are that thing, your attention gravitates toward seeking reassurance that you are the thing you want to be, and it does that by looking *externally*.

The trouble with seeking it externally is simple: that's not where it's to be found. The external world is finite and can be taken away. What we're looking for is something infinite that cannot be taken away. That's how you anchor yourself against a whole world of things you cannot control.

For example, a Four, the Individualist, is defined by their struggle to perceive their own significance. Because they struggle to perceive it internally, they seek it externally, sometimes by trying to create art that will ensure no one forgets them, and sometimes by trying to create bonds with others that are so strong they can never be broken. Fours can end up building their lives around not being forgotten —attempting to be so unique they could never be replaced, forging connections through shared trauma and struggle, and longing for an unattainable assurance against abandonment.

All of this is attention the Four is failing to aim inward to practice perceiving their innate significance that will always be there, whether the external world remembers them or not.

Because these patterns show up in every part of our life, they also show up in our approach to writing and marketing. The Four's need to be remembered can make it almost intolerable for them to conform to existing creative guidelines like familiar plot structures or well-defined genres and tropes. If they are like everyone else, they fear they'll never stand out enough to create a lasting impression.

While this can certainly lead to groundbreaking art that propels forward our understanding of genre and form, it more commonly leads to a confusing path for any potential readers to walk. The Four asks a potential reader to go from not knowing who the author is to understanding enough about the book's promise to decide it might be for them to getting through the first five pages of the book to finishing the book with enough understanding of what happened to go onto the next one. The unhealthy Four might confuse authenticity with obfuscation, and the reader gets lost along the way.

It's also why Fours are at the forefront of rejecting the "write to trend" or even "write to market" approach. Giving a Four this advice is essentially telling them "settle for being like everyone else and easily forgotten." That's fundamentally repulsive for a person who is desperately seeking to be significant and memorable.

So, for a Four to begin reining in the incomprehensible creative expression enough for it to be properly comprehended by the people who would love it, they must first address this fear of insignificance. And to do that, *they must remember that they are already significant without trying.*

Easier said than done, obviously, but mindfulness practices —ones that recognize when the core fear is acting up so that we intentionally turn our attention inward—are what the doctor ordered for this, and they're something everyone can learn to do and then master with practice, practice, practice. Once you know *to* do it, which most people do not, it becomes a matter of remembering to do it and then doing it in ways that are believable to you.

Regardless of your type, when you begin to feel like things in your life are spinning out of control, or you notice yourself becoming emotionally dysregulated, or you simply don't like the way you've been feeling about yourself and the world lately, try giving yourself the gift of thirty uninterrupted seconds somewhere peaceful for you, close your eyes, and try to feel the truth of the following statement for your type:

Ones: I am already built with goodness at my core. I am perfect in my imperfections.

Twos: I am already filled with unconditional love for myself, and I am deserving of compassion.

Threes: I am already endlessly valuable and will never be more or less so than I am right now.

Fours: I am already irreplaceable. The impact of my life will live on in indescribable ways for eternity.

Fives: I already possess all the capabilities necessary to manage each moment as it comes.

Sixes: I am already equipped with a powerful inner guidance. I know what to do in each moment.

Sevens: I am already bursting with abundance. This moment already has everything I need.

Eights: I am already strong enough for this moment. My vulnerability proves my strength.

Nines: I am already a whole person. There is no

part of me that needs to hide to remain connected
to the world.

Closing your eyes and remembering these truths will
present you with new options in your career. Rather than
your efforts flowing outward to *seek* the thing you already
are, you can turn your attention toward more important
things like building a meaningful career and getting your
books out to all the people whose lives would be improved
in some small way by reading them. Hell yes!

When I remember that I am already built with goodness at
my core and am perfect in my imperfections, I feel liberated to say, "I wrote a series about God's daughter trying to
find her way through weird Texas purity culture," and not
rely on the external response to tell me if I'm still a good
person or not. (This is immediately useful because lots of
people don't like that a series like Jessica Christ even exists
and have tried to tell me I am a very bad person for creating
it.)

However, in those moments when I get caught in the
seeking of being good and perfect, it is almost impossible
for me to talk about that series without worrying about
receiving criticism of my character. And that's a shame,
since those books explore the question of "What does it
mean to be a good person?" which I think we all know
cannot be summed up by a simple "Go to church every
Sunday." By forgetting my inherent goodness and perfect
imperfection, I hobble my ability to bring my Type 1 gifts
of wisdom and integrity to the world through my writing.
I don't want that for me, and I don't want it for you,
either.

So, try it out: close your eyes and remind yourself that you are already the thing you seek to be. Feel the relief move through your body as the truth settles in and you reconnect to that part of yourself. If you can access that for a single moment, you can build your connection to it over time.

WHERE DO YOU FIND YOUR RESILIENCE?

In one of my certification classes, the instructor, Dr. Jerome Wagner (of the Enneagram Spectrum of Personality Styles) asked each of us by type where we found our resilience.

Strangely, I'd never considered this question so bluntly. Yet I knew almost immediately where I went looking for the strength to get back up when I was knocked on my ass.

It was quickly apparent that not everyone knew this about themselves, though.

One of the gifts of struggling with depression your whole life, as I have, is that you get a lot of practice in dragging yourself out of bed. If this sounds familiar, I encourage you to focus your attention for the duration of our resilience chat on all the times you did the same, rather than all the times you found yourself crawling back *into* bed while it was still light outside.

After years of deep contemplation and paying my therapist's bills, I've decided that I don't get much out of beating myself up about the times my depression sets in. Instead, I view it as "Of course you find yourself in bed midday sometimes, Claire. You have the depresh. That's what people with the depresh do." There's no need to be ashamed about my body's coyness around serotonin production. Some people have a peanut allergy, and I have depression. We all have our thing, right?

Instead, if you're in the same boat, I want you to think about all the times you got back out of bed, even if it was ten p.m. and you were only doing it to take a leak or scrounge in the pantry like a feral raccoon. The fact that you got out of bed is what matters.

Over the years, through help from therapy, learning about my body chemistry, and letting go of the patterns of my type that kept me miserable (not great for producing more serotonin!), I can proudly say that each time I get out of bed it's a little bit faster than the time before. That's miraculous, especially considering, ya know, the world we live in. I'm frankly shocked more people don't get in bed and stay there for days. But I digress.

Resilience looks like a lot of things. Sometimes it's getting out of bed on the other side of a depressive slump. Sometimes it's showing up to painful physical therapy following an illness or injury. Sometimes it's falling in love again after loss or heartbreak. Sometimes it's publishing the next book after the last book flopped or got panned by critics.

You cannot live a life without setbacks. Trying to lands a person in a life of inaction, timidity, and emptiness. What a waste!

This is why it's so important to not only learn resilience but become familiar with your own source of it so that you can stop worrying whether it will be there for you when the worst comes to pass. Trust in your ability to get back up again, and you can spend much less energy on worrying about getting knocked down.

The **One** can recover when they make a colossal mistake.

The **Two** can recover when they do something uncaring.

The **Three** can recover when they publicly fail.

The **Four** can recover when they're rejected.

The **Five** can recover when they make a fool of themselves.

The **Six** can recover when they act cowardly.

The **Seven** can recover when pain becomes unavoidable.

The **Eight** can recover when their vulnerabilities are exploited.

The **Nine** can recover when they fail to show up or speak up for someone they love.

And so on. There are many things that can knock down each type, and the above list is just one example for each.

Imagine if you didn't worry so much about getting knocked down. Imagine if you greeted every fearful thought and feeling with a deep sense of confidence that you could get back up again and still be okay. What new methods and approaches might you experiment with? How might your career expand and evolve in wonderful ways you never thought possible?

I have a sticky note on the edge of my computer that reminds me of where I find my resilience. It says, in my usual loving tone, *What the fuck else are you going to do with your LIFE?*

When I'm knocked down, when I want to give up, when I don't feel like getting back out of bed, I remember this question. The reason that question brings me to my resilience is because what I'm doing now—through my fiction and helping authors—is built on a strong sense of purpose. What the fuck else would I rather be doing than living through a sense of purpose? What the fuck else would I rather be doing with my life than trying to leave the world a better place than I found it?

So, now I challenge you to think about the last time you got back up after being knocked on your ass. Where did you find that resilience? Is it a stretch to believe that if you found it once, you might find it again and again?

RESILIENCE TOOLS OF EACH TYPE

Where you find your resilience will vary depending on factors from your history, upbringing, skills, and connections. Discovering the sources of your unique resilience over time and through quiet reflection can be a rewarding process, and if you're one of those people who has to arrive at the conclusion yourself before you can get onboard with it, then this might be the best route.

But if you're feeling like you don't even know where to start, like when you ask yourself where you get your resilience your mind starts to *beep* like there's a test of the emergency broadcasting system, don't worry. We can look to our Enneagram type as a starting point.

The internal motivation of each type is strong, and if you know where to find it and you give it some space, it will surge back again and again.

Here are some of the tools of resilience for each type that can be harnessed to help us get back up when we've been knocked down:

Type 1: The Principled Writer
Sources of resilience: Purpose, moral courage

Remember that you can't control things outside of yourself, but you can influence them through love, courage, and standing up for what is right and just. If your ego takes a hit from criticism, return to your sense of purpose, and remember that you have the gift of moral courage that many others don't; when you know in your heart what the right action is, you'll take it, often at a personal cost. The world needs that, so lick those wounds, sure, but then put on your armor, grab your sword, and show up again to inspire readers with your vision for how things could be made fairer, and more righteous, and just.

Type 2 – The Helpful Writer
Resources for resilience: Love, compassion

Remember that the source of your love for others is entirely unselfish. Sure, your ego might've slipped into giving for the sake of receiving, but beneath that, you have too much love to offer to call it quits. Start by practicing compassion for yourself—resting and tending to your own needs for a while the way you would tend to the needs of others—and soon you'll find that the love you have for those around you is too intense to hold in. When you let that compassion shine through your words, your readers will feel it, and it might be exactly what they needed to get back up again, too. You may not make the whole world a more loving place, but you'll certainly make *your* world and your reader's worlds brighter and more nurturing.

Type 3 – The Productive Writer
Sources for resilience: Vision, drive

Remember that you can accomplish whatever you set your mind to, even if you must extend the timeline somewhat. If your ego has taken over, you might be chasing things that wouldn't fulfill you in the end, but that's not your only option. There are so many worthwhile projects that will help others who struggle with the same fears that you have, and if you focus your drive toward those, you can inspire countless readers to follow their dreams rather than letting fear hold them back. The world needs everyone at their best, and your vision for that world can inspire countless others. There is no such thing as failure when you're pursuing a meaningful vision like that.

Type 4 – The Authentic Writer
Sources for resilience: Inspiration, self-expression

Remember that your voice is irreplaceable, and while there may not be original stories, there is always a unique way to tell a familiar tale. What story of your life are you crafting with your decisions? Do you want to play the tragic victim at the first sign of rejection, or would you rather dust yourself off and use your voice to express to all the other people who don't feel like they belong that they matter, that the world would be worse off if they kept small and silent? You can't help but see the beauty in the darkness and the mundane, and what a waste it would be if you didn't help readers see it, too.

Type 5 – The Rational Writer
Sources for resilience: Curiosity, discovery

Remember that no matter how draining or intrusive the world may feel, it's only by going out in it and getting your hands messy that you can truly answer the questions your mind can't stop asking. Your powers of observation and curiosity lead you to ask questions others don't. Think back to how good it feels to explore those questions in your writing and to meet readers who are asking the same kinds of questions. Following your curiosity will lead you to even more interesting questions, and there are so, so many to ask and explore during your short time on this earth!

Type 6 – The Faithful Writer
Sources for resilience: Loyalty, community

Remember that your fears and anxieties don't have to be a disadvantage but can instead be a magnificent call for courage. The more afraid you are, the more potential for courageous acts you have in front of you. Betrayals are no joke, but who knows better than you do what brave love there is behind loyalty, friendship, and our inherent responsibility to one another? Who better to write stories that remind readers that they can get back up again, trust others again, and, through doing that, can create communities that are so much stronger and braver than the sum of their parts? When you reconnect to your loyal love for those in your life, is it even possible to stay down?

Type 7 – The Enthusiastic Writer

Sources for resilience: Possibilities, enjoyment

Remember that your ability to find the magic doesn't live solely in the future but is also with you in the present moment. You can get back up when you fall not just based on a future promise, but because *this* moment is enough to inspire you and refill your well. Because people of your type are among the most naturally resilient, on those rare occasions where you get knocked down so hard that you notice it, the best thing you can do is refocus on the present. Reground yourself so that your mind can start to unfurl the endless possibilities of how you will triumph over the unfinished projects, live at a less frantic pace, and find satisfaction in each moment of writing again. There is too much for you to experience and enjoy in this world for you to stay down.

Type 8 – The Bold Writer
Sources for resilience: Justice, stubbornness

Remember that even strong people get knocked down from time to time. It's not a sign of weakness but a sign that you are not so armored up that there is no humanity left in you. True strength means getting back up *without* adding fresh armor. While falling might be a novel experience to you, your stubborn refusal to let someone else exercise control over you can be a huge gift for resilience. Turn your attention to all the justice that still needs to be fought for in this world, and you'll find your feet in no time and be back up and running. Continuing to be vulnerable through your writing as you do so is a show of power and strength that will inspire others, including your readers, to tap into their own kindhearted boldness to fight alongside you.

Type 9 – The Harmonious Writer
Sources of resilience: Unity, perspective

Remember that you are inextricably connected with the world around you whether there is conflict in your immediate field of vision or not. If you're feeling disconnected and unable to move forward because things you've put off addressing have gotten very big and scary, don't forget to tap into your gift of perspective and zoom out. The universe isn't torn asunder every time a star explodes. Connection exists even in the heat of conflict, and it is, in fact, what allows for resolution. Your ability to feel that deep thread of unity and to see the big picture are exactly what your readers need to guide them through their dark moments. You are never disconnected and can never be cut off or cast out of the bigger picture, so tap into the part you are here to play to get back up again and keep going.

The next time you're down, I hope you'll remember these resources at your disposal. It's certainly okay to take a moment to dust yourself off, lick your wounds, and rest. Allowing yourself that space might be exactly what you need for the kindling of your type's motivation to catch fire. The only thing I ask is that you don't indulge in despair. Try to remember these things before you reach that point. Write them down somewhere you'll see in those dark moments or when you're thinking about giving up. Ask your friends to remind you of your sources of resilience when you fall and do the same for them when they need it. Resilience is not only easier but also more effective as a team sport.

And because our Six friends teach us that you can never be too prepared, let's keep looking at where we can build resilience for our author careers.

PURPOSE AS THE FIRST STEP

There will be times in your career when you feel stuck in inaction. You won't know what the next best move is, and you're worried about picking wrong, investing your time in something that doesn't pan out, having your readers turn against you, or any number of other legitimately scary things happening.

By now, you understand what's happening in this kind of situation:

1. Core fear: Your fear is creeping in and trying to take over.
2. Certainty: You're expecting to have a level of certainty about the future that no one can have.
3. Resilience: You don't have confidence in your ability to recover when you get knocked down.

Great news, though: you are now empowered with the knowledge of what might be stopping you, so you can pause, look over the possibilities, and see where you're running into problems. That process alone can help clear a path forward.

At least... *intellectually*. But to intellectually understand and analyze the problem is not the same as having internalized the solution.

So how do you go from knowing intellectually that you're stuck in a loop made of fear, unreasonable need for certainty, and lack of faith in your own resilience to *actually escaping the loop*? How do you take that first step out of the established patterns?

This is where a sense of purpose comes in handy.

Finding something to set your mind on that is more important than preserving your own ego can propel you forward *despite the fear loop*, and that will very often provide the necessary escape velocity to get out of your loop and moving forward again.

The biggest achievement is that first step out of the loop. Once you've done that, the next one gets a little easier. Before long, you're moving at a steady pace and can't remember why you were feeling so stuck before.

Purpose is a place for us to get a little spiritual, perhaps even a little grandiose. It focuses us on our *contribution* to the world rather than what the world can give us and how it makes us feel about ourselves.

For instance, I want to do what I can to leave the world a more loving and connected place. That's my guiding purpose in building not only my career but designing my life and doing all this hard work on myself. I want the people and systems that I encounter to be fairer and more humane once I'm gone than they were before I arrived. That purpose helps me frame my decisions so that they leave little space for my fear to seep in. And when my need for certainty sneaks up on me (*Am I sure this is the right way to pursue my purpose?*) I remind myself that I am perfectly imperfect, and I will make mistakes along my path. My fear of screwing up comes from my ego's need to protect itself, and that's not a good enough reason to opt out. After all, what the fuck else am I going to do with my life?

A purpose is not the same as a goal.

Goals draw us toward "success/failure" measurements, which jab our ego right in the ribs. But there is no finish line with a purpose, so there can be no failure. Instead, when we shift our attention toward our purpose, we approach our work with curiosity as to how we can shape it to support that established purpose.

It's okay for your purpose of publishing to change as you change and the world around you shifts. That doesn't mean your previous purpose was wrong or not worth the time. It's okay to allow the new version of you to be drawn toward new things.

A metric you can use to decide if your purpose is strong enough to be worth your time on Earth is asking, "Will this inspire to me to get back up and keep trying when I've been knocked down?" If it will, then for shit's sake, hold on to it!

Purpose means living for something greater than ourselves. It means finding a way to take that first step even when it poses a risk to us and the ego we live alongside.

Noticing the patterns we're trapped in is only the first step (albeit a big, important one). While it allows us to see that we have a choice in front of us, that doesn't mean choosing something new is suddenly easy. It can be incredibly tricky to break the patterns and cycles we've lived in for most of our lives. The more we repeat a pattern, especially one based in self-protection, the stronger our neural pathways for that pattern become. We create deeper and deeper tracks each time we repeat the pattern, and those tracks become difficult to move away from.

Interrupting established patterns is essential for creating new pathways that better serve us.

But once we establish those new pathways, we must also repeat the process again and again to create strong pathways where we *want* them to be.

This is the basis for neuroplasticity. Thankfully, it exists, and it's wild that we can change so much about our brains simply by telling ourselves different things about the world around us and our place in it. It's handy as hell.

Our ego, that is, the armor of personality we wear that protects our sense of who we are and eventually traps us, has a single aim: protect itself. To be clear, your ego does not protect you; it protects itself. The interests of you and your ego may align from time to time, but when push comes to shove, if you're letting your ego drive the car, it will sacrifice your happiness, if need be, to protect itself. A deep sense of purpose is one of the fastest ways to interrupt the patterns of our ego so that we can unstick ourselves from inaction and take that first disruptive step.

This is why it's crucial to develop a sense of purpose for something greater than your own interests. Make sure the purpose reasonable and not overwhelming—erasing racism from the world, for instance, might not be a one-person job —as well as applicable to all parts of your life—a purpose of writing books that move people isn't applicable to your life outside of writing, but a purpose of helping people wake up to their true nature might be. And lastly, develop one that sustains you enough to form the basis of your resilience when—not if, but when—you get knocked on your ass.

It's also important to keep an eye on your ego, which will try to hijack this process. If your sense of purpose is, say, covertly based around your ego's need for everyone to revere you, then that's a no-go. Your ego will take the wheel almost immediately.

If you're struggling to come up with what your purpose might be, try asking your friends about their sense of purpose. You might be surprised by what you hear. And if you find that none of your friends have a clear sense of purpose in their lives, well, then maybe you need to add a few new people to your list of friends.

To recap, when you feel stuck and don't know how to take the first step out of the loop:

1. Notice where your core fear is flaring up.
2. Ask yourself if the degree of certainty you want to have about the future is even possible to attain prior to taking action.
3. Remember how you've found resilience in the past to remind yourself that you'll have it in the future.

4. Turn to your purpose for clarity on the next step and the courage to take it.

Admittedly, getting stuck in thought loops of inaction is less common for certain Enneagram types, but no matter your type, you'll find yourself there from time to time. When this happens for folks who don't normally experience things like self-doubt, it can be *especially* unmooring. So, no matter who you are, remember this process, because it will get you through the tough days, weeks, months, and years that are a part of staying in the writing game.

FROM MOTIVATING WITH FEAR TO MOTIVATING WITH PURPOSE

When you stop letting fear motivate your decisions and stop dipping into fear-based adrenaline for energy to cross tasks off your list, you may find that you get slightly fewer things done each day. This is normal, and I encourage you to view it as a signpost that you're on the right track.

The experience of decreased productivity is going to be especially frightening to Threes, and likely also to Ones and Eights. If you are one of these types and teetering on an existential crisis because of accomplishing fewer tasks in your day, I ask that you not immediately snap back into the fear motivation. Sit with the discomfort of this transition and keep reminding yourself of the value of letting your digestive system, endocrine system, nervous system, circulatory system, and even your immune system rest after the long-term stress that's been putting them under so much strain. Notice the anxiety you feel about slowing down and where it's manifesting inside of your body. Watch it as an interested observer would, but remember that you don't have to let it take the wheel. And please, for a little while, resist the urge to go back to the level of activity you were doing before.

If you can hold off on falling back into those fear-motivation patterns, you *will* discover deeper sources of motivation blossoming from a healthier place inside of you, but you *must* give these new, more refined and mature sources of motivation space to unfurl. You must trust this process. You must let your body, mind, and heart reset to a sustainable rhythm.

Motivating yourself through fear is not sustainable.

There *are* things that can motivate us outside of our core fear and core desire, things like a sense of purpose that will sustain us by being more durable than our fragile ego. But only once we commit to rejecting fear as our motivator do we create the space we need to connect things like meaning and purpose in a deep enough way that they compel us forward.

The energy of purpose is often not as intense as the energy we're accustomed to from fear. Our bodies are exceptionally sensitive to fear for obvious biological and evolutionary reasons. Adrenaline is a rush, as it were. You get flooded with it. Your alertness of your surroundings increases, and the blood rushes away from your core to your limbs. The same thing happens when we put ourselves under chronic stress, and it can become such a familiar state that interrupting that cycle can make us feel incredibly low on energy for a while as we endure a crash.

This crash isn't limited to physical energy. It can tank our mood and drag our thoughts down with it, so we must be aware that we're experiencing a crash so that we don't *believe* the moods and accompanying thoughts. They are simply chemical reactions associated with kicking our adrenaline addiction.

If we anticipate this crash, it's easier to detach ourselves from the negative thoughts that can accompany it and take proactive measures to alleviate some of the effects. Taking no measures at this point is letting the plane crash. But there is another option: understanding that the rapidly decreasing elevation is unavoidable, we can take steps to land the plane smoothly and safely. We can be proactive about doing healthy things for our bodies that will keep the chemicals like serotonin, dopamine, and endorphins from crashing and burning.

Consider focusing on building a healthful diet during this time. Choosing foods rich in vitamins and minerals while avoiding foods that we know tank our energy even further is an important step and an act of deep self-compassion. This is going to be easier said than done, as crashes in adrenaline and cortisol send signals to our body to load up on sweets. If surrendering to these cravings were a crime, I'd admittedly be on death row by now, though I will say that the more times I choose the healthful alternative, the easier the choice becomes to do it the next time.

To be clear, I'm *not* telling you to launch into a juice cleanse or go vegan or start on keto here. Radical changes are probably the *last* thing you need as you make this transition away from fear. But when you are deciding what to make yourself for dinner, you can start by asking what the most nurturing thing for your body would be. You probably already know that a Double Whopper and a salmon fillet with sautéed spinach do not carry equal health benefits. Providing your body what it needs to be healthy is a loving act, not a punishment. (And sometimes just eat the Whopper.)

In other words, all those basic dietary recommendations from your doctor about eating more vegetables and healthy oils and fiber and avoiding processed foods? Actually follow them when you're anticipating the adrenaline crash of shifting away from fear-based motivation.

During this process, we can also be proactive by putting time in our schedule for gentle exercise. Hard workouts can increase cortisol levels, which is what we're trying to let decline in a gentle way. So, if you've been exercising like the devil's chasing you with a hot poker, consider temporarily transitioning to something gentler for your body, like going for long walks, yoga, or tai chi.

And finally, as you approach this motivational transition, look honestly at the sleep you're getting. Poor sleep or not enough of it puts every system of your body under stress, which puts you at great risk of reverting to fear-based motivation just to keep yourself awake with adrenaline.

So, clearly it's not as simple as "stop letting fear motivate you," although I wish it were. It's tricky to decompress from the stress levels you're used to. It takes time and trust, and unless you support yourself with healthy practices around food, exercise, and sleep (and ask those around you to support you), you may find yourself feeling so low that you aren't willing to stick with the process.

One more thing to bring your awareness to ahead of this transition: when you disengage from fear as a motivator, you might feel like you've slipped into a void until you can develop the sense of purpose that will carry you forward, which can take some time. The more you've judged yourself based on your productivity, the larger and deeper the void may first appear. This will be especially difficult for Threes, but don't forget that we *all* have a bit of each type in us, and if you live in a capitalist system, you have likely learned to adapt to the Type 3 overlay of that system that says your value equals your accomplishments and output. If either of your parents or early-life caregivers were Threes, then you will have adopted some of these ideas as well. It can all add up to even non-Threes feeling terrified of slowing down and interrupting the fear-based cycle of activity.

But what about the other types, you might be wondering. All types will face a void when they disconnect from fear as a motivator, even if constant activity wasn't your way of seeking what you wished to be.

I warn you now: don't look too deep into the void all at once. That way lies despair. That's because fear-based motivation can feel a lot like a purpose, and in some ways it is—the purpose is to avoid our fear—so letting go of it can feel like losing a sense of purpose, at which point the mouth of the nihilistic void opens in front of us. Remember that you are only losing a *false* sense of purpose. And in doing so, you're making room for a deeper sense of purpose to emerge, a purpose that is greater than yourself, one you contribute to but are not solely responsible for bringing into reality.

The motivational energy of purpose is often described as richer than that of fear. Fear is like eating sour candy. A single, intense flavor profile dominates everything, but over time, you can grow used to it and it doesn't taste so sour. If you switch immediately from something like an extremely sour Warhead (this may be an American Millennial-specific reference, so just imagine the most extreme sour candy you know) to a delicate dish with fig, fresh goat cheese, and honey, you're not only going to miss many of the subtler flavors, but you may not enjoy what you do taste because it's not as sharp and overpowering as you're used to.

And just like you don't become a sophisticated food critic overnight, you're unlikely to discover a meaningful purpose this quickly.

Purpose is something you piece together, bit by bit, as you become more connected to yourself, your gifts, and the world around you. That's why I say you must commit to it, because if you give up at the first sign of trouble or discomfort, you will relapse time and time again into the old motivational patterns of fear.

But once you connect with a sense of purpose, your path forward in your career will become clearer to you. When you make decisions throughout your day based on "What action could I take today to support my purpose?" rather than "What all needs to be done?" you're likely to find that your to-do list gets much shorter. A few small steps each day that support your purpose will take you much further than completing dozens of tasks that only help you avoid confronting your core fear for a little while longer.

So, yes, this is 301-level stuff here. It's hard, it takes a long time and a lot of commitment to discomfort, but if you want to stop the reactive fear cycle that's been driving your writing career in all different directions, this is the process.

You will need support for this. Possibly lots of support, and definitely more support than you expect or feel like you "should" need. If you try to take this process on alone, you're almost guaranteed to fail. Support can look like friends, your spouse, an accountability group, a therapist, working with me, working with another coach (who has overcome their fear-based motivation, which many have not), or even hiring a chef or personal trainer if you have the cash for it.

> **There is certain work that only you can do, but you will need support from others if you stand a chance of continuing forward when the road ahead of you is dark and you still have the option to turn back.**

So, if the practices of building support for yourself are unfamiliar—looking at you especially, Twos, Threes, Fives, and Eights—then start there. Begin strengthening your support network. Tackle that issue first. Twos will need to practice asking for help. Threes must practice allowing others to see an unflattering and messy side of them without packaging it as something more flattering. Fives must challenge their belief that they could be completely self-sufficient if they try and that there's even any value in trying at all. Eights must practice showing vulnerability about their struggles to others who will not leverage that against them. Even if you're not any of those types, now is a good time to start asking if you truly have the support you need to transition away from your fear-based motivation.

To sum up, the process for transitioning from fear motivation to purpose motivation may look something like this:

1. Assess what support you currently have and where you could build more.
2. Think you have enough support? Wrong. Build more. Let those people know what you're planning to do, and ask them to help you keep from falling into the void. Make sure they will hold you accountable when you backslide to fear motivation. Educate them on what you look like when you're functioning out of fear so they can help spot the signs.
3. Make a plan for how you will support your body through food, exercise, and sleep, and tell others about this plan to create accountability and set new boundaries.
4. Begin executing that plan with simple adjustments to your daily routine.
5. Okay, let's do this shit: identify the ways that fear has been motivating you.
6. Keep identifying the ways (there are a lot of ways; so, so many ways).

7. Learn what your body feels like when it's engaging in fear-based motivation. What emotions and thoughts arise?

8. Practice visualizing those thoughts, feelings, and sensations as separate entities that move through you. They are not you. You are simply observing them.

9. When you become aware that you're working out of fear motivation, pause and assess whether the task, thought, or emotion is truly a meaningful one or if it's merely an artifact of your old patterns and you can let it go.

10. Repeat this process until you find that it's becoming easier to recognize the pattern before engaging with it.

11. When you feel the void creeping up on you, don't look into it; instead, remember that I told you it would be there and it's a necessary part of this process. Noticing the void, as scary and alluring as it is, is a sign that you are on the right track.

12. As you continue to practice these steps, give yourself space to think about what you want to contribute to the world around you. What are your gifts? What does the world need? How can you best contribute to it a little each day in how you talk to your friends and strangers and the words that you write and publish?

13. DO NOT LOOK INTO THE NIHILISM VOID.

14. Keep going. You're doing great. Isn't this getting a smidgeon easier now?

It may be months, and it may be years, but eventually you will have a moment where it occurs to you that you are living a purposeful life at a sustainable pace, and—good lord!—look how far you've come from that older version of you who let fear guide your every step! Look how much you've accomplished without working yourself to the bone! Take a look around at how your purpose has manifested not only in your writing career but in your friendships, your home, and your community! And when people ask you your secret, you'll answer them genuinely, "I don't really know. I wasn't always like this." But, boy oh boy, will you be glad to be who you are.

A LIFE OUTSIDE OF WRITING

This is probably one of my more controversial takes because friendships can be such a sore spot for so many people. But here it is: opting out of a social life is not a healthy option. Having a strong network of friends outside of your writing world is crucial to building resilience in your author career.

We've all been hurt and betrayed by friends, rejected by people who we thought accepted us, and it may take a lot of effort for you to develop new friendships. Maybe you're a little awkward around new people. Maybe meeting new people drains your battery quickly. Maybe you live in a remote area or don't have reliable transportation. Maybe you're immunocompromised. There are all kinds of obstacles that might stand in the way of you making more in-person connections, but what stands in the way most frequently is our devaluation of friendship. If we truly understood how important it is to a long and healthy life, we would spend as much, if not more, time cultivating and deepening our friendships as we do trying to hit the best-seller lists.

The negative health effects of loneliness and disconnection aren't limited to the mental and emotional, but also impact our physical health in a roughly similar proportion to smoking and physical inactivity.[*] Meanwhile, those studying longevity and well-being state quite plainly that the key factor to a long and happy life is the quality of our relationships.

If you don't care about living into old age, that's okay. Not all of us want to. But building a life outside of writing is still crucially important to developing resilience to the ups and downs of the business. No more using your work as an excuse to hide from that. No more "I'm too busy." That excuse might hold for a week or two here and there, but if you're too chronically busy to have a life outside of work, then work has become an excuse to hide from life. That'll catch up with you, I promise.

The reason I'm harping on this is because so many of our core needs as humans have to do with feeling accepted by the group. We want security and support and to know that even if we mess up, we won't be left all alone. If all or even most of our eggs of relationships are in the single basket of our writing career, then even the most basic writerly decision can feel extremely high stakes. A misstep could cost us income, sure, but if our only community is the writing

---

[*]   Source: https://www.cdc.gov/aging/publications/features/lonely-older-adults.html

community, then it could also cost us our sense of belonging.

Involving ourselves in multiple communities outside of our work essentially diversifies our portfolio of identity. That is, we feel like we belong to more than one group. You may self-identify less strongly as "writer" if you feel like you are many things to many people.

This idea scares some people, I'm sure, because I know that lots of folks who write stories or nonfiction hand-wring over whether or not they are a "real" writer. And yet here I am suggesting you take steps to feel like less of a "writer."

Go ahead and call yourself a writer if you want. People try to gatekeep the term, yet no one seems to agree on the exact definition, so... maybe do whatever you want? Call yourself a writer today but not tomorrow or vice versa. Who's going to stop you?

As far as your own health goes, though, you might want to transition your thinking from "I am a writer" to "I am a person who sometimes writes" so you don't teeter on the edge of an identity crisis every time you take a little break from the actual typing.

But back to the making friends thing. Consider this: if eighty percent of your attention is going toward your writing career and the writing community, then when something goes wrong (and it will if you stay in this game long enough) then eighty percent of your world is in peril. However, if only forty percent of your attention is going toward your writing career and the writing community, then when something goes wrong, only forty percent of your world is in peril, and you can still feel anchored and secure to the other sixty percent where everything is fine and nobody seems to care much about your book sales. In that case, *most of your world is going fine!*

Often when I talk about this, people will argue that the friends they have in the industry would still be their friend even if their career blew up. That very well might be true. But this isn't a matter of whether people would be your friend so much as it's a question of how you would feel when engaging in that relationship. Could you trust that they would really be on your side when you needed them? Would every conversation with them, no matter how benign, poke at your unpleasant feelings related to writing and publishing? If you're facing a failure, would you be able to tolerate their successes, or would you feel envy creeping in? It's important to be real with yourself on these answers, because once you are, you'll recognize that I raise a damn good point.

When I was first getting started in my writing career, I thought the only acceptable way to proceed for someone who was truly committed to it was to give their career all of their attention. My hobbies dwindled down to almost nothing, and definitely nothing that required me being part of a community. The writing community was my only community, because that was the only seed that I bothered watering. Everything else died of neglect. When a book launch fell flat on its face or I made a massive mistake like uploading the wrong manuscript, the results felt overwhelming and all-encompassing, much more than I had the tools to deal with effectively at that time.

The pandemic brought that isolation into stark contrast for me, and as soon as it was safe to be in public without too much risk to myself or others, I went hard into developing new communities and reconnecting with old ones whose leaves were turning yellow from neglect. (I understand that if you're immunocompromised, leaving the house to meet strangers may not be available to you; online communities can still go a long way to fill this role.)

Now, when a book launch flops or I don't make my money back on a promo, or any of the many other disappointments we face in this industry, it's a pain in the ass, but it doesn't ruin my day. I can stand up from the computer, stretch, and text some of my non-writer friends to see if anyone wants to go kick a ball around, watch some sports, or go for a hike. Or I can pack up and head to the pottery studio; nobody there gives a shit that I'm an author, and I love that about them. To those folks, I'm just a beginning potter who has a long way to go but will gossip about celebrities with the rest of them. One of my soccer friends even confessed to me that he's only read three books since college, all sports biographies. He asked me, "Is that bad? Should I read some books?" to which I replied, "I don't care. If you don't enjoy reading books, then don't read books. I'm not offended." No one on my soccer team has read any of my books, and I very much appreciate that.

You don't need to join a sports team or enroll in a pottery wheel class, but one of the best resilience tips I can give you is to build your identity outside of your career. Have other things going on in your life. Not only will this help inspire your writing (my latest cozy mystery series is set at a pottery studio), but it will help you make the best decisions for your career. You won't have to worry that a publishing mistake will also cost you your entire social life. You'll be able to make the best decision for your business, rather than feel pressured to go along with whatever your author friends are doing. Their best interests might not be your best interest, and that's okay, but it's hard to diverge from that when you feel like your only relationships are also at stake.

You are not just a writer. You may be a person who writes sometimes, but you can also be a person who does many other things. A crucial piece of navigating our ego in this business, so that it doesn't start calling all the shots, is to not over-identify with our career as who we are.

Our ego makes dumb decisions for our bottom line. It can be extremely vain. It cares more about increasing the book's ranking in the Kindle Store than focusing on profit, which is what pays our bills, feeds our family, and can allow us to experience the world in wonderful ways. Focusing too strongly on rank so that we can post about how high our book reached on the charts is often what causes authors to burn through money that they aren't necessarily earning back just to play that ego game. It's a seductive game, sure, and it's normal to fall victim to it from time to time. Ultimately, it's one of those stupid games with stupid prizes. (We might couch the urge for a high rank under the nebulous benefits of "visibility," but it's important to be honest about how many books that sells versus how much money it takes to gain said visibility.)

Our ego may also have us accept an invite to an anthology because we feel loyal to the person organizing it, or because we want to be seen as helpful, or because a successful person is also involved, and we want to be associated with them. Are those solid reasons to commit to it? They might be, but we won't know so long as our ego is in charge. Maybe you don't want to be part of that anthology. Maybe it would require you putting in extra hours of work that don't contribute to pursuing your purpose, hours that won't be spent either building your business productively or building a life outside of your business.

If too much of our identity is wrapped up in the writing community, then saying no to these sorts of opportunities can be too tall of an order, no matter how much the opportunity may not be in alignment with us. It becomes much easier to say no to the things that aren't a fit for us when we know that we can always turn to different friendships and communities if our fellow authors respond poorly to our boundaries (and people often do respond poorly to boundaries; that doesn't make boundaries not worth setting and enforcing, though).

If you're trying to imagine going out and turning random strangers into friends, and the thought terrifies you, I get it. I spent my life up until my early thirties with intense social anxiety. I noped out of so many social events, arrived at parties but couldn't bring myself to get out of the car, and found just about any excuse not to be around strangers. The only way I could be around people who weren't in my inner circle was by knocking back a couple drinks first. If you were to have asked me what I was anxious about, I couldn't have told you. Being around people and having to make small talk felt like torture—that was all I knew.

I am by no means an expert in curing social anxiety, but I'll tell you about how I lessened mine to the point where it only feels like a little shadow that follows me around rather than my whole existence when I'm around others.

First, I started going to therapy in my late twenties. Anxiety doesn't stay in one place. My anxiety about other things in my life spilled over to my social life, and I noticed that the more anxious I was about, say, money or John working overnight patrol shifts without enough sleep in between, the worse my social anxiety became. My mindfulness therapy helped me discover my own resilience, and in doing so, my overall anxiety went down, including my social anxiety.

Along with the therapy, I did all this Enneagram work. As I examined the ways my core fear was dominating my life, I was able to see how much of my social anxiety was wrapped up in my fear of not being good enough, being seen as irrational, and feeling like the authentic version of me wasn't how "good girls" acted. I stopped wasting energy trying to tightrope walk between how "good people" acted and how my authentic self wanted to express itself, and that helped tremendously.

And finally, I practiced, practiced, practiced. I reminded myself that folks around me probably felt uncomfortable too. I chatted people up at the store, made small talk with servers at restaurants, and practiced getting out of my head by shifting my attention away from how I came off (fear) and onto my life purpose of learning how to love people better. That meant I needed to really *see* the human being I was speaking to so my humanity could connect with theirs. The experiences I gained from this last practice, which I couldn't have made it to without the previous support and learning, were so fulfilling and lit me up so much that social anxiety didn't have as strong a hold on me; what it had held me back from all these years was way more precious than worrying about how I came off to people.

That's not to say I beat social anxiety and it's never coming back. It comes back every time I'm in a new group of people. At every conference, every party, every social gathering. Sometimes it even shows up at the start of gatherings with people I know very well, and it takes a minute for me to shake off the cobwebs. But when I look at the progress I've make, it feels like I've shucked a whole-ass straitjacket.

When I first signed up for my soccer team a few years ago, I signed up as an individual player. I didn't know a single person on the team prior to our first game. For whatever reason, I was convinced that I would be stuck on a team of a bunch of twenty-somethings who already knew each other from church and would judge me harshly for the words coming out of my mouth on the field.

You know why I thought that? Because it was the worst-case scenario for me. It would've put me on that old tightrope between being who I am and being a "good girl." It would've made me choose between being relaxed and myself and living up to someone else's purity standards. I also believed that would be the case with the team because *it gave me a solid out for not showing up.* Why would I even want to, if they were all just going to judge me and keep me on the outside?

If you're following along at home, folks, I had conjured up a team that was essentially a form of my own Inner Critic to justify not taking the *legitimately minor* risk of meeting new people. I reckon most folks with social anxiety have done something similar. Anxiety is often a creativity malfunction, and since we're creative people, we're at an elevated risk of our imagination turning against us.

Rather than backing down against my worst-case scenario, I dropped a message to the roster with my name and phone number and asked if anyone wanted to meet up early before the game (we played at a brewery, so easy enough to meet up). Again, I wouldn't have been able to take this step without all the previous steps, and it was a huge sign of progress for me. As a response to my initial message, another teammate (who I later discovered also has social anxiety) created a WhatsApp chat for the team that still exists today.

I was *so close* to concocting an excuse not to go to that first soccer game, but I knew that if I missed the first for no good reason, I'd probably skip out on the whole season, and that would be a shame because I missed playing and wanted more friends. The only way forward was through. And if it turned out that my worst-case scenario was spot-on? I simply would've been right all along, and I love being right all along. Going was a win-win, then.

I met the other eight teammates for our five-on-five league on day one, and discovered that basically *all* of them had signed up individually and had anxiety about who they would be greeted by. After our first match (we won), we decided to share a round of drinks together. Someone suggested we go around the table and say why we decided to sign up. Every single person admitted to being lonely and wanting to make more friends. Can you imagine that? A bunch of adults meeting for the first time and sharing honestly in that way. It was worth the risk of being vulnerable. It was worth the risk of pushing through.

We became a gang shortly after, winning multiple championships, celebrating birthdays together, and showing up for one another in grief. Even after we got suspended from the league for the rest of a season after fighting another team (I described us as a "gang" intentionally) and our schedules grew so hectic that we couldn't find a single night each week to play together, we've stayed in touch. We still show up for each other on birthdays, watch sports together, grab dinner and coffee, and, on those rare occasions when all of us can make it, we do check-ins with each other—one highlight and one lowlight in life since the last time we got together. The way we care for each other as humans is something I cherish.

I would've missed out on all of that if I had let that anxiety win and skipped out on the league.

I'm not saying every community you enter or friends you attempt to make will work out this well. Certainly not. Some communities turn toxic, and then you might want to grab the people who aren't like that and scram. But there are folks in this world who will appreciate your weirdness, awkwardness, and intensity who are not writers. And the more connections you can create that aren't dependent on what decisions you make in your author career, the more viable options you'll see for said career.

You don't have to turn into a social butterfly overnight, but if you suffer from anxiety that keeps you from meeting people outside of the writing community, today seems like a great day to take the first step toward loosening that anxiety's grip on you. Schedule with a therapist, talk to your doctor about meds if you're up for it, and plunge deep into the resilience work I have laid out for you in this book. Life is so short, and there are so many wonderful humans out there to help you build richness in your time on Earth. I hope that you can meet them and that they get the pleasure of meeting you.

SECTION 6: HOW WE GROW

ACCEPTING THAT YOU'RE GROWING BUT NOT GROWN

Making the decision to start changing your life in ways that may not feel as instantly pleasurable as the old ways is undeniably laudable. Much of this work, in addition to helping you build a sustainable author career, will break generational cycles of unhealthy thinking, feeling, and behaving. Whether or not you have children of your own, you will probably spend time around children in some capacity, and through doing this work, you can begin to rest assured that you will not be passing along the same attitudes that tripped you up for so long.

You will also be spending time around other adults, and breaking these patterns inside yourself is so powerful that people of any age who witness it may be inspired to try the same hard work. Becoming less reactive and more grounded in yourself can be world-changing for other people to see, if they've never been surrounded by people who behave that way.

You may become somewhat of an enigma to certain people who didn't know your way of living was an option. People may be inspired to follow your example, which is the ultimate compliment and a sure sign that you've been doing your work well.

None of this is *intended* to be performative, though. If you catch yourself closing your eyes and taking deep breaths for the sake of being seen closing your eyes and taking deep breaths, for instance, you've slipped into performance. No need to feel ashamed if you notice yourself falling into this pattern, because if we give our ego an inch, it can nudge us into this. However, when we do notice that we've slipped into a performance of the healthy patterns rather than the embodiment of them, it's a good piece of data to collect, as you can use it as your cue to pause, turn your attention inward, and ask why you felt the need to perform growth rather than giving yourself the true gift of it.

I like to remind myself that I am growing but I am not grown. This helps keep me from slipping into my old Type-1 pattern of judging others. I've been working on the practices laid out in this book for years with the intensity that I bring to most things that I do—that is to say, more than some people enjoy being around—and I still constantly make mistakes, slip back into my ego, and feel frustrated with how slow the progress is going. My Type-1 patterns pop up everywhere—I can still be critical of myself and others, it still pains me to think that I can only control myself, and there are certain situations where my anxiety whispers, "If that happens, I'll never survive."

As humans, we can dedicate our lives to growing and expanding toward Liberation without ever completing the work. The impulses of our past patterns will keep testing our fortitude, but we can become better at recognizing them and redirecting them, or simply saying, "Thanks, but no thanks."

To remember that we are growing but not grown also acknowledges that others are growing but not grown. As they say, we are all a work in progress, and remembering that can inspire us to give more grace to people where they fall short. When we learn to do that for others, we learn to do it for ourselves.

Remembering that we are engaging with a process that will never end so long as we live also opens the door to be able to laugh at ourselves when we do that thing we always do. Gotta love human folly, especially our own. Having a sense of humor about yourself is one of the most important tools you can have in your toolbox. When we laugh at ourselves, it shows that we are well adjusted to the fact that we are not our personality. We are something deeper beneath that armor, and so it's no threat to who we are to point out the silliness of the patterns our ego develops.

Some of those patterns are objectively silly. Sometimes we behave like children throwing a tantrum. I don't know when the last time was that you watched a three-year-old absolutely lose their shit because of something unfathomable like "you broke my banana!" but it's really fucking hard not to laugh when this happens. The toddler's reaction is so over the top that it slips into parody. Our reactions to the world can be similar in how disproportionate they are to the situation we're facing, and once we start to notice and observe our patterns more, it becomes easier to laugh when this happens.

That laughter is a beautiful thing. That laughter is us letting go and remembering that things will be okay. It's arguing with your spouse in the kitchen about the dumbest little thing because you both had stressful days, and then one of you says something so overblown that you both realize the argument you're having is pointless and that the feelings you're experiencing are related to something else entirely. It's locking eyes with that person you love, sharing a moment of understanding, then cracking up together.

The human condition really is ridiculous, and when you spend less time mindlessly engrossed in it and more time mindfully present and observant, you get to enjoy the spectacle.

Since we are growing but not grown, we don't have to become upset when we realize that were not as far along as we thought. This process is not about reaching an end goal —it's about committing to forward movement and letting go of what's keeping us trapped and disconnected from ourselves and the world. Sometimes we backslide. That's a part of this process, too.

If you ever notice that you're beating yourself up during this process, rest assured that that is entirely unnecessary to your progress, and you can let go of the pattern of beating yourself up.

The most sustainable way forward is not through recrimination and punishment but through love and compassion.

You don't need those ugly tools of torment anymore. You can throw them out and you'll never miss them.

The only time it may be beneficial to measure our growth is when we are looking *backward* and recognizing how far we've come. It's that moment when you notice that the things that used to upset you and derail your workday no longer do. It's an abysmal book sales month that doesn't poison your interactions with your family or your outlook on life like it might have years ago. Don't be afraid to feel gratitude for yourself and all the honest work you've done to get to where you are today. Because as I'm about to describe in the next section, not of all of this process for building a sustainable version of you feels particularly flattering. Sometimes we're called to travel into the darkness to discover the full spectrum of light inside us.

THE REJECTED PARTS OF YOURSELF

So much of the work we do with the Enneagram is sorting through what we consider to be "me" and what we consider to be "not me."

I am this way, but I am not that way.

We often define ourselves in this manner without even knowing it. Sometimes it's because we grew up hearing that we were X but we were not Y and Z. For instance, I grew up hearing that I was stubborn, a high achiever, and a perfectionist. I did not grow up hearing that I was sweet, loving, or fun to be around. You better believe that I internalized those things about myself. In doing so, I focused my attention specifically on downplaying my stubbornness (it was painted as a bad thing, but I now believe it can be a great quality), being an even higher achiever, and... I didn't really know what to do with the perfectionism thing. It was usually described as a flaw, but I was constantly rewarded in school for the fruits of it. I didn't have any attention to spare for how it was destroying my joy and tainting my relationships.

When we adopt these ideas about ourselves, what we are doing is putting ourselves in a box. We are limiting our options in ways that may not make any good sense. Even into adulthood, I struggled to rectify the label of "perfectionist" with the reality of my life where I was terminally unable to proofread my own work, would let my home get quite messy before cleaning it all at once, and not enjoying the more detail-oriented aspects of writing and publishing like I thought a good perfectionist would.

To be clear, I did struggle with perfectionism in many, many ways. The tug of it is still there in my everyday life, though I've long since stopped watering those seeds. My attention still flows naturally toward what might be fixed or perfected, and my skin crawls if a picture frame in my field of vision is crooked. In that way, the description of the Enneagram One struggling with perfectionism did apply to me, no matter how much laundry I let pile up before tackling it. But I was *so many* more things than just a perfectionist. That limiting box didn't fit many parts of me.

The box you're in doesn't fit all of you either. That's why the Enneagram was not designed to put us in a box but rather to help us identify the box that we are already in and help us escape it. The goal of Enneagram work is not to make you more of your type; it's to free you of patterns associated with that type, so that over time you in fact resemble the type less and can witness the parts of yourself that correspond to the other eight types.

That being said, you will never *not* be your type, so get cozy there. There's no reason that you should ever hope to not be your type. Your type has gifts that can only be found in people of your type, and the world needs you to bring those out and share them.

The first stage of learning about our Enneagram type can seem like a fun time. We get to read the general descriptions and see ourselves described in ways that we always kind of knew we were but hadn't necessarily put words to. It can feel great to be seen in that way. "Ooh! There I am! Oh, that's so me!" It's why people enjoy following the meme accounts that show them who they are over and over again.

Inevitably, though, we come upon a moment where we say, "Okay, but what now? Here are these things that describe me that I don't necessarily want to keep doing. How do I stop doing them?"

This is where the truly uncomfortable work begins. We never want to use our Enneagram type as an *excuse* for our unhealthy or even harmful patterns of thinking, feeling, and acting. They certainly serve as an *explanation*, but it's best not to use them as an excuse if someone is holding you accountable for them. You are still accountable for your actions, even if they are typical for your type.

Part of the process of taking accountability is looking at ourselves honestly. This requires learning about our blind spots and confronting our shadow parts that we usually keep out of sight of others but also ourselves.

It can be tricky to see what we can't see, which is where the teachings of the Enneagram come in very handy. There are well-documented and established blind sports for each type, so while we may not see them on our own (they are, by definition, blind spots), it's important that when we read about them we believe that they are there.

It usually doesn't take much poking at one of those blind spots to realize that not only is it there, but it's been there the whole time, wreaking havoc. Only when we shine a light on it do we have the option of confronting it in such a way that it holds less power over our moving forward.

A lot of people will not get to this point of the process because it is not fun work. Truly, it can throw our life into an upheaval for periods of time because we have to sort through so much, oftentimes confronting forms of harm that we have committed without meaning to. We must look honestly at where we weren't the good guy in situations, where the intention of our actions was not the outcome of them, where we meant to help but instead hurt people we loved, and where we flattered ourselves while truly appearing foolish. This is, as Gen Z might say, very *cringe* work. You are almost guaranteed cringe at yourself throughout, but remember, that pain and the commitment to moving forward shows an admirable sort of strength that not everyone has. And before you get big-headed about that, remember that you didn't have the strength previously either, so this is not an invitation to judge other people who are not doing this work.

Our shadow has been hiding in plain sight for a long time. Our dear, sweet Enneagram 9 Peacemakers, for instance, may not imagine themselves as control freaks, but when they look at their shadow, there's no denying that they've been grappling for control for a long time. If we were to casually observe their patterns, we would see them *appearing* to give much of the control over to other people in an attempt to avoid conflict. What's hiding in plain sight is that the Nines seek control in other ways, like passive resistance and passive-aggression. Withdrawing and not speaking their mind plainly can also be a power move in that this pattern causes those around them to exert extra effort to find out what the Nine wants. When Nine says yes when they mean no, it might make the other person initially happy to get their way, but halfway through the process, the Nine may begin giving passive resistance to reassert control. They do it in such a way that they can deny that it's happening, but make no mistake, that's still what it's about.

It's unlikely that Nines will acknowledge, even to themselves, that they're doing this. That's why we call it a blind spot. Acknowledging blind spots takes reading books like this or talking with people like me who are trained in this to point them out. And once you see yours, you can't unsee it. It starts to appear *everywhere*. It's the water that you've been swimming in AND you never realized you were a fish until now. The experience of seeing it appear everywhere can be distressing, and this is where you want to make sure that you have people around you who can support you through it, like good friends or a therapist. There's going to be a lot of unpacking involved in this process.

The first step is starting to notice it, and you could easily spend days, weeks, or months creating an inventory of all the ways your blind spots have been operating outside of your awareness. You'll probably keep discovering new forms of it years and years into your work on this.

Every type has something like what I described with the Nines and their passive-aggression, and I'm sure you're wondering what some of the blind spots of each type are and how they may be showing up in your author career without you even realizing it. Below I've included two big ones of each type (there are many more, but these are useful places to get you started). Thankfully, Beatrice Chestnut, PhD, MA, and Uranio Paes, MM, have already done a magnificent job of explaining these blind spots in detail in their book *The Enneagram Guide to Waking Up*, which is a must-read for anyone who's decided it's time to venture into this territory.

Rather than providing a detailed explanation of each with a series of exercises (which Chestnut and Paes already include), I'll shine a light on how these particular blind spots might show up in our writing and publishing, so that you can begin to understand the true pervasiveness of the things about ourselves that we have hidden in the shadows for so long. Then the first step toward making a change in those areas is to start noticing them. Give yourself time to keep noticing them, without judgment or self-recrimination if you can, before you try to change them. Remember that simply noticing the patterns that we've missed for so long is massive progress.

Once you feel like you understand the pervasiveness of these blind spots in your life, then you can either pick up a book like Chestnut and Paes', or you can schedule a call with someone like me to learn how to liberate yourself from these blind spots.

Now, make yourself comfortable, grab an emotional support blanket and a warm beverage (unless you're an Eight, in which case simply slap yourself in the face a few times or however you rev yourself up), and let's dig in.

Blind spots for type 1

Criticism—You are blessed with the most notorious Inner Critic of all the types. Our Inner Critic was developed to protect us from the painful criticism we felt from the outside world. It monitored our behavior more closely than anyone else ever could.

In writing and publishing: Look at how that critic has its hand on your throat when you try to write and how that keeps you from getting deep into the flow state. Is the Inner Critic's promise of helping you avoid totally fixable and low-stake mistakes worth allowing that nightmare to stick around?

Swallowing emotions—What don't you allow yourself to feel? Which perfectly natural and essential human emotions have you labeled "bad" and put on your emotional terrorist watchlist? Is anger allowed? Rage? Frustration? Self-compassion? Your idealism means you always see what's broken or "not right" first, and years of that may naturally lead to some of those "off-limits" emotions. While you've been busy seeking the "perfect" time, place, and way to express your anger, it's been sitting in your body, poisoning you and fueling your Inner Critic.

In writing and publishing: Think of all the ways pent-up emotions have led to unproductive circular thinking, imagined conversations where you say what you *really* think, and wasted energy that you could be pouring into your manuscript. Where have you been restricting your characters' emotional range? Where have those repressed emotions been poisoning your persona without you knowing?

Blind spots for Type 2

Ignoring your own needs—"What do you need?" is a question that makes your skin crawl. You long ago stopped trusting that people would meet your needs if you stated them explicitly. The idea of asking for what you need, if you even have enough time to figure it out at this point, is about as appealing to you as sticking a fork in your eye. But because you're deeply caring and know what it feels like not to have your needs met, you go around meeting the needs (and then some) of everyone and everything you encounter.

In writing and publishing: Think of all the things you do for others every day and how much energy you have left for meeting your own writing needs. How long have you been running at a deficit? Writing is likely a source of fuel for you if you'd only disconnect from the needs of everyone else long enough to attend to the needs of you and the characters you're creating. Are all of the ways you're giving others your energy necessary (i.e. they couldn't do it without you)? Or are you helping others in non-meaningful ways to *feel* helpful while downplaying the positive impact your books will have once they're finished?

Forced reciprocation—After years of neglecting your needs, you might've lost touch with them. Without meaning to, you're giving in the same ways you'd like to receive rather than meeting the person's specific needs. You've developed the expectation that the only way for you to receive is to give, so when your tank is empty and you could really benefit from asking for what you need, you instead kick the helping into high gear in hopes that someone takes your hint and gives you exactly what you're giving them. How's that working?

In writing and publishing: Think of all the ways you're giving too much to your readers and other authors who are not returning equal amounts of energy. Probably, they don't realize there's an expectation, and they're not mind readers about your needs. If a reader buys your book, that's an even exchange: you get paid, they get a book. Are you giving away too much for free? Is your idea of a "fair trade" one where you get significantly less than the other author or reader?

Blind Spots for Type 3

Human doing—When was the last time you let yourself feel something deeply without launching into action? Emotions can be a pain in the ass because they don't work on our ideal schedule, and they don't always require action. Your need to constantly be in motion makes your relationship to your Heart Center fraught. But make no mistake, you cannot keep disconnecting from emotions without disconnecting from everything that motivates you to keep striving. You can only stay on autopilot, where you *do* without attending to your accompanying thoughts and feelings, for so long before you run out of gas completely. It's time to find a way to stop existing as a human doing and remember how to be a human being.

In writing and publishing: Think of how much you do in a day. Is all of that necessary, or are you doing much of it to *feel* busy and productive? What emotions are you trying to outpace with activity and achievement? How much of your marketing is ineffective for book sales but instead serves to distract you from those emotions? Where might your walls against "disruptive" feelings be limiting your writing range, making certain characters feel superficial and your plots "feel tropey" because you're missing out on the richer parts of life?

Presenting success—Who are you? Not what have you accomplished, but who are you beneath the projection of your successes? And whose definition of success are you measuring yourself by? The desire to meet *all* metrics of success held by people you respect (and even some you don't) may be running your life and causing you to shapeshift constantly, leaving no time and energy for the kinds of things that make life worth living (hint: they're not external markers of success).

In writing and publishing: Think of who you're trying to impress. Is it anyone and everyone you might cross paths with in person or online? Are you subconsciously trying to win over the haters? Has your need to appear successful caused you to pursue publishing achievements that present the image of success but don't lead to more book sales or deeper connection with the readers who love your books? How much energy are you putting toward ignoring, disguising, or reframing your failures because you've attached your self-worth to your success? When was the last time you focused instead on what you wanted out of life rather than what others want you to want?

Blind spots for Type 4

Identifying with emotions—What are you anchoring your sense of self to? If you feel like a different person from moment to moment, it's likely because you're anchoring your identity to your emotions. Emotions come and go, and while it's important to acknowledge them, it's equally as important to let them go rather than identifying with them as a sign of who you are. If you feel sadness, that doesn't mean you are a sad person. If you feel joy, that doesn't mean you are a joyful person. Just because someone makes you sad does not mean they are a cruel person. Your emotions are information, but they are not the full truth, and if you loosen your grip on them as a hard and fast reality, you might find that fewer people accuse you of being oversensitive.

In writing and publishing: Think about how your emotions, particularly negative ones, are determining your relationship with your WIP from day to day. Consider how your emotions, and protecting yourself from possible unpleasant ones, has kept you from telling others about your published book(s). How are you holding on to emotions as truth rather than letting them be the transient experiences they really are? What would you write if you didn't worry about what feelings might arise in the process and could trust that emotions are separate entities from yourself? How might you market more assertively if you weren't scared of what your emotions reflected about you to yourself?

The positive—How much weight and truth do you assign to positive emotions and experiences? What about compliments? Now consider how much weight and truth you assign to negative emotions and experiences and criticism. Your belief that the negative is somehow more "meaningful" than the positive is blinding you to half of the information coming your way. If you scroll right past the good news and read every bit of bad news word for word, *of course* it feels like the world is a dark and hopeless place. Think about the people you surround yourself with. Do positive people feel phony to you? Do cynical people feel more trustworthy and intelligent to you? Who and what you let in versus who and what you keep out determines your worldview, so if the world feels grim, there's a good chance you've built this perception by assigning more relevance to the grim parts.

In writing and publishing: Think about how much attention you're giving to your rejections and attempts that fell short. How much attention are you giving to the parts of your story that you feel are lacking something as opposed to the parts that you think readers are really going to love? How is ignoring the positive depriving you of an important energy source? How are you allowing yourself to be discouraged by your preliminary marketing efforts not amounting to massive success? How might your expectation of failure and rejection be causing you to make decisions that will fulfill that expectation? What are you afraid would happen if you focused on the positives in your writing and marketing, like positive reader reviews and any growth you've seen in the last year? Is there any validity to that fear, or is it old armor you can now remove?

Blind spots for Type 5

Scarcity—You're not as separate from the rest of the world as you'd like to believe. There is a natural flow to things that you have likely cut yourself off from to protect what you have. Your fear of not having what you need when you need it—money, knowledge, energy—can lead to patterns of isolation. You give sparingly. You hoard those same resources you think you might need later. You stop trusting that you have what you need or that what you need might show up when you need it if you simply trust the natural flow of things. Whatever protection isolation has brought you, it's also cut you off from connections that could be essential resources. You don't have to have and know everything yourself—you simply need to know someone who has or knows it and is willing to share. The focus on scarcity also leads to an aversion of abundance— when you do open the door to connection, the natural flow can feel like a firehose after so much time cut off from it. That only causes you to retreat again, leading to more isolation and a stronger need to make sure you can take care of everything on your own without needing anything from anybody.

In writing and publishing: Think about how much energy you're expending maintaining walls around your life. How might boxing yourself in be cutting yourself off from the richness of life that creates captivating writing? What wisdom in marketing and writing craft might not be available to learn through books? Who might be an untapped source of help (or friendship) that you're not reaching out to, causing you to spend extra effort reinventing the wheel yourself? If you write fiction, how do you expect to write rich and believable characters if you're not getting your hands dirty in deep relationships with a diverse set of people?

Intellectualizing—Unfortunate as it is, you can't think your way to the best solution a hundred percent of the time. There is essential data that can only be gained from lived experience through your body and deep feeling through your heart. Your need to create a clean theory around everything is overlooking the messiness of the world. The tendency to intellectualize is yet another way you create distance between yourself and the world around you, watching the action from the safety of the bleachers rather than jumping onto the field. You still have three Centers of Intelligence like everyone else, though, and giving more weight to thoughts than feelings and action is likely to cause you to arrive at an incomplete or simply wrong conclusion, since you're missing crucial data.

In writing and publishing: Think about how many courses or books you've read on marketing or the art of storytelling, hoping you'll reach a point of intellectual certainty before you proceed with the *doing*. If you fall into the pattern of thinking about feelings without *feeling* the feelings, how could you possibly write deeply feeling characters? Have your characters become 2D in that they all proceed logically? Are you always defaulting to the logical appeal in your marketing? What emotional information about the human condition are you discounting or ignoring to the detriment of hooking new readers?

Blind spots for Type 6

Risk aversion—While you might have intellectually accepted that there is no such thing as one hundred percent certainty in an outcome, what if I told you there's no such thing as ten percent certainty in an outcome? How would you live your life then? When your mind is specially trained for locating the risk in a situation, how likely is it that you'll ever get to the point where moving forward carries no risk with it? How much certainty in an outcome are you seeking before you'll give something a shot? There is a limited amount of data we can gain through imagination, which is what risk prediction is. The rest of the crucial data can only be gained from experimenting. Are you able to accept the reality that some experiments don't go as planned?

In writing and publishing: Think about how you perceive others in the industry to be more confident than you. Do they have more theoretical information than you, or are they simply focusing less on the risks and able to move forward with experiments as a result? How might your book sales be better at this point if you took more "risks" and allowed yourself to be okay when they didn't pan out? Who exactly are you, an autonomous adult, worried you'll get in trouble with if you try something new and it doesn't work out the way you planned? How might your own risk aversion be showing up in your characters who aren't Sixes?

Testing others—The problem with trusting others is that you have to trust them. Your impulse to sort people into allies and enemies to keep yourself safe means your attention scans for signs that someone might not have your best interest in mind. Every interaction can become a subconscious test that the person must pass again and again if you're to continue trusting them. One slip-up can mean losing your trust forever. If others were testing *you* all the time, would you pass a hundred percent of those tests? Is it fair to expect everyone to have *your* best interest in mind and not occasionally look after their own? Is that truly a betrayal? And if it is, might you eventually find yourself without a single person you can trust completely? What if you learned to trust certain people with certain things? What if the actions of others that you perceive as betrayal might simply be a misunderstanding?

In writing and publishing: Your need for support and guidance will undoubtedly have you looking to other authors for learning and collaboration. Think about how constantly testing others might isolate you from important relationships over time. Does someone you view as an authority have to pass every test of infallibility before you'll take their advice? How might this subconscious process of testing everyone around you be affecting your options for collaborations with other authors? How might it be straining your relationship with readers if they don't show up for a book release like you'd expected them to?

Blind spots for Type 7

Avoiding responsibility—The fastest way to find oneself trapped in misery is to commit to something ahead of time. Or at least that's how the avoidant thinking pattern goes. Even something that seemed fun ahead of time might turn out to be not the vibe you're going for when the time comes. Combine that with all the possible fun diversions that might come up between the planning and the execution, and you have a whole host of reasons to be wishy-washy. The problem, of course, is that making plans can be incredibly fun and has its own associated dopamine hit. Not everyone, however, sees showing up for said plans as optional as you do, though. Has your aversion to commitment extended to your responsibility to yourself? How much of your life is based around not sticking to a commitment as a way of creating unlimited options and escape routes from pain?

In writing and publishing: Think about all the ways you avoid taking responsibility for your business. Do even self-imposed deadlines cause you to feel restless? Does planning your launch feel great but when it's time to execute, you can't make yourself sit and do the work? Do you love outlining your story but then find yourself uninterested in writing it? Have you passed on opportunities for collaboration because they required too firm of a commitment? Or did you say yes to the opportunities because they sounded fun at the time but now you're regretting it? How might the novel allure of a new platform be spreading your marketing efforts too thin? Are you trying the next hot marketing trick because you think it might work or because it gives you justification for not following through on your existing projects?

Pain aversion—Of course pleasure is better than pain, right? What you might not see is how sensitive you have become to pain through refusing to sit in it. Even boredom and silence might register as pain to you, keeping you on a nonstop quest for pleasure. Often, this is found in novelty and distraction, but both of those wear thin before long. All pleasure wears thin over time. Without pain providing a counterweight, pleasure seeking turns into a search for a stronger hit followed by a stronger hit. Things like relationships are often deepened through sitting in pain with others, and when you've lost the tolerance for that, you may find yourself with a lot of superficial relationships. The crux is that you are not searching for pleasure, but for satisfaction, and those two pursuits are not achieved in the same way. Pain and loss are essential ingredients to experience gratitude for and satisfaction with what you have—rather than focusing on what you *could* have.

In writing and publishing: Think about how many half-finished projects you're facing. Did your attention run screaming from them as soon as you got to the painful part of the process? How has your intolerance for pain caused you to shut off ads or pull away from marketing campaigns because they didn't immediately show returns? Do you find yourself giving up on manuscripts rather than putting your protagonist through the necessary pain of a strong character arc? Do you find yourself on social media or other dopamine machines as soon as you hit a bump in the road with your work?

Blind spots for Type 8

Denying vulnerability—Our vulnerabilities are what make us human. They are why we need each other and have lived as social animals for as long as we've been a species. Why are you expecting yourself to have no vulnerabilities? Doesn't the desire to avoid betrayal, hurt, embarrassment, loneliness, and all those other unfortunate emotions present as a vulnerability in itself? The problem with armoring up with strength and power is that if you allow for no weak points in your armor, you won't be able to move. Expecting that you can somehow orchestrate a world around you where you will not be hurt, or if you are, you can exact your own justice for it, is a sign of fear, not strength. How much energy are you spending trying to shore up all your vulnerabilities? When did you learn that you would be blindsided if you showed the smallest sign of vulnerability? What are you missing out on in life by wearing your armor all the time?

In writing and publishing: Think about how much you insist on doing it all on your own. Is no one coming to your aid because the publishing industry is hostile or because you are showing no recognizable signs of being a person who would willingly accept the offer of help? Are you limiting yourself to the kinds of stories "strong people" would write? Are your protagonists easily handling every obstacle you throw their way because you reject the idea of vulnerabilities making people stronger? Are you burning fuel trying to force certain marketing methods to work, rather than asking for advice from others? Are you giving your readers the impression that you couldn't give two shits about whether they read your books or not?

Hurting others—Where do you draw the line between people you want to harm and people you want to protect from harm? Might your bluntness and forcefulness be leaving unintended victims in your wake? Might your tunnel vision in defending the innocent be blinding you to the collateral damage? How might your belief that the world is generally uncaring or even hostile be causing you to assume the worst of others' intentions whenever there is ambiguity of intent? How might your daily actions contribute to the world being inhospitable to vulnerability?

In writing and publishing: Think about the ways you assume the worst intentions of those around you. Are you taking on causes in the industry that may not be any of your business? Are you firing help based upon presumptions of guilt and malicious intent rather than offering generous assumptions? Could you write more allies into your stories to foster a feeling of safety in your story world? Could your bluntness and unsolicited advice be creating a trail of hurt authors and readers in your wake that may deal with their own sense of powerlessness and victimization by mobilizing against you?

Blind Spots for Type 9

Not showing up—While you may be physically present, that doesn't mean you're mentally and emotionally present. The pattern of not showing up means neglecting your own needs, not fully engaging with the world around you, and feeling out of touch with your desires. You may not even notice you're doing this, but the more sensitive people around you do, and they can become frustrated with you being physically present without contributing. It can feel to others like you're showing up to the metaphorical potluck without a dish to contribute.

In writing and publishing: Think about the ways you don't show up fully for your readers and author community but rather "go along." Did you ask your readers to join your email list but then never email them? Or are the emails generic and lack any hints of your personality? How is your belief that your presence and the things you make don't matter quashing your motivation to write the book? How have your anemic efforts at marketing failed to hit escape velocity and reinforced your belief that it doesn't matter if you show up?

Conflict aversion—You probably already realize that you hate conflict, but you might not see just how much that aversion is running your life. Your sensitivity to conflict means you may view things as "conflict" that others would never consider as such. Is speaking up when your friend has something in their teeth conflict? Most would say not, and most people are appreciative when someone lets them know. When meeting your basic needs could create conflict with others who are trying to meet theirs, your default will be to disconnect from your own needs. Who, then, will meet them, if not you? Your reluctance to address conflict both externally and internally could be causing you to take an approach of "it's fine" when it's very much not fine. Neglect and peace are not the same thing.

In writing and publishing: Think about how you're letting your high conflict aversion keep you from talking about your book. Does marketing feel like "bothering people"? Does highlighting what your book is about feel like alienating people who might be looking for something else? Is this aversion blocking you from adding in necessary conflict to drive your stories forward? Does writing conflict poke at inner conflict you've been disconnecting from?

ALREADY KNEW ABOUT YOUR BLIND SPOTS? THINK AGAIN.

The blind spots I've touched on here might be something that you've already noted about yourself. But I encourage you not to dismiss them as "Yeah, I already knew that," because I assure you that you haven't yet witnessed the pervasiveness of these patterns in your life. That's the real work: seeing the blind spot and then not quickly averting your eyes. These patterns run deep, and you likely have no idea how they are boxing you in through limiting your emotional, intellectual, and physical options in life.

If you've ever wondered how others are able to do things that you just can't seem to do, the fact that they are not working with the same blind spots, and therefore the same underlying patterns of attention as you, could very likely be why.

But once we start to understand how much these patterns have taken over, we can experiment with new options. A simple change of direction away from the patterns of our blind spots can rock our world in ways we couldn't imagine. If that scares you, I understand. But small changes in this area can also yield massive positive results that open your eyes to a whole new world of possibility that's been waiting for you with open arms.

When the **One** shifts attention away from flaws, they experience a whole new world of richness and feel gratitude and joy for things exactly as they are.

When the **Two** shifts attention to their own needs,

they witness a whole new world of beautiful complexity in and around them.

When the **Three** shifts attention away from achievement, they see a world of worthy people showing up to support each other in both success and failure.

When the **Four** shifts attention away from their own emotions and longing, they can accept the perfect imperfection of everything in existence, including themselves.

When the **Five** shifts attention away from patterns of isolation, they feel the intense flow of life around them that connects all things.

When the **Six** shifts attention away from their need for certainty, they discover peacefulness and trust in the universe.

When the **Seven** shifts attention away from pleasure seeking, they experience how the present moment is not only enough, but plenty.

When the **Eight** shifts attention away from armoring up, they see the many beautiful ways people care for one another and can receive some of that nurturing.

When the **Nine** shifts attention away from conflict avoidance, they can envision the truer peace on the

other side of conflict and are compelled toward
clear action.

Poking at the sore spots is, unfortunately, one of the best
ways to catapult yourself toward growth. Our blind spots
are the sore spots. So, my best advice is to remember that
you are brave, then start jabbin'! If you find that it feels like
too much, it's okay to take a break and reach out for support
along the way (we are not built to go at anything alone).

Then prepare yourself for the world to look very different
from how you ever imagined it could.

HOW TO MAKE DIFFERENT DECISIONS

The logical question to ask after learning about your blind
spots is "What do I do with this information?" The first
step of the process is always giving yourself time to notice
where the patterns are showing up. Then you can decide if
you're ready to tackle that area of your life. If you're not, no
big deal; you have a lifetime to work on this. But it could
also be that the pattern you've noticed isn't causing many
problems currently, so it doesn't need to be addressed.

In the areas where you notice that your blind spots have
been wreaking havoc, though, the process for making
adjustments is fairly straightforward: try something else.
Anything else.

It's best to frame these changes as an experiment. We
experiment when we have a hypothesis but need to see if
it's true or not. If the experiment doesn't get us the results
we'd hoped, we can try something else. Either way, inter-

rupting our existing patterns is the first step toward building different patterns.

There are a couple of approaches one can take here. The first is to make a minor adjustment and give it lots of time to unfold so that the results are clearly visible. Another option, and the one I prefer, is to do something completely different from the usual pattern, almost the complete opposite, to help snap our brain out of its rut. The added benefit of this is that if we do something completely different, we'll experience entirely fresh results and gain confidence quickly that our patterns of thinking, feeling, and behaving aren't the only right/caring/successful/authentic/wise/safe/pleasurable/strong/harmonious ones available.

So be clear, I'm not telling the Six to go be completely reckless or the One to commit violent crime. Instead, I'm looking more at suggesting the Six make their next decision based on the assumption that the universe is benevolent and has their best interest in mind, rather than deciding based on the assumption that the worst case is also the most likely situation to play out. And I'm suggesting the One try choosing the option that is the most enjoyable from time to time rather than the *least* enjoyable, which tends to be the default when Ones learn to associate "right" with "unpleasant."

If the experiment doesn't work out the way you'd hoped, I encourage you to try a different experiment rather than snapping back to your old patterns like a taut rubber band.

Pay attention while you experiment with new patterns, too. Notice where the fear lives in your body, observe it, and let it know that you see it, but you're trying something new anyway. Keep an eye out for how the world starts to look and feel a little different as you try on the new patterns. It's not uncommon for us to have a shift in our worldview as we intentionally shift our attention toward different priorities. Check in with yourself and see where you feel lighter and less constrained and where you're starting to see new options for your author career that had existed outside of your narrow field of vision previously.

If you stick with these experiments long enough, the restrictive patterns of your type will hold much less appeal. You've now had a taste of freedom, of liberation, from them, and it's incredibly hard to go back to the way things were after that.

And if you ever see the thought pattern of "this will never work" floating through your mind, remember that the patterns that may be new for you are familiar to plenty of other people who have used them to great effect as they miraculously survived into adulthood and built careers of their own. For instance, the idea of choosing the enjoyable path rather than the most "right" path seemed like a bad idea to me. It triggered my core fear as a One, which told me that if I let myself slip even once into enjoyment, I would regret it. I might never come back, in fact! I might turn into a complete hedonist until my life fell apart!

Then I remembered that there are Sevens out there whose default is to choose the more enjoyable thing, and they're doing just fine. In fact, they generally appear to be having a good time, which I would also like to experience. I decided I'd give it a shot. I started making different decisions, questioning my long-held belief that the easy thing was never the right thing, and the right thing was never the easy thing.

You know where this experiment landed me?

Smack-dab in the middle of a very enjoyable career.

My principled nature will never disappear, and I wouldn't want it to. But when I loosened my grip on it and stopped worrying that one small slip would land me in the gutter, I was able to build a principled *and* fun career for myself. Whether you are the Principled Writer like me or another type, you too can loosen your grip slightly and discover what other wonder layers your author career may be capable of carrying.

SIGNS OF GROWTH THAT MAY NOT FEEL LIKE GROWTH

It's important to bring our attention to the fact that growth doesn't look the same for everyone.

For the person who uses their author career as a distraction from dealing with major life problems, growth may look like slowing down, publishing fewer books each year, being more selective about what marketing tasks make the to-do list, and building the support outside of writing to handle those problems before they get too big.

For the person who is struggling to set boundaries that allow them the time to write their book, growth might look like spending more time writing rather than prioritizing every little non-urgent thing that comes up in life outside of their career.

For someone who's been using their audience for their own emotional regulation (this never ends well, by the way), growth might look like sharing less about their personal life with strangers and building better communication and deeper connections with the people close to them.

For someone who's been shut off and terrified of relating to their readers, growth might look like discovering and leaning into more ways of communicating with readers that feel comfortable (or uncomfortable in a muscle-building kind of way).

For someone who tends to start a new pen name every few months, growth might look like sticking with one pen name and genre for long enough to get traction in the market.

For someone who's been writing under the same pen name for years and put off writing in the genre their heart desires, growth might look like pausing the hamster wheel to take a risk on a new genre and feed that part of themselves.

You get the point. And yet we constantly hear that authors "should" do this or that. There is no universal advice in this industry, though. Not even close.

While I can't tell you the specifics of what growth looks like for *you*, I can tell you that "growth" is an expansion of you. It is loosening your grip on the way you've always done things as you become more aware of how your core fear has been vining through the dark and unexamined parts of your life, causing you to bend into weird shapes as it constricts your movement.

Regardless of what growth looks like for you, the path to growth is paved with new options.

Many of the big decisions we make in building our career don't even feel like decisions to us. Instead, they follow the standard operating procedures of our established patterns of thinking, feeling, and doing. Without our conscious minds having any say in it, our subconscious mind rules out all kinds of options for us so that there's only one left: the way we've always done things.

And what happens when the way you've always done it stops working because the industry changes or your life situation changes?

Your sales dip.

Your readership shrinks.

You struggle to get the words down.

Your career feels like it's closing in around you.

Generally speaking, *not great things.*

Growth, then, looks like our ability to adjust to the changes, to recognize the decision points, and to adapt our thinking, feeling, and doing to the reality of the situation so that we can be at peace with what is and keep moving forward.

Growth is a letting-go process. Growth is a liberation from thinking, feeling, and doing what no longer serves us.

If you're thinking, *That's great, Claire, but can you give me more specifics?*

As you wish.

Signs of growth in your author career by type:

Ones may find that the Inner Critic is less frequently invasive when they're writing. They may also find that their need for that final revision pass isn't as strong, and they're comfortable sending the manuscript to the editor without it. Criticism of their work doesn't sting as much or for as long as it used to, and they are more comfortable making decisions because their attachment to the idea that there is a right and a wrong decision in every situation has lessened. Their confidence in the fact that they are good and human and get to be perfectly imperfect has humbled their ego so they can simply enjoy more of the writing and marketing process without anxiety in the form of judgment and criticism ruining the fun.

Twos may find that the appeal of saving people from themselves has lost some of its shine, and they are much more comfortable letting others handle their own problems when it's writing time. They may see their word counts go up and be able to focus more on their own rich emotional experience as they write. They will become more in touch with what fills them up emotionally in their career and how to meet their needs, and they will do that without experiencing shame for having needs. Their marketing strategy may shift away from trying to earn the love of their readers through freebies and hours responding to emails as the Two connects to the inherent value of the work they're producing.

Threes may find that packing their calendar full of work-related tasks is much less fun than it used to be and leaves them feeling totally spent at the end of the day. Instead, they may shift their strategy and tactics to more of a quality-over-quantity approach that allows them to build fulfilling relationships outside of the industry. They may start to feel a stronger connection to their stories than they ever imagined, losing themselves in them and fulfilling their own desires for once, rather than focusing on everyone else's. In unlocking the unique parts of their imagination, the tone of their marketing might shift from self-aggrandizing to an invitation to connect deeply.

Fours may feel their longing to be "special" or "not like anyone else" lessen as they experience the simple joy of being comprehended and appreciated by others. The idea of writing within set genre expectations might not feel so repellant or may even start to feel like a welcome relief and a comprehensible container in which their creativity can dance around as much as it wants. Moods will stop dictating their schedule as strongly, and they will find ways to anchor themselves to something more constant to get the words down consistently, rather than waiting for the right mood to strike. As they deconstruct their complexity-as-armor, they may begin to appreciate the feeling of being comprehended, and marketing will become less of a dirty word and more like a wonderful way to share their creation with those who can relate.

Fives may start to recognize the emptiness in isolation and become more open to the natural give-and-take of being interconnected. They may discover new, energizing ways to connect with readers on shared topics of interest, or may take charge and organize something like a genre meetup at an in-person author event. As they begin to appreciate the knowledge of their body and their heart, their writing will become richer and their marketing will become more compelling. Perhaps without even meaning to, they will grow a much more robust network of authors, which may result in delightful new opportunities to expand their audience. As the desire to be competent in every area of their career lessens, they may feel comfortable outsourcing tasks to experts rather than spending the time and energy to become an expert in everything themselves.

Sixes may relax into the idea that most of the decisions they make are fairly low-stakes and that doubting and rethinking each one doesn't necessarily land them with a better result. They'll also begin to hear their gut instinct speak up more frequently and will gain confidence in making decisions based on its voice instead of listening to the projections of their Head Center. As they stop worrying so much about future outcomes, the Six will find themselves more frequently slipping into flow state in their manuscript as they can focus their attention back on the present. Their belief that an outer authority always knows better than their Inner Authority will dissipate, allowing them the courage to experiment with new marketing techniques that feel right for them and spend more time connecting with fellow authors and readers based on criteria *other than* the promise of safety, security, and certainty. They will find themselves feeling the industry, and by extension their career, is in peril much less frequently as they gain perspective and remember that they are, in fact, quite good in any true crisis.

Sevens may find that all those "missed opportunities" don't take up as much real estate in their mind. They remain more connected to their WIP because when they get to the tough spots, their attention isn't being lured away and offered refuge by the promise of starting a whole new project. As they build their tolerance for delayed gratification, they learn that all those new ideas for books or series can wait until they finish the current projects. And if the ideas lose their luster before the Seven can get to them, then they were probably dead ends to begin with. The Seven may feel comfortable switching back and forth between two or three projects while also seeing each of those through to its completion, understanding that only with the pain of sticking with something will they experience the satisfaction they're seeking. They will experience more flow states throughout their day as they ween off so many cheap dopamine hits. The same focus and ability to deflect the latest shiny object will apply to their marketing, and they will feel much more comfortable sticking with a tactic or strategy long enough to reach the tipping point where it becomes effective, rather than skipping onto something new before the tactic or strategy has a chance to break through.

Eights may begin to see less hostility and fewer obstacles in the industry and begin to value not only their own vulnerability, but that of other people. In doing so, the Eight might start to experience more warm feelings toward their readers and other authors as their circle of "my people" expands. They may feel drawn to sharing more personally and vulnerably with others, which will strengthen their networking and show that they are more of an ideal ally than they are a threat. As the intensity of their presence softens, they may find more people willing to work with them, either through one-off collaborations or partnerships, and their empowered energy will spread to those around them. Readers may feel more empowered to be leaders themselves and take on responsibilities of rallying the troops for the next book launch. Eights will also find that rest becomes a possibility where it wasn't before as their self-compassion blossoms.

Nines may finally understand their integral contribution to the world through their writing. The sense that they have something important to contribute will energize them to be more connected to their WIP, their marketing, and their readers. The tendency to slip in and out of naps or lethargy will lessen as the veil of neglect keeping them from the conflict-laden reality of the world lifts. They may begin to feel an increased sense of urgency without the accompanying catastrophizing they usually associated with a burst of energy. As that happens, they can expect to feel more clearheaded about the top priorities for getting their project across the finish line. The Nine may also become more attuned to how much their readers genuinely want to hear from them, which can invigorate and inspire them to send more engaging emails... or any emails at all. Nines may feel compelled to seek out opportunities to improve their skills in craft and business not as a diversion tactic but as an investment in themselves and the stories that only they can tell.

. . .

While I say that many of the above symptoms "may" occur, what's described above is a well-documented journey by type (and some added specifics about writing and marketing). You may only notice nine out of the ten possibilities showing up in your life, but isn't that plenty? Isn't that fantastic? If you don't see all of them developing, try not to grow impatient. Keep working on the areas I've described in this book, and then one day a miracle will happen. It may look like waking up rested when that never happens. It may look like someone describing you as "calming" when you've always felt like you had zero chill. It may even look like being in the middle of a business-related shitshow and being able to have a good laugh at it all rather than melting down. Whatever the form your growth takes, and however subtle, when you notice it, I hope you celebrate it. You did that. You got yourself there, bit by bit. But don't stop now. There are so many wonderful surprises left inside of you waiting to be witnessed.

SECTION 7: PROGRESSING FROM HERE

WITNESSING NEW PARTS OF YOURSELF

I was standing at my kitchen island prepping some food while John worked at the dining room table a few feet away. I paused in my cutting, looked up, and said, "Do you think I'm a loving person?"

He looked at me like he always does when I say shit like this out of the blue: cautiously, as if this might be a trap. Then he said, "Yeah, I do."

It wasn't a trap. I had just, for the first time in my life, had the thought *You're a really loving person, Claire. You love the people in your life intensely.*

You might be wondering how this was the first time it had occurred to me, and I was wondering the same. It seemed so obvious once I'd put it into words. My actions said it all. I go out of my way for people I care about *and* strangers I'll never see again. I check in with my friends when they're in grief. I even spent years believing the world was shit and managed to show up for my friends in meaningful ways despite that. But no one had ever *described* me that way, as loving. Intense, sure. Hardworking, yes. But never, "You're such a loving person, Claire."

Maybe that was because I don't come off particularly maternal, and I've never had anyone describe me as "warm," which are the two ways people usually frame what a loving woman looks like. But once those words had popped in my head seemingly out of thin air—*You're a really loving person, Claire*—it was like turning a key in a lock for the first time. *Click.* I saw so many of my everyday actions as obvious acts of love. Counseling my friends when they're in trouble, prepping food for John when he has a long week, showing up to my nieces' soccer games on Saturday mornings, caring for my dying dogs with complete dedication, writing characters that I know will help readers heal parts of themselves. Hell, writing nonfiction like this! My whole goddamn life purpose is to learn to love people better, yet I didn't think of myself as a loving person. I viewed myself as many other things, but not yet that.

Wow! There I was, a little bit of me that I was seeing for the first time. And I liked her!

This is an example of the absolute joy of doing this work. Yes, sometimes it requires looking at parts of yourself that are unflattering, but the reward, outside of no longer burning energy to pretend those parts aren't there, is that sometimes you get to witness wonderful, new parts of yourself *that no one told you about*. Once you see those, it's like the clouds parting to reveal a warm sun and blue skies. The sky was there the whole time, but you couldn't see it behind the clouds.

Now, when my Inner Critic tries to get a word in to accuse me of corrupt motives, I have one more piece of evidence to present to her: I love people fiercely.

The Vietnamese monastic Thich Nhat Hanh talks frequently about his approach to receiving both criticism and praise, and we can apply it to that which we receive from others (readers, authors, etc.) as well as from ourselves. He suggests that you respond to both criticism and praise the same way: "You are partly right."*

This is what witnessing new parts of yourself allows you to do. Maybe you did do something out of self-interest. We all do that. If someone calls you selfish for it, you can rest easy knowing that you may be partly selfish, but you are also caring. Maybe someone praises you for your strength and perseverance, and you can remind yourself that you are partly strong, but you are also soft and vulnerable. You are so much more than your lens has allowed you to see of yourself. You have range. You have options. You *are* options.

One exercise that can get you started on seeing some of these new things about yourself is to go through each of the nine types and think about what gifts they bring to the world.

Here are just some of them:

---

* Source: https://plumvillage.org/articles/accepting-ourselves-and-being-partly-right

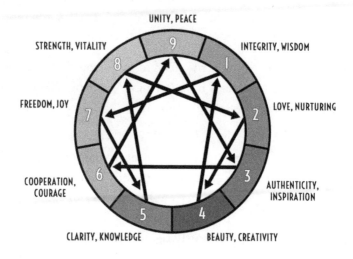

Start with a type you rarely identify with. Look at those words and rather than asking, "Am I those things?" ask, "How am I those things?" Remember, you have all nine types inside of you. So maybe the trait isn't a *defining* one that you're frequently recognized for, and maybe it doesn't come as naturally as your type's gifts, but that doesn't mean you don't possess it.

The Six might ask, "How am I peaceful?" and the Three might ask, "How am I wise?"

I've only included positive traits because that's a nice, safe place to start with this exercise, and I don't want to provide those who are prone to self-recrimination an excuse to build a case against themselves.

Also, identifying our positive qualities that we haven't yet seen is the fastest way to bring more of them into the world. Once you recognize yourself as a giving person, you are more likely to do what giving people like to do. Once you recognize yourself as a brave person, you are more likely to do the brave thing in your career because that's what brave people do.

It's okay to leave the darker work for later. Start with the positive parts of yourself that have gone unrecognized for far too long, and then see what interesting new options present themselves to you in the coming weeks to bring those positive attributes to the world.

RECOMMENDED READING

While I applied and included plenty of specific knowledge, insights, and examples from my years of writing, publishing, and working with authors, I by no means invented the Enneagram concepts in this book. The underlying concepts I discuss are derived from the Enneagram, which I've learned from some of the best teachers around, not only through my certifications and guided workshops, but by reading the words of much smarter people than me on the topic. A lot of words. So many words.

While my point of writing this book was to deliver the most relevant concepts for you and your writing career in a context that could be most immediately useful, I know some of you will want to go even deeper in your process, and I love that. I'm happy to point you to some of my favorite Enneagram books.

I've also found that books can be a fantastic pillar of the support we need to do this work. I constantly revisit certain titles that remind me of the truths I know but have lost sight of due to my ego, pop culture, the news, and the other various temptations of being human. I reread these books to help me connect to my heart, head, and body more deeply. I visit them again and again to remind myself to look to purpose over fear, and to make the difficult but necessary decisions that build a meaningful life. I've never been lucky enough to have a real-life mentor, so books by wise people have filled that place for me. My guess is that they fill that place for many people reading this book, as well.

To keep things simple, I've put together a recommended reading list. When you need some guidance, fresh insight, or a helpful reminder, you can browse this list for something that calls to you in the moment. Just go to www.ffs.media/reading-recommendations. These books are essentially a collection of deep dives (along with much more of the science behind the concepts I cover) into what I've discussed in this book. If you're struggling with your connection to your Body Center, go check out the section of books about the Body Center. If you're struggling with focus, go grab a read from the Head Center section. And if you're simply hurting in the ways we all tend to hurt from living in a complex world with imperfect people, then maybe something in the Healing Your Hurts section will call to you.

I don't permit myself many magical beliefs, but one that I'll stand by is that the right book will find you at the right time. Perhaps my reading list will find you at the right time, too.

HELPFUL QUESTIONS FOR GROWTH

When our days are packed full of activity and responsibility, it's easy (and convenient in many ways) to slip into autopilot in our author career. We defer to our default patterns of thinking, feeling, and behaving, and "just get through it." *Just* make the graphics. *Just* write the next damn chapter. *Just* answer the cursed emails.

Or maybe you can't *just* do it. Maybe your current default patterns are those of *avoidance* rather than pushing through. So you avoid sitting down with your manuscript or put off getting the graphics completed. Maybe much of your day is spent *not* thinking about your inbox. That's pretty typical, too.

But the more frequently we interrupt our autopilot, the more we'll grow. Autopilot—that is, defaulting to our existing patterns of thinking, feeling, and acting that we more or less passively developed in our younger years—is the antithesis of mindfulness. We are not observing our thoughts, feelings, or actions when we are on autopilot; we are simply riding them and hoping they take us somewhere nice.

It's fine and normal to be on autopilot sometimes. Even if it weren't, there ain't jack shit you can do about it. You'll never be one hundred percent mindful. Ain't gonna happen. So the point will never be to eliminate autopilot completely, but rather to practice accepting a little bit less of it than before. And a dash of extra mindfulness goes a long way over the course of your life.

One of the best ways to knock yourself out of autopilot is to ask intentional open-ended questions. If you give yourself a moment to really consider them deeply, they can lead you to new ideas that yield fresh results, especially after you've read this book and begun implementing some of the practices that work for you.

Here are some examples of questions that can lead to new ideas:

"What am I missing here?" What information don't you have that could prove insightful? What assumptions are you working on that might not be true? Whose feelings or motivations haven't you considered that might be relevant?

"Who can I reach out to for a fresh perspective?" Have you tried to solve a similar problem on your own before? Who has a different lens from you and might provide insight you would never have thought of?

"What patterns am I defaulting to?" Examine what beliefs you hold on the matter, what emotions you're experiencing about it, and what actions you plan on taking. Do they fall into the typical patterns of your type? Are you ready to try on something new instead?

"What emotion is making it hard for me to be present?" Emotions are a chemical reaction resulting from the situation and our beliefs about it, ourselves, and others involved. If the result of the chemical reaction is an emotion that you don't allow yourself to feel, sometimes the only option left is to check out and disconnect. Is that happening, and might you intentionally lean into that feeling to address it so you can become present once again?

"What thought have I accepted as truth that might not be?" Beliefs fall under this "thought" category. What are you subconsciously assuming about the people and factors in the situation that might be a result of unhealthy thought patterns or past trauma but may not apply to this specific situation?

"What sensation is making it hard for me to be present?" Is there tension in your body or pain somewhere that makes you want to distract yourself? What emotions or habits might be causing this sensation? What, if anything, might this sensation be calling you to do?

"What parts of myself am I failing to witness?" Are you suspicious of other's kind words or desire to be with you because you're failing to witness some of your better qualities? Have you checked in with your blind spots lately? How might the parts of yourself you're not witnessing be covertly altering your perception of the situation?

"What boundaries do I need to create and enforce?" These can be boundaries with yourself or with others, but when we don't have the time we need to rest, think, feel, and do what needs to be done, it's usually because we forgot to set the necessary boundaries or we thought we could set them once and they wouldn't need frequent enforcement. Where is someone asking too much of you? Where are you asking too much of yourself?

"Where do I need more support?" Adults don't get extra credit for doing things all on their own. What areas of your life and career are exhausting you because they don't play to your strengths? Where would it simply be *nice* to have more people supporting you with their knowledge, love, resources, or wisdom? How can you start cultivating more support in those areas?

I keep a few of these questions that are most relevant to my patterns written on sticky notes that are stuck to the top of my desktop computer. When I get frustrated, tired, or angry, I turn my attention to these, and it reminds me that the situation might not be of my making (though it often is), but the way I feel about it and am functioning as a result of it are still well within my control.

And then there are essential questions that can be profound for each Enneagram type. Asking these will challenge your established patterns, hitting at the heart of the matter and broadening your lens almost instantly.

Here's one question for each type to get you started:

Ones: What would I do here if there were no right or wrong to guide me?

Twos: What would I do here if there were no selfish options?

Threes: What would I do here if I knew no one would praise me?

Fours: What would I do here if I wanted to keep things simple?

Fives: What would I do here if I had endless resources and energy?

Sixes: What would I do here if I was boldly courageous?

Sevens: What would I do here if I also enjoyed the painful parts?

Eights: What would I do here if I believed the best of everyone?

Nines: What would I do here if I felt safe enough to bring my whole self?

As you do more of this work, you'll develop new questions that are relevant to your patterns, and I encourage you to write those somewhere you'll see them every day—your computer, the mirror, by the coffeemaker. If you were to pick one of these questions and asked yourself to answer it every day for a month, your life would look very different at the end of that month.

For instance, if you're a person who loves to figure things out for yourself, but you asked, *Who can I reach out to for a fresh perspective?* each morning while you waited for your coffee to brew, *and then you asked that person for their perspective*, not only are you much more likely to solve the problem in novel ways that provide fresh results, but after a month, there might be dozens of people who realize for the first time that you value their perspective. They'll probably feel good about that. Maybe you valued their perspective the whole time, but if you don't ask them for it, they won't know. Or maybe you didn't value their perspective before, but after learning about how narrow your own lens can be, you now do.

(Note: You will not get this benefit if you shout the question into the online void, so consider doing the more vulnerable thing of asking just one person at a time.)

In engaging with these folks about their perspective, you will undoubtedly also be creating deeper bonds with them, bonds that could bring unexpected and delightful developments to your life. Maybe you find that one of your acquaintances is way more enjoyable to be around than you expected, and now you have a new friend. All of these things could transpire in a month from simply asking the same question every day, giving yourself time to really consider it, and then taking simple action on it. Now imagine what could happen over the coming years if you ask a few of these questions regularly.

The possibilities are literally endless.

CREATING DAILY PRACTICES

By this point in the book, you've ingested a lot of new information, seen new parts of yourself emerge, and started asking the hard questions that move us toward growth. You probably have a much stronger intellectual understanding of the Enneagram, your type, and how your lens has been limiting you in its narrow scope.

You've also been presented with a variety of exercises and questions to consider, more than can really be ingested in a single pass through the book, frankly. Some concepts will hit like an arrow to the heart on your first time through, and others will fly completely under your radar. But when you revisit this book in a few months or years, those concepts that you thought weren't for you might be exactly what you need at that time. That's what I love about the Enneagram framework. It's so rich that it has something useful to offer you no matter where you are along the path, and when a particular concept isn't what you need in that moment, you can just skip over it and move along.

All of the learning you've done so far is only twenty percent of the work, though. The other eighty percent is practice.

There's a difference between "knowing" something conceptually and knowing something deeply. For instance, I know I shouldn't eat so many potatoes in their various delightful forms because the starch is bad for my blood sugar, but I clearly don't know it deeply, or else I wouldn't keep eating so many potatoes. (Or maybe I love potatoes more than I love having energy?)

This means I haven't *integrated* the knowledge. I haven't put it into practice until it becomes such a part of me that I no longer feel a deep longing when I look at a side of fresh waffle fries (spoiler: I'm not currently trying to integrate this knowledge).

You'll hear people talk about the terms "stress" and "growth" in the Enneagram, specifically what particular type we begin to resemble when we're under stress or start to grow. There are schools of Enneagram that call stress "disintegration" and growth "integration." I think those are fine terms, but they're not as clear for the average person, and at this point a lot of New Age cults have co-opted them to mean other weird things.

What, exactly, are we integrating? And what is becoming "disintegrated"? Is it when we find ourselves under prolonged stress?

Essentially, it's our understanding of our Essence, that is, what's beneath our personality. Disintegration is losing touch with our Essence, and integration is connecting deeply with it, a.k.a. integrating it into your reality.

As we integrate the truth of who we are, the armor we've been wearing starts to fall off us, allowing us to move and exist more freely. We are liberated from the patterns that have been weighing us down.

I tend to think of integration as more of an unlearning process than a learning process. This is where I get a little woo-woo, I understand that, but I believe we were born as our Essence, even before we had words to put to it. We just were it. And then the world taught us some harsh and untrue lessons that we've used to protect that Essence when it comes under attack. Those lessons were created by young brains thinking in oversimplified terms and assuming that every time an adult mistreated them, the adult had a good reason to. When certain hurts poked at what we were guarding, we built up defenses against those hurts.

All of our defense mechanisms, all the lessons we learned about surviving in the world, all of the fears and pleasures we adopted, are what we call "personality."

That's how I can justify saying that your personality is not you. It's a set of rules and tools you learned throughout your life to protect your Essence from your core fear.

I say this because I want to demonstrate that you are currently taking part in an unlearning process, and beneath all the trite sayings, creeds, and attitudes you've learned throughout your life, there is something substantial underneath, and it's an absolute delight to learn what it is and to know it more fully.

The process requires regular attention, though. The concepts you learned in this book will fade beneath your deeply ingrained patterns that are constantly reinforced by the world around you. That's why eighty percent of the work is practice. A commitment to growth means working on it every day in small ways.

Thankfully, the practices I recommend take almost no time at all, and you may develop some of your own that are similarly quick and easy. The quicker and easier the better, frankly, as a practice you don't actually do will never be effective.

So, let's brainstorm some practices for moving forward. I encourage you to try out as many as you'd like and see which few work best for you and your lifestyle. Then do them.

(I can't tell you how frustrating it is when people come to me with "I've tried absolutely nothing and none of it has worked!" energy. If you don't incorporate new practices, you'll never get new results.)

PRACTICES FOR THE THREE CENTERS

What I love about focusing on the three centers (head, heart, body) for practices to incorporate is that you don't need to be an Enneagram aficionado to get started. All you need to remember is that *you have three centers*. Then you find one way to connect to each of them at the start of your day or whenever you feel like you need a bit of a reset.

It can help to remember that these are three Centers of Intelligence. They have information for you, and all you have to do is ask what they need, then they'll tell you.

Practices for the Head Center:

- Jot down a list of all the things you need to do. Letting it rattle around in your brain unmanaged makes focusing on your writing harder.
- Write down one repeating thought you're having about yourself and objectively assess whether it's helpful or harmful.
- Remove one task from your schedule for the day. Strike it right off. The odds are, you're trying to do

too much on too little. Give more attention
to fewer things.

- Assess evidence and data to evaluate something
  objectively. Are your fears and emotions
  substantiated with hard facts?
- Practice putting boundaries around the
  information you ingest. Use an app like Freedom
  App to block websites that steal your attention.

Practices for the Heart Center:

- Ask yourself what emotion you're feeling. Feel it
  without trying to judge or fix it. (I reference the
  emotion wheel on my wall for this.)
- Listen to a song that engages your heart.
- Express your feelings to someone rather than
  holding them in.
- Practice boundaries around your emotions. Close
  your eyes and ask your heart whose emotions it's
  holding on to. Visualize letting go of every
  emotion that you've taken on for others.
  Experience how light your own emotions are
  when it's just them in your heart.

Practices for the Body Center:

- Go outside. Even if it's cold or rainy, dress
  appropriately then go outside.
- Exercise however you are able. Dance, go for
  walks, stretch, hit the gym, play with your dog.
  This will take the edge off the daily stress cycles.
- Stretch. Hold each one for ten deep breaths.

- Laugh, sing, gargle water, and practice deep breathing to tone your vagus nerve, which helps your nervous system transition quicker from fight/flight to safe/relaxed.
- Do what your doctor tells you. Take your vitamins, get those booster shots, and practice setting boundaries with people who are carelessly sick around you.
- Organize your writing environment. If you're at risk of knocking a cup over with your elbow, your body will be in a state of tension. Give yourself physical room to move.

BUILDING A MANTRA

This next practice is one of my favorites. As you've learned about your Enneagram type, you've started to decode what beliefs of yours were created out of self-protection and which ones are truth reaching out to you through the mire of modern life.

Building a mantra is a technique I learned from Dr. Jerome Wagner, who developed the Enneagram Spectrum of Personality Styles and whom I studied under during my certification.

The gist of the mantra is that we recognize truth when we listen deeply to ourselves. So, when you create your mantra, you want to speak from what you know is true. That way it will connect with something deep within you, even when you don't feel particularly in the mood to connect with that part.

This is what sets apart this practice of a mantra from most daily affirmation practices. If I look at myself in the mirror first thing in the morning, remnants of mascara smeared around, bags under my eyes, hair looking crazy, and I tell myself, "You are a beautiful, powerful woman," because I read in a book somewhere that I should say that to myself, that practice will do literally nothing for me and might in fact make me feel the opposite, triggering negative thought patterns instead.

We must dive into ourselves and pull out the truth on our own. It must be something that comes from us.

That's why I'm not going to tell you what your mantra should be. I want you to develop it with the truths that you are starting to connect with more deeply. The *process* of designing your mantra holds great value.

Instead of telling you what it should be, I'll tell you how I designed mine and why, and I encourage you to create one for yourself.

I repeat my mantra many times a day. Any time I'm feeling restless or blocked, when I step outside for a walk or work in the garden, when I'm stuck in traffic, and when I arrive somewhere early (or on time but other people are late). I use it when I'm disappointed with an outcome, when I feel overwhelmed by grief, and even when I have a migraine set in. It feels like a secret weapon.

And as reluctant as I am to share this mantra, because I like it being a little secret I keep with myself and loathe opening it up to possible judgment from the outside world, I'll do the brave thing now and put it in print so that you can see how simple and true a mantra can be.

Here's mine:

> *Everything is exactly as it should be.*
> *There is nothing required of me in this moment.*
> *I am so glad to be here.*

My mantra will not be your mantra, even if you're a fellow Type 1 Reformer. Now, let me take you through the journey of how I built this so you can follow the process if you'd like.

Everything is exactly as it should be – This is tapping into the truth that everything is perfectly imperfect and there is an order and balance to the world that is bigger than my ego could ever orchestrate. It accepts the belief that if something is, then there was no other way for it to be. Therefore, all my personal beliefs about what "should" be can kick rocks, because if something really "should" be a certain way, then it is that way. This is letting go of my notion that I know better than the universe and Mother Earth, better than the complex and countless causes and effects happening around me. It tells me that my judgment of what is, is not necessary to the unfolding of the universe... and is irrelevant anyway. Once I stop fighting this truth, I get a great deal of relief from it.

There is nothing required of me in this moment – This is a gift for my nervous system. The weight a Reformer carries around of all that could be "fixed" in the world (according to our egos) and what we "should" be doing can make it very difficult to just be. The stress is also a result of time compression; we see all that needs to be done in the future, and then it suddenly feels like it all needs to get done now. The truth, however, is that if you pause and really feel into the moment, nothing is required in any true sense. The world will not collapse if you pause and exist. I've even tested this out in the airport security line. The person ahead of me moved forward, and I reminded myself that nothing was required of me, not even moving forward myself. It reminds me that I have the option to be present at any time, that I have a choice. That obligation does not loom over me in any sense other than the one I assign myself. Telling myself that nothing is required of me in this moment reminds me that I am free. I am already the thing I seek to be without doing a thing or needing to earning it.

I am so glad to be here – The ability to be grateful for the moment regardless of the moment is truly a talent. But think about it—you could also be *not* here. You could not exist, and some day that will happen, more or less. You'll die. Your time on this planet is so finite that every single experience is a gift. We lost one of our dogs to cancer a year and a half ago, and in the process of her dying, I woke up every morning, saw her at the foot of the bed, and felt true gladness along with the grief. I told her every morning, "I'm so glad you're here," and I meant it truly. I knew she would soon not be here. And I did the same for my other dog each morning as she aged and struggled with health issues until it was time to say goodbye to her earlier this year. I was so glad she was there. My gratitude for it was overwhelming. And as I write this today, neither dog still around, but I can connect back to that gratitude and feel its overwhelming glow. I am so glad they were here. Why, then, wouldn't I feel that gratitude about myself? I'm here now, and I eventually won't be. My mind, heart, and body are luxuries that will end. How amazing is it that I exist and have gotten to love this world so deeply!

This final line of my mantra also taps into the values of joy and gratitude of my growth type, the Enthusiast, and that's why I save it for last. For me, I have to clear away the clouds with the first two lines before I can see the blue sky.

To sum up the structure I use (and you're free to structure this any way you want):

Line 1: Reel in my ego, allowing me to...

Line 2: Reconnect to the present, clearing the way for me to...

Line 3: Reach for the gifts of my growth type.

When I put this mantra into practice, I usually have to repeat each line a few times before I feel it and then move on to the next. My ego can fight back, for instance, against the idea that everything is as it should be. *But what about war and famine?* my ego demands. *I don't have to approve of the way things are to accept that they could be no other way given what led up to them,* the truth replies. If things seem wrong, I can work to change them, but I can never change what is, and my judgment of right and wrong doesn't change anything, it only separates me from the wonder of it all.

I encourage you to take some time to be silent and construct your own mantra. It can change over time, as most things do. If one of the lines of mine struck a chord, you can borrow it, but don't look for shortcuts.

If you're struggling to come up with something, think of your favorite poem. You can borrow lines from there. Just make sure that you're speaking the truth and not speaking from a place of hurt and fear. It's easy enough to access *those* parts of us without creating a mantra.

BREATHING

The practice of deep, controlled breathing is so easy, it's usually dismissed or overlooked as an effective tool for overall health. But the effects of it on your nervous system are scientifically documented, so don't overlook it. What's especially helpful about developing a breathing practice that works for you is that, like the mantra, you never have an excuse not to do it. You're already breathing, so why not make it a little more beneficial to your well-being?

I'm by no means an expert on this, but there are a few go-to techniques that work well for most people (if you are not one of these people, that's okay). If you ever feel yourself getting lightheaded as you do these, please stop. Seriously. I'm not a doctor, so you don't have to take medical advice from me, but, like, don't do things that make you pass out? I hope that's not too much to ask.

That being said, here are a couple gentle breathing practices that can immediately reset your body, heart, and mind.

> **Belly breaths.** When we get stressed, our body shifts from breathing into our belly to breathing

into our chest. We don't activate our ab muscles but instead make our shoulders do all the heavy lifting, raising up and down with each breath. This causes shallow breathing, less oxygen intake, and tension in our shoulders, neck, and head. Meanwhile, breathing into our belly so that it expands on the inhale and retracts on the exhale while our shoulders remain relaxed activates our parasympathetic nervous system. Our parasympathetic nervous system tells our bodies we're safe and protected. Breathing into our chest keeps our sympathetic nervous system alert, which tells the rest of our body that we're in danger. With the low-level stress of modern life that never gets resolved, it's not uncommon to spend years breathing into your chest without realizing there's an alternative. If that's you, and you're transitioning to belly breathing, it's going to feel weird at first. Keep practicing.

Box breathing. This is a great tool for troubleshooting when you're feeling overstimulated. It requires inhaling to the count of four, holding the inhale for four seconds, exhaling over eight seconds, then holding the out breath for four seconds. Repeat a few times, and your body and outlook on life will look completely different on the other side. But again, if this gets you lightheaded, stop.

When you practice these two techniques, no one even has to know you're doing it. You can be mindful of breathing into your belly when dealing with a relative who makes a hobby of stirring up feelings of shame in you, or you can do some box breaths after you park your car to help you transition from the stress of the road to whatever is waiting for you next. Breathing exercises are so effective it's almost unbelievable. There are many other options, but these are two of the simplest and ones I feel confident recommending as not-your-doctor.

Side note/rant: Two covert attitudes that keep us from a healthy connection to our Body Center are ableism and fatphobia. You may be generally healthy now, but you will eventually get sick, injured, or chronically ill. It's not a matter of if, but when. Staying connected to our Body Center means loving ourselves no matter our physical capabilities or challenges, no matter the pain our body might be causing us. It doesn't hate us. It's doing the best it can, and it's all we got.

Additionally, fatphobia has likely caused a rift between us and our bodies from a young age, and there was no winning at it. We already know about the well-documented trauma that it causes for people whose body weight and size exceed the arbitrary standards of society and are therefore subject to all sorts of insidious and ignorant stigmas. That is certainly enough damage to argue a case for why we should all do better. But even those whose body size falls within the range of "acceptable" suffer from the persistence of fatphobia. Before you compliment your friend on all that weight they recently lost, are you certain that it didn't result from a serious illness, depression, grief, or disordered eating? You wouldn't want your faulty and simplistic ideas about what large and small bodies indicate about a person's character to cause harm to your relationships with others, but fatphobia will do just that eventually, if it hasn't already.

The harm it causes between each of us and our own body runs deep as well, and starts at a frighteningly young age. For example, back when you were a school-age kid, perhaps somewhere around middle school, you probably learned to suck in your stomach to appear as small around your midsection as possible. Regardless of whether you were considered "fat" or "skinny," this seed was likely planted in your psyche. First of all, I'm sorry that your younger self learned that lesson and felt like your job was to take up as little space as possible. It's truly a hurtful subconscious belief to take on at a young age. But on top of the harmful belief, think about this consequence: in trying to keep your middle appearing as small as possible, you were training your body to expand your chest instead of your belly as you breathed, especially if you were a woman. Fatphobia has altered many people's lifelong breathing patterns in this way. You deserve to breathe deep into your belly wherever and whenever you want to, no matter how snug or loose your clothing. In fact, why not be rebellious as hell and take a few deep belly breaths right now? Stick it to The Man!

Whatever practices you do choose, continue with them for a while before deciding whether they're helpful. While we sometimes get to experience revelations in this work, most of the progress is slow, and progress reliant on daily commitment. Belly breathing to start your day for a few weeks will not make you an enlightened person. Sticking an emotion wheel on your wall then never referencing it will not increase your EQ.

The most enlightened, wise, and vibrant people you know, the ones who seem to hold secrets to life that others don't, all have practices like these that they have incorporated into their day. The practices are not silver bullets, but they *are* the secret.

Our personality is, after all, a collection of attentional patterns—thinking, feeling, and acting. We must swap those deeply ingrained patterns that no longer help us with new ones. Ones of our choosing. Ones that move us toward Liberation and away from fear motivation. We're up against a lot, not just in the publishing industry, but in this world, and our practices are our tools for pursuing our purpose regardless of the setbacks. Choose ones that feel right for you, and then learn to use them well.

HOW I CAN SUPPORT YOU

As you develop practices for growth and build your author career into more than you ever dreamed it could be, you'll also want to create support for your growth so that one step backward doesn't end up turning into a complete backslide. Finding friends who are committed to the same process helps tremendously, so the more authors who read this book and the more these concepts become part of the average author's lexicon, the easier it will be to gather those people to you.

A few friends and an encouraging spouse are rarely enough to support you through the long nights and tedious stretches, and sometimes your friends can mean well and want the best for you, but that doesn't mean that they necessarily have the most enlightened advice tailored for you and your motivation.

This is where it can be helpful to bring in professionals like me. When we work together, we develop a relationship that puts your mental, emotional, and physical health at the forefront of your author career. Sometimes just having the knowledge that I'm here when you need me can be a great reassurance when it's time to take the scary but brave next step in your career. If it doesn't work out, I can help you pick up the pieces—you don't ever have to do that alone. When your story's stuck, no need to freak out. Book an appointment with me, and rest assured that you'll be unstuck on the other side of it. When you hit a wall in your career and don't know the next best step, you don't have to worry about it, because the next best step can be coming to see me, and then I'll help you find what to do afterward.

This writing and publishing thing can be quite pleasant once we know who to call for help (and accept that we are allowed to ask for help). You don't even have to wait until it's an emergency! You can reach out to me before the existential crisis sinks its claws in.

Here are some of the ways I can help you:

- **The 5-Day Indie Author Supercharge (free course)** – www.ffs.media/5day

This course helps you explore the concepts of *Reclaim Your Author Career* and includes reflection exercises about your type.

- **Reclaim Your Author Career (book)** –
  www.books2read.com/RYAC

This book explains strategies for building an author career aligned to your particular Enneagram type and how to decide what kind of stories will fuel you.

- **The Liberated Writer 5-Week Course** –
  www.ffs.media/liberated-writer-course

Not only will you develop individualized practices for yourself and explore more advanced aspects of your Enneagram type, but you'll have two group calls with me each week to ask your questions about the material and get live coaching. It's also a great place to meet other authors you click with who are as committed to this as you are.

- **The Liberated Writer Retreat** – www.ffs.media/retreat

This is a boutique workshop and retreat for authors. The mornings are spent workshopping your career and learning how to write stronger characters, and the afternoons are for relaxing, enjoying time with the other ten attendees, and planning for success. Your ticket includes all meals and board, a typing interview before the event, as well as a one-on-one with me during the retreat.

- **The Author Alignment (individual career & Enneagram coaching)** – www.authoralignment.com

Spend an hour with me problem solving and getting individualized coaching about your author career.

- **The Story Alignment (individual story consulting)** – www.storyalignment.com

Spend an hour with me problem solving and leveling up your WIP with my story expertise from years of editing fiction, coaching authors on their manuscripts, and writing dozens of books myself.

If you have questions about which is the right place for you to start, send me an email at contact@ffs.media, describe where you're at in your career and what you'd like support with, and I can help you find what's right for you.

YOUR FUTURE SELF IS PROUD OF YOU

I want you to think about yourself twenty years ago (or ten if you're younger than thirty). Think of the mistakes you made, the pain you didn't know what to do with, and the way you carried on anyway. Lean deep into appreciation for how you persevered. That version of you was doing the best they could with the tools they had, and even though their progress wasn't perfect or even all that flattering at times, they got you here, to where you are today with all the wonderful things you have in your life. If you can find a picture of yourself from back then, take a look at it. Can you believe how self-conscious you were about your appearance? Can you believe how much you took for granted your youthful energy and overlooked your gifts?

When I think about myself twenty years ago, I see a girl who was making all kinds of mistakes, hurting people without meaning to, being hurt in ways she couldn't put words to, and hurting herself because she didn't think she deserved better. It breaks my heart.

I also see someone who worked her ass off for other people, stood up for what she believed in despite it being unpopular, and didn't give up on her dream of writing when everyone told her it was irrational. I am so thankful for the work that young woman did twenty years ago and in the twenty years following.

I hope you're proud of your former self, too. They carried your traumas, disappointments, loneliness, and despair long enough so that you could build yourself a place to transform and heal. Allow yourself a moment to experience a profound sense of gratitude for that messy, scrappy younger you. They found a way to carry on, learn, do better, and love others.

Now I want you to time-travel forward. Imagine yourself twenty years from now. How would that version of you feel about you today? What fortitude and imperfect growth will they see when they look back over their past twenty years? Close your eyes, reach a hand toward them through time, and receive how proud they are of you for your commitment to facing your fear, experimenting with new ways of being, and building a writing career that not only sustained itself, but sustained you. Imagine the pride your future self feels for your resilience and the compassion you showed to yourself when things didn't go according to plan or you were hurting and tired and decided to take a rest instead of beating yourself up. How does your future self feel about those times you reached out to others for help and support even though it felt scary to you? Twenty years from now, how much gratitude do you feel for the times you tried something new and uncomfortable that made your life worth living in ways you can't yet imagine today?

Each of those versions of you through time exist inside of you right now, and every one of them has looked fear in the eye and said, "I choose to keep going anyway. I couldn't possibly stop now. I have too many gifts to share with the world."

ACKNOWLEDGMENTS

When I stop to think about how much support I have in my life and career, it knocks me speechless.

My support system is woven from an uncountable number of threads to create a wonderfully soft net to catch me every time I fall, and I fall so fucking much. I am endlessly grateful to everyone who has shown me love in their own way, even when I was disconnected from self-love.

My biggest thank you is to my husband, John. Your kindness and non-judgment baffled me when we first met, and our years together have taught me two important things: I was and am worthy of that kindness, and you are actually low-key judgmental AF. Thank you for both things.

This will sound weird, because neither one could read when they were alive and they especially can't now that they're gone, but thank you to my dogs Penny and Senga for swapping soul parts with me. A sliver of me died with each of you, but a part of you lives on in me, and I'm incredibly pleased about that last bit.

To Alyssa Archer, who edits all this stuff and does such a wonderful job preventing me from making a total ass of myself through the written word, thank you for your diplomacy in the edits and for being my warm and compassionate invitation back to the Enneagram all those years ago after my first brush with it was less than appealing. I am so lucky to be your friend.

Teachers are what keep the world working, and I've had the honor of learning about the Enneagram from a few of the greats. Thanks to Dr. Jerome Wagner of the Enneagram Spectrum of Personality Styles, Diane Ring and Dirk Cloete of the Integrative Enneagram, and Michael Naylor with the Enneagram Institute for your insights and expertise and for modeling how to create healthy and unforgettable learning environments for growth.

I don't know when, if at all, I would've overcome my subtle but invasive fears around writing this book if it weren't for the support and encouragement of my dear friend Becca Syme. Our connection has been such an unexpected gift. Thank you for letting me fall asleep on your couch to football and for texting with me about nothing in particular during some of the harder nights of my life lately.

Hi, Bryan. Are we still friends? Phew! Thanks for still being my friend.

I hope to never need to hide a body, but thank you to all my friends who make it clear that you would help me do it. I would name you individually, but that would be such an easy lead for an investigator to follow up on. You know who you are, anyway.

There's a whole parade of people in this industry who I simply love as humans and whose mere presence brings so much joy to my life. So, thank you for existing and for chatting with me about non-writing things, Amy Teegan, Crystal Shannon, Damon Courtney, Dan Wood, Donovan

Scherer, Ember Casey, Erin Johnson, Ernie Dempsey, Jami Albright, Kalvin Chinyere, Kerri McQuaide, Mike Stop Continues, Monica Leonelle, Nathan Van Coops, Oliver Altair, Traci Andrighetti, Trixie Silvertale, and so many others who I like and wish I could chat with more often. And yes, I did it in alphabetical order of first names because I don't want it to seem like I'm picking favorites (although you're clearly my favorite, Amy, don't worry). (Also, there are some duplicates between this list and the hiding-a-body one, but I'm not saying who.)

Lastly, thank you to everyone in this industry who trusts me enough to ask for my help and support, who hires me to speak, coach, and consult. I am so grateful that the unintended side effect of the work I do is meeting so many courageous, hilarious, intelligent, and fascinating people who also happen to be authors. Why would I ever stop doing this? You were my inspiration to keep writing this book through various health issues and the weighted blanket of grief. It was a no-brainer for me to keep going because I love what I do, and you are the reason I love it.

And to you, dear reader, whoever you happen to be: **I am so glad you're here.**

ABOUT CLAIRE TAYLOR

Claire Taylor is an independent author and the owner of FFS Media. She offers courses, coaching, and consulting for writers who want to supercharge their fiction and align their career using the Enneagram.

She still lives in her hometown of Austin, Texas.

Find her author services and fiction at www.ffs.media.

To receive tips and tricks to make your next story unforgettable, sign up for the FFS Media Story Nerds: www.ffs.media/join.

Printed in the USA
CPSIA information can be obtained
at www.ICGtesting.com
CBHW030812200524
8695CB00011B/14